Discursive Navigation of Employable Identities in the Narratives of Former Refugees

Studies in Narrative (SiN)

ISSN 1568-2706

The subject of SiN is the study of narrative. Volumes published in the series draw upon a variety of approaches and methodologies in the study of narrative. Particular emphasis is placed on theoretical approaches to narrative and the analysis of narratives in human interaction.

For an overview of all books published in this series, please see *benjamins.com/catalog/sin*

Volume 27

Discursive Navigation of Employable Identities in the Narratives of Former Refugees
by Emily Greenbank

Discursive Navigation of Employable Identities in the Narratives of Former Refugees

Emily Greenbank
Victoria University of Wellington, New Zealand

John Benjamins Publishing Company
Amsterdam / Philadelphia

The paper used in this publication meets the minimum requirements of the American National Standard for Information Sciences – Permanence of Paper for Printed Library Materials, ANSI Z39.48-1984.

DOI 10.1075/sin.27

Cataloging-in-Publication Data available from Library of Congress:

LCCN 2020003876 (PRINT) / 2020003877 (E-BOOK)

ISBN 978 90 272 0556 8 (HB)
ISBN 978 90 272 6117 5 (E-BOOK)

John Benjamins Publishing Company · https://benjamins.com

Dedicated to my parents, for their constant generosity and support, and for teaching me empathy and kindness by example.

Table of contents

CHAPTER 1

Introduction and aims

Research motivations

A little over a decade ago, I volunteered with a local refugee resettlement agency to assist newly-arrived former refugee families settling into their new homes. It was a humbling experience for me which first hinted at the challenges of forced migration and the enormity of what resettlement entails. It also destabilised my preconceptions of what it meant to be a refugee. This work would begin before the families arrived, sourcing furniture, bedding, appliances, clothing, books, and the like to set up the homes the families would arrive to, as well as gathering useful information about local schools, public transport, and services. Before we began this work, all volunteers were required to attend a short training course to prepare us for what was to come. Ten years later, two things remain in my mind from these training sessions. The first of these was a brainstorming activity which we did in groups. Reminiscent of craft activities in primary school, we were given large sheets of paper and a variety of coloured pens and told to draw and write all of the things that meant *home* to us. So, we took up the challenge, drawing colourful renditions of our families, friends, jobs, leisure activities, pets, and so on, chatting and getting to know one another as we did. Eventually the woman running the training session gathered up all of the groups' creations, took them to the front of the room, and wordlessly tore them all to pieces. Although we had all been expecting that our work would be used to illustrate the things refugeehood might threaten, this simple act with no real-life consequences shocked us all to silence. The trainer explained that this is what refugeehood entails: everything that was home is gone, just like that. The other moment that has remained with me was the trainer talking about meeting the families we would work with, telling us *don't expect them to them to be grateful*. Although I have come to see this as common sense, at the time it surprised me. A younger me would have wondered, 'would these forced migrants not be grateful to be safe and welcomed in their new homes, after their original homes had been irreversibly taken from them, as so dramatically demonstrated to us in the earlier drawing exercise?' The reality, I would come to learn, is much more complex than such a danger/safety or gratitude/ingratitude binary would suggest.

This complexity and apparent contradiction, along with the humbling experience of the volunteer work with the newly-arrived family itself, has stayed with me and has in part motivated this research. The complicated and ongoing resettlement struggles that I witnessed first-hand are only the beginning of what can be a very long journey from society's periphery to full inclusion and participation in a new society. Involvement and belonging in a given social context is negotiated and co-constructed in interaction, as newcomers and oldtimers take up and assign various and dynamic discursive identity positions, which may be affirmed or rejected by others. Thus, in this study I approach this issue from an Interactional Sociolinguistic perspective, exploring former refugees' discursive enactment and negotiation of employable identities in New Zealand. Such an approach allows for close examination of the challenges and obstacles that forced migrants can encounter in their attempts to navigate new social worlds.

Research context: Refugees and resettlement

Before former refugees face navigating liminality and belonging in new societies, they experience refugeehood: leaving a country of origin, claiming asylum, and being granted official UNCHR refugee status. A refugee is someone who "is unable or unwilling to return to their country of origin owing to a well-founded fear of being persecuted for reasons of race, religion, nationality, membership of a particular social group, or political opinion" (UNHCR, 2018c). There are around 68.5 million forcibly displaced persons in the world today, around 25.4 million of whom are refugees (of the remainder, 40 million are internally displaced, and 3.1 million are asylum seekers who do not (yet) have UNHCR refugee status (UNHCR, 2018b)). The magnitude of refugee numbers became more visible in 2015, when the so-called European refugee crisis dominated media worldwide. As civil war forced millions of Syrians from their homes, and increasing numbers of people fled conflict, persecution, and poverty in Afghanistan, Iraq, Eritrea, Kosovo and other nations, more than one million people crossed into the European Union via the Mediterranean Sea and Southeast Europe (BBC News Service, 2016). The global political climate regarding refugees and migration became further complicated by the President of the United States taking a controversial hard-line stance on migration from Muslim-majority countries and refugees. The predominant media images of this crisis (outside of far-right tabloids) are those of desperation and trauma (Schwöbel-Patel & Ozkaramanli, 2017). However, the very wording 'refugee crisis' hints at the ideological assumptions underlying this term, and in political discourse, "what is often meant… [by 'refugee crisis'] is the threat posed by refugees" (Faist, 2018, p. 418). That is, the 'crisis,' in commonly circulated discourse, refers not to the situations that lead to mass forced migration, but to the perceived "threats to peace and security in the Global North" (Schwöbel-Patel & Ozkaramanli, 2017, p. 4). *Global North* and *Global South* are alternative terms to economically-based terminology (e.g. *first/third/developing world*), based on "social relations and cultural difference *and* political and economic disparity," broadly based on mapping a wealthier Global North and poorer Global South. This broad definition has "immediate exceptions" including the fact that New Zealand, Australia, and sometimes South Africa are generally considered part of the Global North (Del Casino, 2009, p. 26).

While nations in Western Europe scrambled to deal with growing numbers of refugee arrivals, it is worth noting that the vast majority – 85 percent – of the world's displaced persons are not hosted in the West: the top refugee-hosting countries are Turkey, Uganda, Pakistan, and Lebanon (UNHCR, 2018b). In fact, in Lebanon, one in four people is a refugee (BBC News Service, 2015). The challenges surrounding refugee resettlement are almost guaranteed to increase for many years to come, likely exacerbated by both the environmental and political ramifications of climate change, and a rise in isolationist and xenophobic ideologies across the globe. This 'new normal,' as Schwöbel-Patel and Ozkaramanli (2017, p. 2) note, will continue to "[place] practical pressures on receiving states and spaces, origin states and spaces, and, on a more metaphysical level, general conceptions of humanitarianism."

Due to New Zealand's geographical isolation, it is a country which is largely unaffected by the challenges posed by asylum seekers, that is, those who arrive seeking asylum without having been assigned UNHCR refugee status in another country first (UNHCR, 2018a). For various reason including visa restrictions, most asylum seekers do not fly to the countries in which they wish to seek asylum. Reaching New Zealand by boat is fairly impractical given its distance from refugee-origin and intermediary countries. New Zealand's refugee quota currently permits the resettlement of 1,000 refugees each year (although exceptions have been made such as temporary increases during the ongoing conflict in Syria), if they are referred by the Office of the United Nations High Commissioner for Refugees (UNHCR), an agency which co-ordinates refugee resettlement allocation worldwide. In September 2018 Prime Minister Jacinda Ardern announced a commitment to raise the quota to 1,500 by 2020 (RNZ, 2018). Those who arrive in New Zealand under the UNHCR quota are granted Permanent Residence upon arrival, which entitles living, working, and studying in New Zealand indefinitely, as well as access to social services and healthcare. In this book I make a distinction between the terms *refugee* and *former refugee*. The first refers to those who have claimed asylum and been granted refugee status by the UNHCR but have not yet been resettled. The latter refers to those who have been refugees in the past but are now permanent residents of their countries of resettlement. That is, I use the term *former refugee* to recognise that the process of refugeehood technically ends upon arrival in, in this case, New Zealand. Although the effects of refugeehood can linger indefinitely, the label of 'refugee' no longer applies.

When refugees arrive in New Zealand, they first spend six weeks at Mangere Refugee Resettlement Centre (MRRC), where they take part in a reception programme which "aims to build basic social and coping skills required for refugees' new lives in New Zealand and provide information on work and expectations of employment" (Immigration New Zealand, 2018b). This programme focuses upon health assessments and treatment; planning for living and working in New Zealand; and education, including English language. These focuses are in line with Immigration New Zealand's (2012) five desired integration outcomes for former refugees:

1. Self-sufficiency: all working-age refugees are in paid work or supported by a family member in paid work.
2. Housing: refugees live in safe, secure, healthy and affordable homes without needing government housing help.
3. Education: refugees have English language skills that help them participate in education and daily life.
4. Health and wellbeing: refugees and their families enjoy healthy, safe and independent lives.
5. Participation: refugees actively participate in New Zealand life and have a strong sense of belonging here.

At the end of this six weeks, the former refugees are placed in one of eight receiving regions in New Zealand; Auckland, Waikato, Manawatu, Wellington, Nelson, Christchurch, Dunedin and Invercargill. They are provided with affordable rental housing, and are eligible for settlement support for one year, which includes assistance accessing services they may require as they settle into their new communities (Immigration New Zealand, 2018b). This support from the government and NGOs is invaluable for former refugees in their first months in New Zealand. Nonetheless, forced migrants (along with other migrants) to New Zealand encounter myriad challenges during resettlement, including of course prejudice and discrimination (Butcher, Spoonley, & Trlin, 2006). At the extreme end of this, while many New Zealanders may have believed their home to be immune to the xenophobic violence emerging elsewhere around the world, the Christchurch mosque shootings of 15 March 2019 which left 51 people dead disabused this notion. Acts of terrorism are extremely rare in New Zealand, but less visible challenges to newcomers' full involvement in society are far more prevalent.

Numerous studies have explored the challenges that former refugees encounter during resettlement into their new countries of residence. These have included studies looking at the effects of discrimination and othering (e.g. Butcher, Spoonley, & Trlin, 2006; Hatoss, 2012), gender (e.g. McSpadden & Moussa, 1993;

Warriner, 2004), and social inclusion (e.g. Colic-Peisker, 2005; Correa-Velez, Gifford, & Barnett, 2010). Studies focused on the resettlement experiences of refugee youth have explored issues of wellbeing (e.g. Edge, Newbold, & McKeary, 2014; Montgomery, 2010), and education (e.g. Hatoss & Sheely, 2009; Hek, 2005; Woods, 2009). Further studies explore issues of linguistics such as language socialisation (e.g. S. O'Connor, 2014), language acquisition (e.g. Navarro, 2016; Navarro & Macalister, 2017), and language maintenance (e.g. Bradshaw, 2013; Revis, 2015). The challenges faced by former refugees upon arrival in their country of resettlement are substantial. Initially, the lingering effects of displacement such as separation from friends, family, and home; experiences of war or violence; language competency issues; lack of familiarity with local norms and customs, and so forth, can present various and numerous obstacles for resettlement. However, following the initial hurdles and practical logistics of settlement of these new arrivals, perhaps the greatest challenges for former refugees and host nations alike lie ahead. In particular, for former refugees to meet Immigration New Zealand's fifth 'integration outcome' of actively participating in New Zealand life and gaining a strong sense of belonging, may take much longer, and is linked to success in the first goal of self-sufficiency.

Employment challenges

Governments and resettlement agencies recognise that economic self-sufficiency has a significant influence on migrants' capacity to fully participate in their new societies; without employment, former refugees risk social and economic marginalisation (Immigration New Zealand, 2012; UNHCR, 2002). Research has indicated that within New Zealand, former refugees are some of the most marginalised people in terms of employment opportunities (ChangeMakers Refugee Forum, 2012). This has social as well as economic implications. Meaningful employment is an important contributor to former refugees' self-esteem and to their sense that they are contributing to society, as well as to challenging negative stereotypes and building support networks. As Colic-Peisker (2009, p. 178) notes, former refugee employment and the reality of downward social and economic mobility "have the potential to adversely affect other aspects of resettlement: family life, the creation of social networks, the feeling of belonging and consequently, people's overall emotional well-being and life satisfaction." Accessing and securing such employment is far from straightforward when confronted with trauma, loss of social capital and status, English language proficiency difficulties, and lack of recognition of overseas-gained qualifications and experience.

Navigating employment is an on-going challenge for any migrant, and particularly so for those of refugee-background. It is largely considered by host governments to be the most important factor for social integration (Colic-Peisker, 2009; Colic-Peisker & Tilbury, 2007; Feeney, 2000; Lamba, 2003; Statistics New Zealand, 2004; Wooden, 1991). Accessing and securing stable, long-term employment is also a high priority for former refugees themselves, who frequently report not being able to find jobs commensurate with their qualifications or experience (Colic-Peisker, 2009; Gans, 2009; Lamba, 2003).

Given the importance of employment to both governments and former refugees alike, it is unsurprising that much literature has focused specifically on the topic of former refugee employability and labour market success (or lack thereof). Various studies have approached the issue from the perspectives of (downward) social mobility (Gans, 2009; Koyama, 2013), translating social and cultural capital post-migration (Feeney, 2000; Krahn, Derwing, Mulder, & Wilkinson, 2009; Lamba, 2003; Lamba & Krahn, 2003; Morrice, 2007, 2009; Ricento, 2015), negotiating belonging, including identity (Colic-Peisker & Walker, 2003; Collie, Kindon, Liu, & Podsiadlowski, 2010; F. Tomlinson, 2010), the impacts of policy (Bloch, 2000), the lingering effects of trauma (Montgomery, 2010), the role of agency (Hunt, 2008), personal employability (K. Allen, 2015; Williams, 2009), and discrimination (Colic-Peisker, 2009; Colic-Peisker & Tilbury, 2007). Fewer studies have taken a sociolinguistic or discursive approach to exploring former refugee employment challenges in resettlement, though some have explored the discourse surrounding linguistic isolation and its effects (Nawyn, Gjokaj, LaFa Agbényiga, & Grace, 2012), barriers to employment (Archer, Hollingworth, Maylor, Sheibani, & Kowarzik, 2005), volunteering as an entry point to the labour market (Yap, Byrne, & Davidson, 2010), and employer discrimination (Tilbury & Colic-Peisker, 2006). While the challenges surrounding identity negotiation post-forced migration have been explored (e.g. Baran, 2018; Hatoss, 2012; Hoffman Clark, 2007; Marlowe, 2010; Oo Jin Lee & Brotman, 2011), I have found no literature focusing on former refugee employment challenges from the perspective of an identity which is negotiated and co-constructed in interaction, which is the approach that I take in this study.

Conceptualising employable identity

In order to navigate new, dynamic, and less stable labour markets in the late twentieth century, the idea of personal *employability* replaced expectations of lifelong careers characterised by linear progression within a single organisation, and traditional ideas of education as a conduit to suitable, desirable employment (Boden & Nedeva, 2010; Bridgstock, 2005, 2009; Moreau & Leathwood, 2006; Purcell &

Purcell, 1998). Though expressed in various ways, the concept of individualistic employability, based on "develop[ing] the personal and professional capacity to maximise one's employment potential" (V. Smith, 2010, p. 280), has generally been characterised by what Len Holmes (2001) calls the 'skills agenda,' wherein the extent to which an individual is considered employable rests upon the presumably observable and demonstrable work-related skills and attributes of which the individual is in possession (Boden & Nedeva, 2010; Bridgstock, 2009; Hinchliffe & Jolly, 2011; L. Holmes, 2001; Moreau & Leathwood, 2006). Recent literature, however, has begun to focus instead on the idea of employability as an interactionally achieved, co-constructed, and contextually-dependent *identity*. Discussed variously in terms of *graduate identity* (Hinchliffe & Jolly, 2011; L. Holmes, 1999, 2001, 2013), *career identity* (LaPointe, 2010), *professional identity* (J. Holmes, 2005a; J. Holmes & Marra, 2005, 2017; J. Holmes & Riddiford, 2010; Marra & Holmes, 2008; Schnurr, 2011), or simply *enhancing employability through identity work* (V. Smith, 2010), I adopt and will herein refer to an *employable identity* (cf. Reissner-Roubicek, 2017).

Problematising employability

Conceptualisation of personal employability, at least in white collar professions, was initially characterised by the idea that university education was a secure route to success in the labour market (Moreau & Leathwood, 2006). In a timely study with particular relevance to my research, Brown, Power, Tholen, and Allouch (2016) note that the supposed guarantee of convertibility of tertiary education into employment success only holds up when educational qualifications can maintain their value by virtue of scarcity. Increasing numbers of highly educated individuals from a range of social classes have led to "credential inflation" (2016, p. 192) whereby a qualification's value drops due to its ubiquity on the labour market. This in turn has led to something of a qualifications arms race in developed countries as "those aspiring to join occupational elites add professional, master's and doctoral qualifications alongside their undergraduate credentials" (2016, p. 193). A qualification arms race, particularly in a user-pays context, is a battle that the financially secure are better equipped to wage, which can only contribute to the reinforcement of existing class disparity (2016, p. 193). This is not to say that tertiary qualifications have become irrelevant in the labour market, but rather that in some cases they have become simply a prerequisite starting point to which further so-called 'soft' skills must be added to distinguish oneself (Brown et al., 2016).

Tertiary institutions have thus lent institutional support for supposedly employability-enhancing skills and attributes (Hinchliffe & Jolly, 2011; Moreau & Leathwood, 2006). A widely-cited shortcoming of the employability-as-skills/

attributes approach is the fact that what these critical skills are, and how they might manifest themselves, are neither unanimously clearly defined nor agreed upon (e.g. Hinchliffe & Jolly, 2011; L. Holmes, 1999, 2001, 2013; Moreau & Leathwood, 2006; F. Tomlinson, 2010). Key desirable skills and attributes that are often named include communication skills, adaptability, confidence, flexibility, proactivity, enthusiasm, resilience, and teamwork (Hinchliffe & Jolly, 2011; L. Holmes, 1999; Moreau & Leathwood, 2006; Reissner-Roubicek, 2017; Williams, 2009). Their value is taken to be so self-evident that both governments and universities have encouraged or attempted the embedding of these skills and attributes into teaching curricula (Hinchliffe & Jolly, 2011; L. Holmes, 2001; Moreau & Leathwood, 2006). However, the source of such lists of useful characteristics is less clear, as Len Holmes (2013, pp. 1047–1048) describes:

> In many institutional initiatives, the 'identification' of the skills or attributes... seems to involve little more sophisticated than a task group of staff... engaging in some brainstorming-type activity, producing a 'wish list' of what they desire of their graduates. That list is then distributed for 'consultation,' before making its way through a set of institutional committees for endorsement as a 'strategy' for employability... There is often some consultation with employers, mainly in terms of asking them whether they would agree that the items listed are important to them.

If this is indeed representative of the origins of so-called employability enhancing skills and attributes, they are clearly rather arbitrary. Frequently, Michael Tomlinson (2010, p. 80) notes, there has been a "descriptive labelling of these skills, whereby their meaning is simply inferred through the assumed set of attributes that characterise them." That is, the interpretation of each of these skills, while perhaps seemingly self-evident, may differ from one person to the next, and certainly between jobseekers and employers (L. Holmes, 2001, 2013; V. Smith, 2010; M. Tomlinson, 2010).

Furthermore, how these skills are to be demonstrated appears to be equally imprecise. Len Holmes (2013, p. 1047) argues that the skills agenda makes the assumption that the employability-indexing skills and attributes are observable and are "amenable to *identification* or *discovery*, thereby implying that they have some objective existence" (emphasis original). That is, this approach assumes that an attribute like *confidence* or a skill like *adaptability* can be exhibited, approved, and ticked off a list. This focus on the employment-enhancing attributes that jobseekers and workers are equipped with essentialises and frames employability as strongly individualistic (LaPointe, 2010; Moreau & Leathwood, 2006; M. Tomlinson, 2010), and "overlook[s] features of the labour market that might shape both [job seekers'] opportunities for realising their employability as well as the overall capacity for employer organisations to accommodate them" (M. Tomlinson, 2010, p. 76). It does not take into consideration the relationship between the job seeker or worker and the labour market or employer: it ignores the relational and co-constructed nature of the *performance* of employability. This is important in the context of former refugees whose social and interactional norms may differ from (and/or conflict with) the dominant social and interactional norms of their new circumstances.

Employable identity

A solution to this essential and internalised view of employability is to instead conceptualise the job seeker's relationship with the labour market from the perspective of identity construction. An employable identity approach allows us to view employability as a discursive and socially situated phenomenon, which is interactionally achieved *with* employers, interviewers, and colleagues. Identity, as discussed, discursively emerges from and gains meaning within social and cultural practices (Bucholtz & Hall, 2005; LaPointe, 2010). Thus, as Michael Tomlinson (2010, p. 80) notes, "notions of employability, skills and competence only have meaning when located within socially-constructed channels of inter-employee engagement and interaction," and employable identities must be negotiated between employers, employees, and colleagues. For all the valuable skills, attributes, and experience job seekers may 'possess,' these must be recognised as such by those employing or considering employing them. In order to attempt the performance of employability, then, a person needs to "understand how a particular practice is enacted" and have the discursive skills to do so (Hinchliffe & Jolly, 2011, p. 564; following L. Holmes, 2001).

Enacting a practice such as a job interview or a workplace meeting entails choices of positioning of self and other (Bamberg, 1997b; Lagenhove & Harré, 1999), and the acceptance or rejection of that positioning by other interlocutors, perhaps interviewers or colleagues (L. Holmes, 2001; LaPointe, 2010). The positioning of self and other, Reissner-Roubicek (2017, p. 61) suggests, "is a highly relevant struggle to construct an employable identity… whether explicitly or implicitly achieved." It is important to recognise that an employable identity, then, is not any one 'thing,' but the *doing* of contextually-appropriate identity negotiation. While most research focuses on this identity work in workplaces and job interviews, it is not only performed in these contexts, but indeed may be performed in any context where employability is salient to interlocutors. For former refugees, this salience may be heightened due to their status as newcomers and ongoing employment-related challenges. Particularly in the context of employability-focused research I would argue that for the participants, their own employable identities factor into how they narrate themselves in interaction.

Bamberg (2009, 2011b) proposed three 'dilemmas' involved with the positioning of self and other:

- the dilemma of same vs. difference (aligning with and differentiating the self from others);
- the dilemma of constancy vs. change (presenting the self as the same across time and also as having changed or developed); and, crucially,
- the dilemma of agency (presenting the self as a product of the world or as a 'producer' of the world; or as an actor vs. an undergoer) (these are explored in greater depth in Chapter 5).

In a job interview context, Reissner-Roubicek (2017, p. 63) argues, these three dilemmas underlie the struggles interviewees may encounter in their attempts to establish employable identities.

With this conceptualisation of employable identities as negotiated and co-constructed within interaction, this book aims to explore the following question:

1. How do refugee-background jobseekers and employees enact employable identities in discourse?

A discussion of my theoretical approach in the following chapter will allow me to elaborate and expand upon this research question in light of the conceptual framework that I employ in this study.

Book overview

This book comprises eleven chapters. Following this introductory chapter, I begin Chapter 2 by laying out the theoretical underpinnings of this study. Having established that I intend to approach the idea of employability from the perspective of an employable identity, I discuss the concept of identity as fluid, dynamic, and interactionally negotiated. I proceed to explore the notion of discursive agency as it pertains to the enactment of identity, followed by the discursive attempts to translate social and cultural capital (Bourdieu, 1986) from one social context to another. This discussion leads into another structural obstacle which is especially salient for former refugees negotiating belonging, which is the navigation of ideological social discourses (Gee's (2015) Capital-D Discourses) that are strongly connected to the social distribution of power, and may undermine attempts to enact competent, capable, employable identities. I then discuss the value of an Interactional Sociolinguistic approach to address this study's research questions.

In Chapter 3, the methodology chapter of this book, I first address the refugee context in which this study was undertaken. I review the roots of and ethos behind ethnography, before describing the ethnographically-informed approach I take to my research, including drawing on critical ethnographic approaches. Next, I describe my approach to research ethics, before outlining the process of recruiting participants, and gaining their informed consent. The data collection section of this chapter comprises two sections. Firstly, I discuss the type of semi-structured interviews that I undertook with this study's four main participants. Secondly, I discuss gaining access to and collecting data in the workplace of one of my participants. Finally, I describe the analysis which I have applied to this study's data, exploring identity in narrative interaction. I provide a brief example of the ways that this type of analysis can illuminate the dynamic and co-constructed negotiation of identity in interaction.

In Chapter 4 I introduce the five former refugees who participated in this study: Arwa, Isaac, Kelly, Nina, and Omar (all names in this study are pseudonyms). I also (re)introduce myself as the researcher, in order to reflexively account for my role in the production and co-construction of this study's data.

This book has five analysis chapters; Chapters 5 through 9. In these chapters I move from the wider social context which I have laid out in the previous chapters, to micro-level, Interactional Sociolinguistic analysis of employable identity navigation 'on the ground.' In three of these chapters (Chapters 5, 6, and 7), I provide analysis on interview data from Isaac, Kelly, and Omar. I then provide a case study analysis of Arwa's interview data over a twenty-month period (Chapter 8), and the final analysis chapter explores Nina's workplace data (Chapter 9).

In Chapter 5, the first of my analysis chapters, I discuss the value of exploring identity in narrative, and examine participants' self- and other-positioning in their narratives of flight. Emergent from this analysis is the ways in which former refugee storytellers are obliged to navigate sometimes disempowering wider social discourses of what it means to be a refugee. Navigating such discourses requires exercising discursive agency, which is the focus of Chapter 6, in which I explore how the participants take up, cede, reject, and assign various higher and lower agency positions to others, and to themselves, both as storytellers and as protagonists within their own storyworlds. In particular, I explore an agency 'dilemma' (Bamberg, 2011b), namely the potentially disempowering effects of social discourses of refugeehood which are in conflict with the participants' attempts to enact and negotiate employable identities in the New Zealand context. The enactment of locally-useful employable identities can be particularly challenging in new social contexts, when previous valuable networks, skills, and knowledge (Bourdieu's (1986) social and cultural capital) are devalued. In Chapter 7, I explore the participants' own understandings and discursive navigation of their social and cultural capital, and the implications not only for enactment of employable identities in the immediate interactional context, but also for imagined, future identities (Norton, 2001).

Recognising that the journey towards negotiating a locally-valuable employable identity may be a long and challenging one, in Chapter 8 I take a longitudinal, case study approach to exploring the experiences and narratives of one participant, Arwa, over almost two years. In this time, Arwa encountered numerous challenges to her sense of self as employable, and emergent from the data is a developing appreciation for the negotiated nature of employability.

These negotiations do not end once employment is secured. Thus, in the final analysis chapter, Chapter 9, I explore the negotiation of an employable identity in the workplace, drawing on the methodology and ethos of the Language in the Workplace Project (e.g. J. Holmes, 2018; J. Holmes & Marra, 2004, 2005). In this analysis, Nina can be seen to navigate the same othering social discourses that emerged out of the earlier interview data (see Coupland, 2010 for a discussion of othering), as she skilfully and dynamically negotiates a competent and professional employable identity.

In this study's discussion chapter, Chapter 10, I return to the macro-level of society and explore the wider implications of the structural barriers that these former refugees are facing in their attempts to enact locally-validated employable identities, focusing upon the two-way process of negotiating belonging. Finally, in Chapter 11, I readdress this study's research questions, and discuss the methodological, analytical, and societal implications of my research.

Summary

Having introduced the motivations and aims of this study, I now turn to explore the theoretical and conceptual approach that I take to this research in order to explore former refugees' navigation of employable identities in the New Zealand context.

CHAPTER 2

Theoretical and conceptual framework

Introduction

Exploring the enactment and negotiation of employable identities in discourse requires grounding in a theoretical framework that recognises the discursively and socially-situated nature of identity. A social constructionist approach to identity highlights the mutually-constitutive nature of the individual and the social world, with language being the privileged site of this dialectic construction. Within a given social context, certain pragmatic and social norms characterise interaction in a manner which is tacit and goes unnoticed by those 'native' to it. The ramifications for newcomers to a new social context, of course, are that the 'rules of the game' are not necessarily evident. Former refugees' adaptation to their new environments takes time and personal (discursive) agency, particularly where they attempt to take up identity positions that conflict with wider social discourses of refugeehood. Moreover, the navigation of extant and new forms of social and cultural capital (Bourdieu, 1986) further complexify possibilities to take up, assign, accept, and reject subject positions within discourse. Narrative is an ideal site within which to explore this complex identity negotiation, as it is through stories that we make sense of the world and our place within it (Bamberg, 2011a; De Fina, 2003; De Fina & Georgakopoulou, 2008; Greenbank & Marra, 2020). To examine and account for the navigation of identity at both the interactional (micro) level and the wider social context (macro) level, I follow the philosophy of Gumperz (1982, 2005) and the *interactional sociolinguistic* framework which informs situated, discourse analysis of the negotiation of meaning in face-to-face interaction. An interactional sociolinguistic approach examines identity in discourse, as it dynamically emerges.

Identity

The concept of identity has been studied across a wide range of disciplines, from psychology and philosophy to anthropology and (socio)linguistics. While some approaches have considered identity as a fixed and stable reality located within the individual, interactional conceptualisations of identity foreground identity as a multiple, fluid and dynamic sociocultural phenomenon that emerges from and is negotiated within interaction (Bamberg, Fina, & Schiffrin, 2011; Bucholtz & Hall, 2005; Darvin & Norton, 2015; De Fina, 2003). Identity can be conceived of in many ways, as de Fina (2012, p. 1) notes, as collective or individual, social or personal, cognitive or performative. Furthermore, the role of language in identity can be seen as one of "reflecting, conveying, constructing identities or as carrying out all those functions at the same time" (De Fina, 2012, p. 1). In this study I take a discursive approach to identity which is consistent with an Interactional Sociolinguistic approach, in which identity is negotiated within interaction drawing upon symbolic resources.

Systematic research involving sociolinguistic approaches to identity began with studies of language variation (e.g. Coupland, 1980; Labov, 1972), in which identity was considered a variable (alongside social context) that contributed to the ways in which speakers modified their style of speaking in different contexts (De Fina, 2012, p. 2). Later sociolinguistic research began to recognise the contribution to identity processes of all participants, not just the speaker (e.g. Coupland, Coupland, Giles, & Henwood, 1988; Giles, Coupland, & Coupland, 1991); and to focus on micro analyses of the construction of identity through discourse, and the linguistic strategies that speakers use to index different identities (Bucholtz & Hall, 2005; De Fina, 2012; De Fina, Schiffrin, & Bamberg, 2006). This century, the dominant paradigm of language and social identities encourages the exploration of how identity is negotiated in particular instances of interaction, without presupposition of what identity positions will be taken up and how (Bucholtz & Hall, 2005; De Fina, 2012, p. 3; De Fina et al., 2006; J. Holmes, Marra, & Vine, 2011).

Bucholtz and Hall (2005) provide an influential overview of post-structural, sociocultural linguistic approaches to identity in interaction. They propose five principles as fundamental to the study of identity. The first principle posits that identity is *emergent* in interaction, that is, a rejection of a traditional view of identity as located within the mind of an individual, and language's role as simply reflecting the individual's mental state (Bucholtz & Hall, 2005, p. 587). The authors note that the concept of emergence does not preclude the identity work in a given interaction drawing on 'structures' of ideology and the linguistic system that precede the interaction in question (2005, p. 588). This relates to the second principle, *positionality*. In this principle, the authors posit that speakers dynamically take up, abandon, and reject temporary interactional positions within discourse on a moment to moment basis, allowing them to orient to various and changing identity positions within discourse. *Indexicality*, the third principle, is concerned with how identity is discursively enacted, or the creation of links between discourse and social meanings (2005, p. 594). Indexicality, Bucholtz and Hall (2005, p. 594) note, "relies heavily on ideological structures, for associations between language and identity are rooted in cultural beliefs and values." Identity may be claimed overtly linguistically, but it is also frequently indexed indirectly and symbolically (De Fina, 2012, p. 3). That is, certain words, expressions, and styles of speaking come to be associated with certain ideas, attributes, and ideologies, which themselves are associated with various social groups (within a particular social context). Thus, a given linguistic feature, such as discourse marker *like*, can be employed to index adolescence or youth (De Fina, 2012, p. 3).

The fourth principle draws attention to the fact that identity is *relational*. This means that firstly, identity is not a one-sided affair. Identity positions only gain meaning in relation to alternative identity positions and other people (see discussion of co-construction, in methodology chapter to follow). Secondly, Bucholtz and Hall (2005, p. 598) introduce this principle to highlight that identities "are intersubjectively constructed through several, often overlapping, complementary relations, including similarity/difference, genuineness/artifice, and authority/delegitimacy" (cf. Bamberg's (2011a, 2011b) discussion of the sameness vs. difference 'dilemma'). The final principle, *partialness*, recognises that any representation of identity is necessarily partial, contextually-situated and ideologically constrained (2005, p. 605). This relates to social constructionism's questioning of realism and assumption that any view of the world is necessarily partial (Burr, 2003, p. 7).

Social constructionism

While Bucholtz and Hall (2005) do not explicitly position their discussion of identity within a social constructionist framework, the various modern conceptualisations of discursive identity, as De Fina (2012, p. 1) observes, "have, in one way or another, all been influenced by social constructionism." Social constructionism is an anti-essentialist, critical approach to taken-for-granted or 'common sense' knowledge (P. L. Berger & Luckmann, 1967), which challenges the notion that the true nature of the world may be revealed through observation (Burr, 2003, p. 3). Social constructionism is anti-positivist and anti-empiricist, and seeks to question existing structures and conventions and reveal the ways in which "the social and psychological worlds are made real… through social processes and interaction" (Young & Collin, 2004, p. 375). Thus, the whole idea of 'truth' loses its privileged status within research (Burr, 2003, p. 6).

Social constructionism recognises that the categories and concepts we use to make sense of the world are historically and culturally situated. Furthermore, these categories and concepts are in fact *produced* by that culture and history, and "are dependent on the particular social and economic arrangements prevailing in that culture at that time" (Burr, 2003, p. 4). From a social constructionist perspective, the individual and the social world mutually constitute one another dialectically, and the apparently objective nature of the social world "is in fact constituted through human action and interaction and is not independent of it" (De Fina, 2012, p. 1). Language is the privileged site of the construction of the individual (and reality) in social constructionism and is both "a precondition for thought and a form of social action" in itself (Young & Collin, 2004, p. 377, also Schieffelin & Ochs, 1986). Identity, then, is seen to reside not within the individual, but as a process of and within social interaction (De Fina, 2003, 2012), for language is, as Burr (2003, p. 54) asserts, "a fundamentally social phenomenon."

Research approaching identity as a dynamic social construction negotiated within discourse has been undertaken across a range of research sites, notably workplaces (e.g. J. Holmes & Marra, 2002a, 2005, 2017; J. Holmes et al., 2011; Marsden & Holmes, 2014), and in the study of heritage languages and additional-language acquisition and maintenance (e.g. Dawson, 2017; Miller & Kubota, 2013; Norton, 2000, 2001, 2013, 2017; Norton & McKinney, 2011; Norton & Toohey, 2011; Pavlenko & Lantolf, 2000; Seals, 2017). Locating identity as a social and cultural phenomenon means that a seismic change in one's social and/or cultural situation will have significant effects on processes of identity negotiation. This is reflected in a large number of studies exploring identity negotiation in cross-cultural contexts (e.g. Dawson, 2019; Duff, 2015; Giampapa, 2004; Meadows, 2009; Pavlenko & Blackledge, 2004), including (former) refugee contexts (e.g. Berg & Millbank, 2009; Ngo & Hansen, 2013; F. Tomlinson, 2010; Warriner, 2004). Migrants in a new context will inevitably experience challenges to their sense of self and to their understanding of their relationship to the world around them. Lack of knowledge of and familiarity with local norms (or cultural capital (Bourdieu, 1986); see discussion below) may give rise to 'identity struggles' (J. Holmes & Marra, 2017; Miglbauer, 2017; Reissner-Roubicek, 2017; van de Mieroop & Schnurr, 2017a). This becomes particularly salient in relation to negotiating an *employable* identity, where it may become necessary to "respond to the sometimes competing norms and expectations of the context in negotiating an identity which ultimately need[s] to be accepted and legitimised by other interlocutors" (van de Mieroop & Schnurr, 2017b, p. 1). For newcomers to a given social context, navigating such acceptance and legitimation can be a complicated endeavour.

Intersectionality

Furthermore, social constructionism emphasises that identity is not singular and unique. The dynamic and multifaceted nature of a constructed identity leads me to utilise *intersectionality* in this research, a concept which developed out of appreciation of the fact that black women's experiences and challenges had slipped through the cracks of both the Civil Rights and Feminist movements (Davis, 2008, p. 68). As a framework, it recognises that various macro facets of identity such as gender, sexual orientation, class, ethnicity, age, disability, and so forth, do not exist as standalone 'categories' and are not simply cumulative, but intersect and interact with one another in complex ways (Crenshaw, 1989; Davis, 2008; Yuval-Davis, 2006). These macro identity 'categories' are themselves socially constructed, but their effects are very real in terms of the distribution of power in society.

Intersectionality attempts to unpack how complex patterns of power impact upon the marginalised (Beck, Williams, Hope, & Park, 2001; Crenshaw, 1989; Davis, 2008; McCall, 2005; Yuval-Davis, 2006). Thus, individuals have a repertoire of "a constellation of identities often conflicting with each other… from which they draw when presenting and representing who they are" (De Fina, 2003, pp. 26–27). This concept of conflicting identities is important because meaning, as Burr (2003, p. 54) points out, is always contestable; and language is "a site of variability, disagreement and potential conflict." It is within this conflict, or struggle, that meaning is negotiated between interlocutors, and "power relations are acted out and contested" (Burr, 2003, p. 55). For former refugees, as discussed in Chapter 1, their 'constellation' of identities may be superseded by social imposition of the 'master status' of 'refugee' (Marlowe, 2010, p. 1), obscuring all of an individual's other aspects of self and potential identity positions (e.g. Oo Jin Lee & Brotman, 2011; Pittaway & Bartolomei, 2001; Vervliet, De Mol, Broekaert, & Derluyn, 2013; Yuval-Davis, 2007). Resisting this other-imposed master status requires agentive discursive work in the face of pervasive, wider social discourses of refugeehood, as discussed further below.

Identity in narrative

Narrative is recognised as an important site for the exploration of identity in discourse, because narratives are necessarily "culturally determined versions of personal experience" (De Fina, 2003, p. 217) in which narrators endeavour to create a coherent sense of self through creating and indexing discursive relationships between self and other, and past, present and future, both in the narrative world and the interactive context in which the narrative unfolds (Bamberg, De Fina, & Schiffrin, 2007; De Fina, 2003; LaPointe, 2010). Bamberg et al. (2007, p. 5) describe the importance of narrative to identity construction:

> Narrative functions as the glue that enables human life to transcend the natural incoherence and discontinuity of the unruly everyday… by imposing a point of origin and an orientation towards closure, and thereby structuring the otherwise meaningless into a meaningful life.

Thus, the orientation and indexicality employed in narrative allows narrators to construct "a (more or less) coherent sense of self" (Bamberg et al., 2007, p. 5), and gives analysts rich ground for exploring the moment by moment enactment of socially-constructed identity. Furthermore, a narrative approach is one way to combine the micro and macro levels of social constructionism. Macro approaches (e.g. poststructuralist, Foucauldian and critical analyses), while taking the productive potential of language into account, focus on wider social and institutional structures and the role they play in constituting or impacting upon identity construction (Burr, 2003, p. 22; LaPointe, 2010, p. 2). Thus, attention is placed on power dynamics, and macro social constructionists often explore – and challenge – issues of social inequality.

In the context of research involving former refugees navigating their employable identity, incorporation of the macro becomes particularly salient. The local context of the interactions in this study involve the sociocultural backgrounds of both myself and the participants, located within the wider New Zealand sociocultural setting (and the dynamic power differentials that this situation may entail). Furthermore, social structures impact upon different groups and individuals differently, as well as on their ability to agentively take up or refuse certain identity positions within discourse. For former refugees, as marginalised newcomers to the sociocultural context, these constraints may be more pronounced.

Complementing macro approaches, micro social constructionist approaches to identity locate social construction in everyday discourse and examine in close detail the enactment or performance of identity in interactional instances and contexts (Burr, 2003, p. 22; LaPointe, 2010, p. 2). The two 'versions' of social constructionist approaches to identity are of course not mutually exclusive, and many have argued for working with a combination of the two, in order to account for both the local context of interaction as well as the institutional and social structures within which they are occurring (Burr, 2003, p. 22; citing Wetherell, 1998). I will explore the productive marriage of micro identity analysis and narrative data in greater detail in Chapter 4.

Agency (and structure)

The enactment of identity, as discussed, does not occur in a (social, historical, cultural) vacuum. As succinctly laid out by Cameron (2009, p. 15), social identity construction "takes place within parameters which those engaged in it did not set, and to which in most cases they offer no radical challenge. To make sense of what they are doing… we also have to consider the inherited structures… which both enable and constrain their performance." Burr (2003, p. 7) observes that "we are born into a world where the conceptual frameworks and categories used by people in our culture already exist," and thus our interactions are socially, historically, and culturally situated. The social world is characterised by unequal relations of institutionalised and dynamic power. When we act or exercise agency within the social world we do not do so independent of social structures which impact upon the discursive positions we can or are willing to take up – or those which our interlocutors are willing to ratify.

Agency and structure are interdependent concepts which have been the focus of much academic discussion and theory. As provisionally defined by Ahearn (2001, p. 112), agency is the "socioculturally mediated capacity to act," though as she notes herself, this definition is 'skeletal' and requires further elaboration (2001, p. 109). Discussions of agency often draw upon Foucault's (1977, 1978) definition of power, which has been argued to preclude human agency (Ahearn, 2001; C. Barker, 2008; Giddens, 1984). Foucault's conceptualisation of subjects as "the 'effect[s]' of historically specific discourses and disciplinary practices" (C. Barker, 2008, p. 234) seems to deny subjects the agency necessary for political action or to bring about social change. While he does bring the concept of resistance into his discussion of power, he states that this resistance "is never in a position of exteriority in relation to power" (Foucault, 1978, p. 95, cited in Ahearn, 2001, p. 116), and does not explain the processes that might be involved in resistance, or the 'mechanisms' that would allow speaking subjects to adopt certain discourses or positions and thus employ agency (Ahearn, 2001; C. Barker, 2008).

Post-structuralist sociologist Anthony Giddens's (1984) structuration theory, perhaps the most influential approach to the relationship between structure and agency, focuses on the way that agents, through their actions, both produce and reproduce existing social structures, and positions subjects as "active and knowledgeable agents" (C. Barker, 2008, p. 232). Social order is constructed through the activities and language of social actors who, while skilful and knowledgeable, are both constituted by and themselves reproduce social structures that may unequally allocate resources and competencies between those social actors (C. Barker, 2008, p. 233; Giddens, 1984; Sewell, 1992). This idea, which Giddens (1981, 1984) calls 'the duality of structure' is central to his structuration theory: structures are both "the medium and the outcome of the practices which constitute social systems" (Giddens, 1981, p. 27). In this view, as Sewell (1992, p. 4) notes, "human agency and structure, far from being opposed, in fact *presuppose* each other" (emphasis in the original). Giddens's theory maintains that "people's actions are shaped (in both constraining and enabling ways) by the very social structures that those actions then serve to reinforce or configure" (Ahearn, 2001, p. 117; C. Barker, 2008; Giddens, 1981, 1984). He argues that, as agents, we are aware of societal institutions and understand that our actions have consequences and are constantly making choices with that knowledge. However, these choices are not made a propos of nothing, but within "the boundaries of an evolving structural context" (Lamba, 2003, p. 48). Within this framework, Chris Barker (2008, p. 233) observes, "identities are understood to be a question both of agency (the individual constructs a project) and of social determination (our projects are socially constructed and social identities ascribed to us)."

Furthermore, when exploring agency in this study's data, it is worth noting Ortner's (2006) proposition that there are two, interconnected types of agency. The first, the 'agency of (unequal) power,' involves oppression and/or resistance to oppression, and is "therefore to a large degree defined by the terms of the dominant group" (Ahearn, 2010, p. 36). The second type of agency, the 'agency of projects,' relates to "(relatively ordinary) life socially organized in terms of culturally-constituted projects that infuse life with meaning and purpose" (Ortner, 2006, p. 147; cited in Ahearn, 2010, p. 36). These two 'types' of agency will become salient in the conversational data of my former refugee participants, as they attempt to navigate the "culturally-constituted project" (Ahearn, 2010, p. 36) of a locally-useful employable identity, situated within the power differentials of social structures such as disempowering social discourses.

Turning to the question of agency within discourse, it could be claimed that the very act of speaking is agentive; that "by speaking we establish a reality that has at least the potential for affecting whoever happens to be listening to us, regardless of the originally intended audience" (Duranti, 2004, p. 451). However, this is not particularly helpful for unpacking agency from a discursive sociolinguistic perspective. The extent to which autonomy and intentionality affect action is not so much the focus of this study as the idea that agency can be viewed as "the accomplishment of social action" (Bucholtz & Hall, 2005, p. 606). This conceptualisation, Bucholtz and Hall (2005, p. 606) note, "is vital to any discipline that wants to consider the full complexity of social subjects alongside the larger power structures that constrain them." A dialogic approach to agency, drawing on Bakhtinian notions of answerability in interaction (Bakhtin, 1984, 1990), dismisses the idea of a structure which is *reflected* in action, and takes up instead the idea of structure collaboratively emerging out of situated action (Ahearn, 2001, p. 128; Al Zidjaly, 2009). Agency, like meaning and identity positions, is co-constructed in interaction (Ahearn, 2001; Vitanova, 2005).

From this perspective, agency can be seen to be located in the dynamic taking up, assigning, ceding, and rejecting of discursive positions and (dis)alignments, situated within social structures which both impact upon and are reinforced (or challenged) through language use (Ahearn, 2001; Al Zidjaly, 2009; C. Barker, 2008; LaPointe, 2010). Social actors, then are "neither free agents nor completely socially determined products" (Ahearn, 2001, p. 120) but perhaps could be thought of as "loosely structured" (Ortner, 1989, p. 198, cited in Ahearn, 2001, p. 120). Agency can be seen in the emergent identities that arise "as a result of interaction and negotiation vis-à-vis the available positions and the particularities of a given time and place" (LaPointe, 2010, p. 3). Thus, agency here does not mean that agentive action need be intentional, as "habitual actions accomplished below the level of conscious awareness act upon the world no less than those carried out deliberately" (Bucholtz & Hall, 2005, p. 606). As suggested in Giddens's (1984) structuration theory, all interaction is both constrained by ideological power relations and wider social discourses, and is the means through which these social structures come into existence (Bucholtz & Hall, 2005, p. 607).

Social and cultural capital

Discursive agency becomes particularly important in cross-cultural contexts where 'the rules of the game' are not necessarily transparent. Lack of familiarity with local norms, practices, systems, and social structures can be a challenge to any migrant in a new sociocultural context, not least of all forced migrants (Lamba, 2003; Piller, 2016). Structural obstacles which emerge as particularly relevant in my research context include the 'translation' of a lifetime's cumulative cultural knowledge to a new context, the recognition of extant qualifications and experience, and the creation and maintenance of useful social networks. These are components of Bourdieu's (1977a, 1977c, 1986) *cultural* and *social capital.*

Using an economic metaphor in an attempt to explain seemingly inherited social positions, Bourdieu theorised that cultural and social capital impact upon the enactment of contextually-legitimate identities, and function as a form of social structure. Bourdieu's work focuses in large part upon social power dynamics, including attempts to reconcile structure and agency, and (following earlier theorists including Marx, Weber, and Durkheim) developing frameworks for understanding the often-hidden mechanisms of social order and power distribution. In particular, his interest is in capital's role in the reproduction of society and the subtle ways that powerful groups maintain their social positions across generations (Bourdieu, 1977a, 1986; Brown et al., 2016). An individual's relationship to the world is shaped by their (variously valuable) social and cultural capital, including their imagined future identities (Norton, 2001; Norton & Toohey, 2011). Furthermore, the discursive *indexing* of capital – i.e. referring or pointing to one's (or others') capital directly or indirectly – allows individuals to take up positions relative to that capital and thus make various identity claims. These claims must then be taken up and ratified by interlocutors for that capital to be situationally valuable (Darvin & Norton, 2015; Seals, 2010).

Cultural capital, put very simply, is valuable knowledge of and expertise in culturally-specific practices associated with power (Bourdieu, 1986; Meadows, 2009). It can exist in three forms:

1. The *embodied* form; dispositions and competencies which are inside, or a part of, the bearer. This form of cultural capital assumes a personal investment of time by the holder into learning and acquisition. Thus, as its name suggests, embodied cultural capital cannot be separated from its bearer nor bestowed upon another (Bourdieu, 1986, p. 85). Due to its embodied nature and the fact that "the social conditions of its transmission and acquisition are more disguised than those of economic capital" (Bourdieu, 1986, p. 86), embodied cultural capital is likely to be perceived as legitimate competence or natural talent (Bourdieu, 1986; Weininger & Lareau, 2007). This might include long-lasting dispositions, a particular accent or linguistic proficiency, skills and experience, taste, or values.
2. The *institutional* form; credentials of competencies or skills imbued upon an individual by an external (institutional) body. This is one way that embodied cultural capital can escape the "biological limits [of] its bearer;" through gaining (theoretically) objective value in the form of academic qualifications (Bourdieu, 1986, p. 88). By virtue of having been institutionalised, this capital now bestows upon its bearers a roughly equivalent and "legally guaranteed value with respect to culture" (1986, p. 88). In theory, institutionalised cultural capital allows the establishment of "conversion rates between cultural capital and economic capital by guaranteeing the monetary value of a given academic capital" (1986, p. 88). For example, the (ostensive) worth of academic degrees in the labour market.
3. The *objectified* form; actual goods or objects which represent or stand in for embodied capital. Examples of objectified cultural capital might include art works, musical instruments, or books. I will not be exploring objectified cultural capital in this study, as it is scarcely readily employed via discourse (except via deixis).

Bourdieu first conceived cultural capital as a way to explain disparities in scholastic achievement between children from different social classes (Bourdieu, 1986; Bourdieu & Passeron, 1979). He believed that previous explanations of economic inequality were insufficient to account for these disparities in the "specific profits which children from the different classes… can obtain in the academic market" (Bourdieu, 1986, p. 84). The transmission of cultural habits and dispositions in the home is vital to scholastic success, and Bourdieu (1986, p. 85) describes this as "the best hidden and socially most determinant educational investment." Thus, according to Bourdieu, the way that, at a given time, the different types of capital are distributed "represents the immanent structure of the social world" (Bourdieu, 1986, p. 83), that is, the aggregate of opportunities and constraints which determine the functioning of that social world and determine its inhabitants' chances of success.

Social capital is the sum of all potential resources an individual may be able to access by virtue of their group memberships, and relationships in social networks (Bourdieu, 1986, p. 88). The idea that group memberships grant positive outcomes to individuals and communities was not an entirely novel idea to sociologists, but Bourdieu refined the idea by focusing on the benefits gained through participation in groups, and "the deliberate construction of sociability for the purpose of creating this resource" (Portes, 1998, p. 3). This type of capital comprises both the social relationships that provide access to the resources held by others, and the nature of those resources (i.e. amount, and quality) (Portes, 1998, pp. 3–4). Social capital functions as a source of both immediate support, and of benefits via wider networks (Bourdieu, 1986; Portes, 1998). Like cultural capital, social capital assumes an investment of time (at individual or collective, and conscious or unconscious levels) in the establishment and reproduction of social relationships that are "directly usable in the short or long term" (Bourdieu, 1986, p. 52).

Developing the notion of capital, its accumulation, and its effects allowed for explanation of the out-of-site reproduction of power structures and the social world. When any form of capital is attributed to legitimate competence, or as a legitimate basis of power, it becomes what Bourdieu calls *symbolic* capital (Bourdieu, 1986; Meadows, 2009). That is, the capital's socially-constructed origins are hidden. When the powerful impose ideologies upon the less powerful, particularly ideologies that reinforce and legitimate existing structures of inequality, this is Bourdieu's *symbolic violence* (Bourdieu & Wacquant, 1992; Connolly & Healy, 2004; Lawler, 2009; Swartz, 1997). This symbolic violence contributes to the maintenance of social class inequality, and describes the ways in which the dominated can play a role in reproducing (and internalising) the conditions of their own domination (Bourdieu, 1991; Connolly & Healy, 2004; Swartz, 1997).

Similar to the concept of hegemony (Blommaert & Bulcaen, 2000; Gramsci, 1971; Paltridge, 2012; van Dijk, 1993; Wodak, 2011), symbolic violence is, as explained by Connolly and Healy (2004, p. 15), "an act of *violence* precisely because it leads to the constraint and subordination of individuals, but it is also *symbolic* in the sense that this is achieved indirectly and without overt and explicit acts of force or coercion" (emphasis original). Thus, symbolic violence plays an important role in maintaining the status quo, which may have significant impact upon the experiences of the vulnerable or disenfranchised when attempting to ameliorate their personal circumstances. Furthermore, the 'rules of the game' vary and evolve across different social and physical contexts), and "the value of one's capital also shifts as it travels across time and space" (Darvin & Norton, 2015, p. 44).

Bourdieu conceptualises this context-specificity as a *field*; a setting defined by contextually-specific rules and occupied by agents who possess varying amounts and types of capital (Bourdieu, 1991; Hesmondhalgh, 2006; Hilgers & Mangez, 2014). Or, as described by Thompson (1991, p. 14), a "structured space of positions in which the positions and their interrelations are determined by the distribution of different kinds of [capital]." Movement from one field to another may render a particular type of capital more or less valuable, depending upon the new field's 'rules' and that type of capital's ubiquity in the field. Thus, an individual's investment of time into any type of capital may be effectively confiscated at the border of a new country. For former refugees, the circumstances of their migration may mean that not only do they need to navigate a new and unfamiliar sociocultural context, but that they must do so with little of the pre-migration planning and research that voluntary migrants are able to undertake. Their embodied capital may lose its value in the host society, their institutional capital may be unrecognised or devalued, and their social capital may be non-existent and difficult to recreate (Colic-Peisker & Walker, 2003; Lamba, 2003; Ricento, 2015).

(Capital-D) Discourses

The ways in which newcomers must renegotiate their senses of self within the social structure of the new field (Bourdieu, 1991) are not only shaped by the discursive navigation of both existing and new forms of capital (Bourdieu, 1986), but also by wider social discourses regarding their roles in this new field. It is important to examine the relationships between the immediate identity work being undertaken in a given context, and relationships to wider social ideologies and values, as these are "mediated through wider discursive and social practices that may not necessarily be apparent in individual interactions, or signalled by speakers' orientation towards them" (De Fina, 2003, p. 28). In interaction with present interlocutors, De Fina (2003, p. 30) notes, speakers concurrently address "discourses that are not necessarily uttered in their presence, but that are being socially circulated." Gee (2015) observes that "we do not invent our language, we inherit it from others." That is, our language is imbued with contextually-dependent indexical meaning and connotation before we even open our mouths, and we are able to understand one another because we share background knowledge and norms for language use and interpretation (see discussion of Interaction Sociolinguistics later in this chapter). These socially-circulated discourses are made up of the ways in which we talk and write (etc.) about the world, and they encompass power relations which have implications for the ways people and groups are treated (Burr, 2003, p. 18 citing Foucault, e.g. 1978). This brings me to a distinction which I adopt in this study, between *discourse* (with a lower-case d), and *Discourse* (with a capital D), a distinction coined by James Paul Gee (1990).

Everyday language use – conversations, arguments, stories, or "connected stretches of language that make sense" – are what Gee (1990, 2015) refers to as 'little-d' discourse. The data excerpts from interviews and workplace recordings in the chapters to come are examples of discourse. 'Capital-D' Discourse refers to, in Gee's (1990, p. 142) words, "ways of being in the world." That is, a Discourse is

> a socially accepted association among ways of using language, of thinking, feeling, believing, valuing, and of acting that can be used to identify oneself as a member of a socially meaningful group or 'social network,' or to signal (that one is playing) a socially meaningful 'role.' (Gee, 1990, p. 143)

Capital-D Discourses are made up of not only little-d discourse, but also behaviour, values, customary practice, social identities, gesture, body language, and dress (Gee, 1990, 2015; Hart, 2014). They are "pre-existent sociocultural forms of interpretation" (Bamberg, 2005, p. 287), or as Gee (1990, p. 142) describes them, as "a sort of 'identity kit'" which provides 'instructions' on how to talk and behave so as to fill – and be recognised by others as filling – a particular social role. That is, they are a way of demonstrating socially-recognised membership in a given group or network, or to illustrate that through the demonstration, one is performing a 'socially significant identity' (Gee, 1990, 2015).

Because the interpretation of Discourses is widely shared in a society, they function as "resources which can be used in interaction for identity performances" (Kiesling, 2006, p. 265). Thus, there exist many varied and overlapping Discourses, which, to name but a few examples, include the Discourse of Feminism, the Discourse of Medicine, the Discourse of The Working Class, the Discourse of Theatre, the Discourse of enacting being female or male or a student or a New Zealander, and so forth. They are conventional, often entrenched, ways of interacting, thinking about, and representing the world and its inhabitants, which speaking subjects engage with, are influenced by, and reproduce (Hart, 2014; Lin, 2014; Oliphant, 2014).

Discourses are ideological by their very nature, and bound up with the social distribution of power (Gee, 1990, p. 144). That is, a given Discourse involves "a set of values and viewpoints about the relationships between people" (Gee, 1990, p. 144), and stances on other, potentially opposing Discourses. The values and available subject positions within a Discourse can in some ways be determined by what they are not, i.e., in opposition to the values and available subject positions of alternate Discourses. Gee (1990, p. 145) suggests that we could consider that "it is not individuals who speak and act, but rather that historically and socially defined Discourses speak to each other through individuals." However, while this statement recognises the sociohistorical contexts from which Discourses emerge and are situated, as well as their potential structural constraints upon discourse, speakers do of course have the agency to align with or distance themselves from a given – or a range of – Discourse(s).

Discourses surrounding refugeehood

In this study, two interrelated Discourses in particular become very salient: Discourses of *Refugeehood*, and Discourses of (refugee) *Gratitude* (other Discourses also become relevant in the data (as discussed in following analysis chapters), but it is these two that are most striking in the data and which I will unpack here). Discourses of Refugeehood, of what it means to be a 'refugee,' are likely to take divergent (but overlapping) forms depending upon the geographical, historical, and social context. In New Zealand, as evidenced through prevalent media discourse (e.g. Greenbank, 2014), while such Discourses include elements of threat and criminality, these are less prominent that those that are found in, for example, the United Kingdom and Australia (Baker et al., 2008; Gabrielatos & Baker, 2008; Leudar, Hayes, Nekvapil, & Turner Baker, 2008; Salahshour, 2016, 2017). More common are media discourses that characterise former refugees as vulnerable, needy, and suffering from trauma (Greenbank, 2014) (other Discourses of Refugeehood that are associated with criminality and threat are present in New Zealand (see Greenbank, 2014; Sulaiman-Hill, Thompson, Afsar, & Hodliffe, 2011), but did not become salient in this study's data). This victim-like positioning has been reinforced by debates surrounding rights to claim asylum in various places. This is predicated on the idea of 'bogus' and 'genuine' refugees (where 'bogus' refugees are assumed to be voluntary, economic migrants taking advantage of asylum-claiming rights), resulting in refugee rights advocates placing greater emphasis upon victimhood to justify refugeehood and thus state protection (Korac, 2009, p. 7). While this kind of representation can draw attention to refugees' plight and foster empathy, even if well-intentioned, it can also suggest that refugees are incapable of helping themselves (Marlowe, 2010; Pupavac, 2008), and contribute to the reproduction of social inequality (Araeen, 2000).

Tied up with these ideas of refugeehood is the expectation that former refugees be grateful for the opportunity or safety that the host country has afforded them though resettlement (Colic-Peisker, 2009; Moulin, 2012; Nayeri, 2017; Nguyen, 2013; Rescher, 1992), resulting in Discourses of Gratitude. Indeed, this gratitude (or at least the expressions thereof) may, for some, be an unspoken condition of tolerance of their country's resettlement programme. These assumptions around asylum-as-a-gift and of refugee-gratitude are commonly normative in refugee-receiving nations. These Discourses thus contribute to the social structure (Giddens, 1984) within which speakers must make choices about how to position themselves (and others). Evidence for these Discourse of Gratitude can be seen in newspaper headlines in New Zealand such as *Grateful refugee turned scholar* (The Nelson Mail, 2015), *Settlers grateful for safer lives and careers in New Zealand* (NZ Herald, 2015), *Families grateful for peaceful new lives* (Horrell, 2009), and *Extra intake of Syrians grateful for NZ asylum* (Collins, 2016). Thus, whether or not they feel grateful for their situations in the host society (and I would argue that most former refugees do), people of refugee background may feel obliged to orient to these Discourses of Gratitude; to *express* gratitude in their discourses, particularly when explicitly discussing refugeehood.

Implicit in the idea of gratitude is an expectation of some kind of 'return' on the gift of asylum, the idea that former refugees 'give something back' to the nation that received them, or at least prove that the decision to accept them was 'worth it' by excelling in some noteworthy manner. Dina Nayeri, an Iranian-American former refugee who has written on expectations of refugee gratitude, addresses this 'debt' as follows:

> ... isn't glorifying the refugees who thrive according to western standards just another way to endorse this same gratitude politics? Isn't it akin to holding up the most acquiescent as examples of what a refugee should be, instead of offering each person the same options that are granted to the native-born citizen? Is the life of happy mediocrity a privilege reserved for those who never stray from home? (Nayeri, 2017)

The Discourses within which *others* might position us are not necessarily the same Discourses we would align with, which may contribute to identity struggles in discourse. Instead of aligning with the available culturally dominant or expected identity positions, individuals may agentively construct 'dissident' identities (relative to dominant norms or expectations (van de Mieroop & Schnurr, 2017a, p. 451)). They may draw on other, unexpected Discourses or create "counter narratives" (Bamberg, 2004a) which, if repeated or reconstructed enough, may give rise to new Discourses (De Fina et al., 2006, p. 7; van de Mieroop & Schnurr, 2017a, p. 451). This resistance to social Discourses (as well as the agentive discursive alignment with preferable Discourses) comes into play in my participants' narratives and in their (attempted) enactment of locally-valuable employable identities in the analysis chapters to follow. It is particularly visible in the ways in which they frequently orient away from Discourses of Refugeehood as they construct themselves as competent, qualified, and employable in the interview, workplace, and wider New Zealand context. To explore such careful and dynamic navigation of interaction, particularly in a cross-cultural research context, requires an approach to analysis which allows access to and examination of both micro level discursive features and macro level social contexts. Interactional Sociolinguistics is well suited to this task.

Interactional Sociolinguistics

The socioculturally situated actions and language use of social actors both create and recreate social structure, and reproduce the hierarchies of power already in place in that society (C. Barker, 2008; Giddens, 1984). The socially-constituted nature of structure does not preclude the very real constraints it may have on the discursive self- and other-positioning available to social actors in a given context. To understand the ways in which social structure impacts upon the refugee-background participants in this study requires recognition of their own emic understandings of their positions within society. Etic and emic are two complementary perspectives on the same situation, and correspondingly, two manners of description thereof (Franklin, 2009, p. 1). An emic perspective represents the internal meanings of a given cultural setting or individual, and describes thoughts and actions which correspond to the participants' self-understanding (Morris, Leung, Ames, & Lickel, 1999; Olive, 2014). An etic perspective, on the other hand, is that of the researcher or outsider. Incorporating both these perspectives and taking account of the fact that the social structures within which we navigate our identities are not static or fixed but contextually dependent and vary from one (speech) community to the next, my research requires a framework that allows for the exploration of emergent identity at both micro and macro levels.

Interactional Sociolinguistics (IS), most commonly associated with the work of Gumperz (1982, 2005), is a methodological and theoretical approach to the discourse analysis of face-to-face interaction that explores how meaning is created in everyday communication. Central concerns of IS's development include the formation of a theory that puts language at the heart of social and cultural processes and that includes methodology and concepts suitable for its description. Gumperz (2005) developed IS as a method of qualitative analysis "that account[s] for our ability to interpret what participants intend to convey in everyday communicative practice" (2005, p. 309). It is an approach which seeks to locate discourse in its wider sociocultural context (J. Holmes et al., 2011). It involves fine-grained, situated analysis that draws upon analysts' first-hand knowledge of community norms and the sociocultural context to account for intended and interpreted meanings (including mismatches) of participants in a given speech event (J. Holmes et al., 2011).

Cross-cultural contexts

As Gumperz (2005, p. 218) notes, diversity is a central theme to IS, due to ever more linguistically and culturally diverse modern environments. Gumperz and other researchers in IS (e.g. J. Holmes, 2005b; J. Holmes et al., 2011; J. Holmes & Schnurr, 2017; Marra, 2012; Winn, 2005) have traditionally focused much of their research in cross-cultural research contexts, where meaning-making processes and expectations are not necessarily shared, and where this can lead to misinterpretations and miscommunication that highlight those unshared elements (Gumperz, 1982, 2005; Tannen, 1992, 2005). Interactional analysis in this context aims to uncover how interlocutors use language to achieve communicative goals through examination of the processes of meaning-making and the underlying assumptions that speakers make (Gumperz, 2005, p. 218). The utility and importance of studying cross-cultural contexts is described by Tannen (1985, p. 203): "... the fate of all people, indeed the fate of the earth, depends upon negotiations among representatives of governments with different cultural assumptions and ways of communicating." However, as she goes on to elucidate, a cross-cultural context may refer not only to interactions involving speakers from different countries or linguistic backgrounds, but also perhaps to compatriots from different classes, regions, age groups, or even genders (Tannen, 1985, p. 203).

When communication 'goes well,' the systems underlying that communication go unnoticed. It is only when misunderstandings occur that the taken-for-granted processes become visible (Gumperz, 1982; Tannen, 1985, p. 203, 1992). IS is underpinned by the theoretical foundation that expectations and conventions of communicating meaning are culturally-dependent, and generally below the level of conscious attention. Interaction involves continuous negotiation of inferring others' intentions and monitoring the reception of one's own contributions (Gumperz, 2005, p. 218). Despite shared grammatical and lexical knowledge, interpretive norms and ideas about language use are culturally bound, and what is communicated may be understood so differently by different interlocutors that there is a significant gap between the intended and received messages (Schiffrin, 1996a, p. 307).

Within an IS framework, then, traditional ideas of what 'context' means are revised (Rampton, 2017, p. 3). Rather than referring to a static and external position, context in IS refers to situated interpretation of meaning, implied and inferred though entities and ideas that are indexed but not explicitly articulated (Rampton, 2017, p. 3; Schiffrin, 1996a, p. 215). Frequently, Gumperz (2005, p. 313) notes, interactants' ideas about what is relevant and what that means in the particular encounter emerge out of and during the interaction itself. Thus, IS sees context as a situated, dynamic, interactionally achieved and (re)negotiated understanding (Gumperz, 2005; Rampton, 2017; Schiffrin, 1996a).

Roots of interactional sociolinguistics

IS has its roots in several disciplines, including ethnography, linguistics, pragmatics, sociology, and anthropology (Gumperz, 1982, 2005; Rampton, 2017; Schiffrin, 1996a). Gumperz's thinking was deeply influenced by Hymes's (1964) Ethnography of Communication approach to discourse analysis (initially called the Ethnography of Speaking (Hymes, 1962), later changed to incorporate non-verbal communicative elements), which draws on ethnographic methodology and explores language use within the context of a particular speech community. Hymes's most important insight, Gumperz (2005, p. 309) claims, was to concentrate on situations of speaking (speech events) rather than seeing talk as a direct reflection of a community's beliefs and values.

Gumperz also drew on the work of Goffman (1967, 1981, 1989), whose theory of face-to-face interaction contributes understanding to the situated nature of language in the various contexts of social life (Goffman, 1981; Schiffrin, 1996a, p. 307). Goffman took a microlevel analysis to exploration of the interrelation of self and society, with everyday interactions and activities as his primary research site (Schiffrin, 1996a, p. 308). Gumperz incorporates Goffman's (1967, 1974) notions of *face* and *framing* into an IS framework for the negotiation of meaning in interaction. *Face*, or the "positive social value a person effectively claims for [themselves] by the lines others assume [they have] taken during a particular contact" (Goffman, 1967, p. 7) is a way of considering the socially-constructed nature of the self. That is, the idea that one's 'face' is not an internally-located phenomenon but something which is located, and becomes meaningful, within encounters (Schiffrin, 1996a, p. 309; Goffman, 1967) (cf. the social construction of identity in interaction). Goffman's (1974) *framing* serves to connect the immediate social context to wider values and ways of understanding; to make the interaction in question "... intelligible in terms of prior experience" (Gumperz, 2005, p. 311). That is, framing is the process of discursively translating wider social values and ideologies to be applicable to the current conversational context (Gumperz, 2005, p. 311; Goffman, 1974). This, Gumperz (2005, p. 311) believes, is integral to a theoretical and methodological move away from the idea that community or social beliefs and ideologies are *revealed* in interaction, rather than being *enacted* in interaction (cf. my earlier discussion of identity).

Contextualisation cues and conversational inference

Drawing on the work of these scholars, Gumperz developed his own interactional sociolinguistic theory of communication. He explored how the way an utterance is said allows for situated inference (Gumperz, 1982, 2005; Schiffrin, 1996a), or the ways in which meaning is negotiated and understood in interactional context. How we contextualise language and make inferences is socially and culturally shaped, or as Gumperz (1982, p. 12) says, "what we perceive and retain in our mind is a function of our culturally determined predisposition to perceive and assimilate." Gumperz developed the key concepts of *conversational inference* and *contextualisation cues* in his approach to communication.

Conversational inference refers to the interpretive work interactants undertake in a given communicative situation, matching the conversational content to their background knowledge and the conversational context, in order to determine what meaning the speaker intends to convey, as well as planning appropriate responses, and managing their expectations of what is next to come (Gumperz, 2005, p. 219; Rampton, 2017, p. 3). Rampton (2017, p. 3) notes that the concept of *contextualisation cues* is a complementary one. Gumperz used the concept to refer to both verbal and nonverbal language and behaviour that a speaker uses concurrently with surface level communication (i.e. grammar and lexical content) to create the situated context, or background information, that allows for situated inference of the speaker's intended message (Gumperz, 2005; Rampton, 2017; Schiffrin, 1996a; Tannen, 1992). Contextualisation cues may include code-switching, pronunciation, prosody, and tempo among others, and may invoke such contextual shifts as level of formality, presence of additional potential listeners, levity (or otherwise) of the remarks, shift of intention and so forth (Gumperz, 2005, p. 221; Rampton, 2017, p. 3; Schiffrin, 1996a, p. 318; Tannen, 1985, p. 204).

Thus, speakers use contextualisation cues to display "different aspects of self and other" (Schiffrin, 1996a, p. 318) in order to indicate "not only what they mean to say, but also what speech activity they are engaged in" (Tannen, 1992, p. 10). As noted earlier, these signalling mechanisms, largely culturally specific, are generally tacit, and rarely consciously noted (Rampton, 2017, p. 3; Schiffrin, 1996a, p. 314). Because of this, even a small divergence in behaviour on the part of a speaker from what a listener is expecting can cause confusion about the speaker's meaning or intention (Rampton, 2017, p. 3; Tannen, 1992, p. 11). The ramifications for negotiating employable identities in an unfamiliar context are clear. Attempts to take up various identity positions – or recognise others' attempts to do so – may be thwarted by miscommunication and orientation toward discursive strategies that are not easily transferable between cultural contexts. The ways in which Gumperz's

(1981, 1982, 2005) framework for analysis of interaction brings together the macro level elements of (situated) context, and the micro level elements of discourse make it well suited for the examination of employable identity negotiation in narrative.

Doing interactional sociolinguistics

Gumperz's (1982, 2005) discussion of the application of IS combines his concepts of contextualisation cues and conversational inference with a range of earlier research resources. These include linguistics and discourse analysis (the linguistic resources participants have at their disposal and what this affords them), Goffmanian and conversational analysis (description of the sequential construction and roles of conversational elements) and ethnography (Rampton, 2017). IS research generally takes an ethnographic approach, using the researcher's detailed knowledge of the sociocultural context in which interactional data was collected, alongside micro-level discourse analysis to explore the moment-by-moment negotiation of meaning in interaction (J. Holmes et al., 2011a, p. 21).

Typically, IS methodology firstly involves a period of ethnographic research to gather insight into local communicative practice, identify appropriate types of data for collection and analysis, and observe and interview key participants (Gumperz, 2005, p. 223). Audio or video data is collected and transcribed with high detail, including such communicatively significant details as verbal and nonverbal cues, prosody, pauses, tone, volume and so forth (Gumperz, 2005, p. 223; Rampton, 2017, p. 1; Tannen, 1992, p. 9). Combined with participant observation and post-hoc commentary and reflections from those involved, this data is analysed to glean insight into interactionally-achieved meaning, situated understanding, and communicative contexts.

Analysis focuses on communicative strategies: the conversational inferences and contextualisation cues. The communication is approached as a reflexive encounter, in that "everything said can be seen as either directly reacting to preceding talk, reflecting a set of immediate circumstances, or responding to past events" (Gumperz, 2005, p. 221). As such, often an utterance's response can be more revealing than the utterance itself, in how the response may indicate the utterance's inferred meaning and interactional importance (Schiffrin, 1996a, p. 322). Further discussion of ethnographic approaches is provided in the next chapter.

Summary

Using an IS framework to explore employable identities in interaction allows for the examination of the relationship between micro level discursive processes and the wider social processes and structures that both shape and are shaped by them. The rich analysis offered by this type of approach is well suited to unpacking this study's overarching research question – *How do refugee-background jobseekers and employees enact employability in discourse?* – into more detailed questions that explore emic understandings and micro level identity negotiation. The attention to emic perspectives that IS offers provides insights into the participants' own conceptualisations of what it means to be employable in the New Zealand labour market and workforce. Exploring this at a micro level reveals the minutiae of how employability is actually being enacted in both interview and workplace interactions. Furthermore, the analysis of this identity work in interviews over a substantive data collection period affords examination of participants' dynamic and developing employable identity negotiation, within the constraints of various and dynamic social structures. Thus, the refined research questions of this study are:

1. How do refugee-background jobseekers and employees enact employable identities in discourse?
    a. How do this study's participants make use of narrative to position themselves in the New Zealand context?
    b. What do this study's participants understand to be important to employability, and how is this relevant to the ways that they attempt to negotiate employable identities in discourse?
2. How does a participant's navigation of an employable identity develop over time?
3. How does a participant negotiate an employable identity in a specific workplace context?

Exploring these research questions of identity from a social constructionist perspective underscores the dynamic and changeable nature of identity, co-constructed as it is between speaker and interlocutor(s). This stance "frames communication as a process that is instrumental in the creation of our social worlds, rather than simply an activity that we do within them" (J. Holmes et al., 2011, p. 21). It also illuminates the socially-constructed and socially-reproduced structures which impact upon navigation through the social world and allows for examination of agency within and against that structure. Bourdieu's (1986) social and cultural capital, and the contextually-specific recognition and validation thereof, are particularly pertinent forms of social structure for this study given their implications for negotiating employability in new social settings. Social Discourses, too, become especially important in explorations of the identity work of the marginalised. An Interactional Sociolinguistic, ethnographically-informed methodology is well-suited to accessing the depth and breadth of data and analysis required to address this study's research questions. My methodological approach is the focus of the next chapter.

CHAPTER 3

Methodology

Introduction

A social constructionist, interactional sociolinguistic framework is clearly appropriate for the examination of employable identities as they are negotiated in discourse. The elaborated research questions outlined at the end of the previous chapter, homing in on participants' particular understandings of employability, the ways in which they discursively put them into practice, and the trajectory of employable identity over time, call for a methodological design that provides access to emic perspectives, allows for an investment of time, and requires deep understanding of the context(s) in which data is (co)constructed. Ethnographic research provides an excellent avenue to address all of these needs. An ethnographically-informed approach means that researchers aim to "access and interpret social events of complex modern communities from multiple perspectives" (Marra & Lazzaro-Salazar, 2018, pp. 346–347), resulting in rich, complex data and analysis. This approach is particularly useful when undertaking research with participants who are part of a potentially vulnerable or marginalised community, adding a layer of complexity which needs to be accounted for in methodological design as well as ethical considerations.

This research has two phases in which employable identity negotiation is explored. The first, and larger, phase of this study is made up of ethnographically-informed semi-structured interviews with four former refugees who, at the time of data collection, were either looking for employment or were in part- or full-time employment. The second, smaller phase of the study explores recordings of authentic workplace interactions of one former refugee in her role as a carer in an eldercare facility.

Implications of the refugee context for methodological design

The participants with whom I undertook this research were, for the most part, born in and spent a critical portion of their lives in social and cultural contexts quite different to New Zealand's. Conceptualisations of research and ethical conduct may vary significantly from one cultural context to another and thus the idea of taking part in research may mean very different things to researcher and participant in intercultural contexts. Furthermore, while relations of power are inevitable in qualitative research, these power differentials can particularly affect research with marginalised groups (Bhopal, 2010; Scheyvens, Scheyvens, & Murray, 2003). While, as discussed in the previous chapter, assumptions of trauma and vulnerability can be unhelpful in the discursive positioning of former refugees, the nature of forced migration and its common causes mean that the possibility of vulnerability needs to be accounted for through choice of an appropriate methodological design and attention to ethics.

Groups that are socially marginalised, by definition, have less social power than dominant groups. As a Pākehā (this term refers to New Zealanders of European descent, who comprise the largest ethnic group in New Zealand, and are culturally dominant), native speaker of English in the role of researcher, there are inevitable power differentials between myself and the study's participants. Any potential participants are likely to be non-native speakers of English, (relative) newcomers to New Zealand, and necessarily identified in their (former) refugee role by nature of the study's aims. Furthermore, my study's stated goals of exploring challenges faced by former refugees in the labour market presupposes a certain degree of marginalised status.

Postmodern thinking has come to see scientific practice as intrinsically tied up with power (R. J. Berger & Quinney, 2005, p. 3), following Foucauldian notions of dominant 'regimes of truth' which restrict the creation and dissemination of knowledge to 'experts,' and marginalise other ways of generating and administering knowledge (Foucault, 1977). This new wave of thinking has also challenged the idea that a researcher can achieve objectivity.

The idea of the researcher as somehow outside of the research context, observing an objective reality from a neutral standpoint, is at odds with postmodern recognition that the complex and dynamic nature of any given observed reality is "the outcome of socially and historically mediated human consciousness" (I. F. Goodson & Gill, 2011, p. 18). Ethnography, which has been described as the "quintessential exemplar" of qualitative research (Gottlieb, 2006, p. 48), is an approach to research which aligns with this postmodern destabilisation of objectivity and truth. It involves direct observation of human behaviour in a given cultural setting, in order to gain an understanding of social reality from the perspective of those being observed (Gobo, 2011; Reeves, Kuper, & Hodges, 2008; Starfield, 2010).

Power dynamics can and do shift, and power can arise from various sources (Lammers, 2007), and can be taken up in various ways. This particular research context, the nature of the data to be collected and the theoretical lens and framework within which this study takes place mean that ethnographic methods are an obvious fit to address this study's research questions. Using ethnographic methods is an excellent way to achieve deeper research involvement (Gottlieb, 2006; Marshall & Batten, 2004). While not conducting an ethnography, I borrow ethnographic methods in this study, which I discuss below.

Ethnographic approaches

Fundamental to an ethnographic approach is recognition that the manner of data collection impacts upon the data content, that any researcher's observation of and involvement in the research context is shaped by that context, and that the 'type' or quality of data collected or created is as affected by the researcher as by the research participant themselves (Gottlieb, 2006, p. 48). This research reflexivity aligns with post structuralist conceptualisations of meaning (and thus, identity and agency) as situationally co-constructed in interaction by all participants (Ahearn, 2001; Bucholtz & Hall, 2005; Gumperz, 2005; Rampton, Maybin, & Roberts, 2014). Reflexivity has played an important role in my research design in acknowledgment of the fact that any research I conduct may reflect a bias of my own "values, attitudes and personal agenda" (Bhopal, 2010, p. 193).

Being aware of and responding to a dynamic research context requires, as Karen Block et al. (2012, p. 70) note, "continuous vigilance on the part of researchers." Reflexivity in research improves not only the reliability and trustworthiness of research, but also the "relational and ethical dilemmas" that may come up through the research process (Finlay, 2012, p. 317). Taking this into account in my own study has allowed me to both reflect on my own involvement in, and influence upon, the research. Furthermore, it has allowed me to explicitly describe the research process as well as the difficulties and challenges that arose in the course of the study, along with the research implications of these (K. Block et al., 2012; Mann, 2010; Starfield, 2010; Talmy, 2010).

Participant observation and the prolonged community engagement it entails allows ethnographers to gain deep insight into a particular community, and to "[generate] a rich understanding of social action and its subtleties in different contexts" (Reeves et al., 2008, p. 337). Ethnography allows access to social practices which might not normally be publicly visible, and can draw connections between seemingly unrelated phenomena through 'thick' description of the data (Reeves et al., 2008, p. 337). Furthermore, ethnography is committed to recognising and respecting the irreducibility of human experience (O'Reilly, 2009; Rampton et al., 2014); that is, while data selectivity and idealisation may be to an extent inevitable in any research, a focus on the particularity of a given context allows for recognition that any account will necessarily be partial. Ethnographers often approach their research with the view that "… every story is, by definition, incomplete, and that the richest ethnographic portrait comes from collecting and presenting several stories across divergent lines… rather than seeking just one as the single, authoritative version" (Gottlieb, 2006, p. 61). Data is most typically collected through prolonged participant observation within a community, supplemented by ethnographic interviews.

In-depth, involved research of this kind allows both etic and emic perspectives of the research context and data. Incorporation of both these perspectives into ethnography or ethnographic research allows the strengths of one to counteract any weaknesses of the other and create a fuller (yet necessarily still partial) picture of the research context (Morris et al., 1999; Olive, 2014; Rampton et al., 2014).

For some researchers, as Gobo (2011, p. 16) notes, ethnography "refers to a philosophical paradigm to which one makes a total commitment, for others it designates an instrument that one uses as and when appropriate." My research aligns with an ethnographic ethos and draws on methodology borrowed from ethnography, while not amounting to ethnography proper. In particular I follow ethnography's commitment to reflexive observation of social contexts from both emic and etic perspectives which offers depth of data and analysis over breadth. A distinctive feature of 'true' ethnography is often that the researcher spends a long time – sometimes several years – living in close quarters with participants (Gobo, 2011; O'Reilly, 2009). This may include observation of discrepancies between what participants say they do, or believe, and their actual behaviour (Gobo, 2011, pp. 25–26). In my research, there was no physical research 'site' or indeed one community within which my participants were living or participating (cf. Marra & Lazzaro-Salazar, 2018), but in any case, living in close quarters with them was not the goal. Furthermore, I examined the co-construction of identity in discourse, and thus the situated negotiation of meaning is emergent within the data, not in any contrast with extra-discourse activity.

Ethnographic methods involve drawing upon "a multiplicity of data collection techniques that allow for a holistic approach" (Marra & Lazzaro-Salazar, 2018, p. 347). In this study, participant observation contributes to interpretation and analysis of the data. The main data for this research has been collected in several ways, including the collection of naturalistic workplace interactions (see discussion of Language in the Workplace Project approach, below) and interviews which draw upon an ethnographic ethos. Ethnographic interviews, viewed alongside other qualitative interview styles, "can be distinguished by their duration, frequency of contact… an awareness that the interview itself is a site of meaning construction and that the interview 'produces' a text for interpretation" (Starfield, 2010, pp. 57–58). They occur at regular intervals throughout the research period and are usually informal, conversational types of interaction where although some topics of conversation are pre-determined, other topics emerge naturally and may be explored in a naturalistic manner. This informality allows elicitation, or creation, of rich, complex data between interviewee and interviewer. Thus, borrowing techniques from ethnography allows me the depth and breadth of data emerging from naturalistic situations and genuine relationships (cf. Dawson, 2019; Kidner, 2015; Navarro, 2016).

Drawing on critical ethnography

I enter into this research from a critical position that presupposes the marginalised status of former refugees within New Zealand (and probably all refugee-receiving nations). This is not a controversial position to take, given the well-reported un- and underemployment of former refugees (Butcher et al., 2006; ChangeMakers Refugee Forum, 2012; Jansen & Grant, 2015), along with economic and social marginalisation (Colic-Peisker, 2009; Collie et al., 2010; Gans, 2009; Piller, 2016). While it can be expected that involuntary migration might result in a longer-than-average period of readjustment in a new country, first generation (former) refugees tend to take longer, on the whole, to 'catch up' to their former, pre-migration employment (or social) statuses, if they do at all (Guerin, Ho, & Bedford, 2004; Strategic Social Policy Group, 2008).

While there is plenty of valuable advice and support available for former refugees on how to best 'fit in' and 'adapt' to their new homes, the movement of newcomers from society's periphery towards its centre is not a one-player game (Angouri, Marra, & Holmes, 2017; Giampapa, 2004). The successful resettlement of refugees (from the perspective of both former refugees and the (members of the) host society) is a joint endeavour, in which moves toward belonging by newcomers must be recognised and ratified by 'oldtimers' (Norton, 2001). Furthermore, existent social and institutional structures impact on the possibilities for this process to take place, including but not limited to ideologies of nationhood/the imagined community of the nation of New Zealand (B. Anderson, 1991; Ehrkamp, 2005; Spoonley & Butcher, 2009), language (competence) ideologies (Menard-Warwick, 2005), the gender order (Connell, 1987; Dawson, 2019; J. Holmes, 2006a), the culture order (J. Holmes, 2018), avenues for the recognition of non-local capital (Colic-Peisker & Walker, 2003; Ricento, 2015), and various forms of discrimination (Guerin et al., 2004; Jelle, Guerin, & Dyer, 2006).

For these reasons the ethnographic approach which I take to this research is specifically informed by *critical* ethnography. Critical ethnographic approaches, in keeping with the Interactional Sociolinguistic framework that this study adopts, employ macro level sociological theory to micro level analysis of ethnographic data (O'Reilly, 2009; Starfield, 2010). Research begins with an assumption of the oppression or marginalisation of a given group, based on previous research into the area (Carspecken, 1996; Madison, 2012; O'Reilly, 2009), and aims to uncover, unsettle, and describe typically out-of-site taken-for-granted assumptions and relations of power (Madison, 2012; O'Reilly, 2009). It is an approach which illuminates Bourdieu's (1977b) "... everyday acts of symbolic violence in which all members of a culture are complicit" (O'Reilly, 2009, p. 53). Exploring the particular shape this presupposed marginalisation takes allows a critical ethnographer to "[contribute] to emancipatory knowledge" (Madison, 2012, p. 6), and, potentially, social change (Carspecken, 1996). Applying this critical lens to my own use of ethnographic methodology has allowed me to access former refugees' emic understandings of their experiences in this critical area of resettlement, and their relationship to my own etic understandings of the wider social context (informed both by extant literature and my position as a majority group member in the New Zealand context).

Ethics

Ethical considerations affect all research involving human participants. Qualitative research gives rise to particular, complex ethical issues due to the manner in which it closely examines human existence and allows description of "intimate aspects of people's life worlds" (Brinkman & Kvale, 2005, p. 157; also Patton, 2002). This study was completed as my thesis for a PhD in Linguistics at Victoria University of Wellington (VUW). Undertaking research that involves human participants at VUW requires approval from the university's Human Ethics Committee, whose responsibility it is to ensure that the research is conducted ethically and in accordance with the university's Human Ethics Policy (Victoria University of Wellington, 2018). The ethics application for my research was approved on 14 December 2015 with Ethics Approval number 22190.

While gaining approval from an ethics committee is an important and necessary step in research design, this alone cannot address all ethical considerations than may arise in long-term qualitative research. In adopting a reflexive approach in my research, I have aimed to take into account the possibility of divergent conceptualisations of ethics (Marshall & Batten, 2004), and the dynamic nature of research which may end up in places not predicted (or predictable) at the outset (Bhopal, 2010; K. Block et al., 2012).

Participant recruitment

Participants for the interview stage of this study were all identified by people working and volunteering in refugee resettlement. They were suggested on account of their current status as job seekers (Arwa and Kelly) or having recently found work after a stretch of unemployment after arrival in New Zealand (Omar). In Isaac's case, he was identified as someone who would potentially be able to provide access to further participants through his union work and connections with former cleaning colleagues, but he expressed interest and willingness in participating in the research himself. In all cases, the future participant was emailed by the contact person to request permission for me to contact them about my research (cf. Bloch, 2007a), then upon their acceptance, I contacted them and arranged to meet up to discuss the research. In these first meetings I explained the nature of the research and asked them to initially take part in a series of interviews. I also discussed the possibility of future workplace recording, if and when that became possible and appropriate. As it turned out, I was not able to gain access to the workplaces of any of these four participants, an issue which is discussed further below.

In gaining consent I provided the participants with both the information sheet and consent form in advance of signing (either in person the first time we met, or by email) in order to allow time to read through them at their own pace. At the time of signing the consent forms, all participants indicated that they had already read both and were happy to proceed. Nonetheless I went through the information sheet and consent form with each of them, allowing space for clarifying concepts and answering questions when necessary to ensure they were comfortable with what they were agreeing to take part in.

Upon reflection, it is possible that my insistence upon completing this step could have come across as patronising to the participants, all of whom had evidently already read and understood the material. Given the research context, I had believed it important to take account of the possibility that refugee-background participants' linguistic background, familiarity with local norms, understandings of contextual power dynamics, and potential vulnerable status as members of a marginalised group could affect the provision of truly informed and willing consent. My participants' apparent enfranchisement and language proficiency appears to me now to negate this concern, and suggests that I was perhaps drawing upon and feeding into Discourses of Refugeehood that index incompetence. However, the alternative, ignoring this possibility, risks harming or exploiting ill-informed or unwilling potential participants.

The four participants of the interview stage of this study are Omar, a highly-qualified Syrian engineer in his 40s, married with three children; Kelly, a

Palestinian jobseeker in her 30s with a Bachelor of Business Studies degree, single mother of two children; Isaac, an early 30s Eritrean university student (at the time of data collection) in International Relations and a part-time employee of his university's union; and Arwa, a mid-30s Doctor of Computer Science and jobseeker from a Middle Eastern country. I provide further background information about each of these participants in Chapter 4, to follow. I spent various amounts of time with each of them, and the number of times I interviewed them ranged from two to nine times, each interview typically around an hour. Outside of these interviews I spent time with each of the participants in social contexts, including meeting for coffee, attending parties, school fairs, and dinner with their families, and I have maintained friendships with several of them.

Data collection

Interviews

Research interviews have traditionally been seen as a method of extracting an objective truth from interviewees, in conditions under which interviewers ideally remain as neutral and passive as possible, to prevent or limit affecting the data being collected (e.g. Oppenheim, 1992). Talmy (2010, p. 129) calls this conceptualisation *interview as research instrument*. Following an ethnographic ethos within a social constructionist, interactional sociolinguistic framework, I approach interviews in my research as conversational, social encounters of meaning-making where that meaning is co-constructed by both the interviewer and the interviewee (Holstein & Gubrium, 1995; Mann, 2010; Talmy, 2010). Talmy (2010, p. 129) calls this *research as social practice*, where the research interview "is explicitly conceptualised and analysed as *social action*" (my emphasis), wherein data is created rather than uncovered.

The concept of co-construction is based on the acknowledgement that, because an interview is a social interaction, the ideas, perspectives, details and narratives that emerge from that interaction are produced collaboratively by both (or all) parties (Edley & Litosseliti, 2010; Kerekes, 2007; Mann, 2010; Talmy, 2010). Contrary to the idea that an interview may be 'spoiled' by the effects of an interviewer's involvement, the researcher's contributions do not *interfere* with the data, but rather, *are* part of the data (Eastmond, 2007, p. 261; citing Freeman, 1989, pp. 432–433). Taking reflexive account of the researcher role in the creation of interview data allows reflection on my own involvement in and influence upon the research, and the implications of this. This involves fully outlining the context in which the data was collected and the details of the methodology, and paying close analytical attention to my own contributions to the data alongside those of the participants.

In fitting with an ethnographic approach's assumption that data is emergent, it becomes clear that using a predetermined set of questions may be inappropriate where the researcher "... doesn't know beforehand what is going to happen, who will be present, or what will be important to ask during an event, incident or experience" (Patton, 2002, p. 342). While it is good practice to enter into an interview with a certain degree of planned structure, the flexibility to take an unanticipated direction is important in ethnographic style interviews, as the richest data sometimes emerge out of topics entirely unplanned by the interviewer (Patton, 2002; Reeves et al., 2008; Rubin & Rubin, 2005; Turner, 2010).

This unstructured or semi-structured approach to interviews has been used to explore the (co)construction of meaning and positioning across a range of contexts and topic areas, from children's and adolescents' storytelling (e.g. Minks, 2007; Moissinac, 2007), to workplace conflict (e.g. Miglbauer, 2017), and teachers' identity work in discourse (e.g. G. C. Johnson, 2006). This approach has been used to illuminate the discursive employment of agency (e.g. McKendy, 2006; Tainio, 2002), alignment and disalignment with Discourses of Masculinity (e.g. Kiesling, 2006; Korobov & Bamberg, 2007), as well as the navigation of national identity and political discourse (e.g. Kidner, 2015; Wodak, de Cillia, Reisigl, & Liebhart, 2010; Woodhams, 2015). These interviews have also been used to explore reported experiences of resettlement and othering in the narratives of migrants and former refugees (e.g. Colic-Peisker, 2009; Collie et al., 2010; De Fina, 2003; Eastmond, 2007; Hatoss, 2012; Paoletti & Johnson, 2007; Revis, 2015; Tanyas, 2016). The flexibility that this approach to interviewing affords is well-suited to research with vulnerable communities such as former refugees, as it allows for responsivity to the dynamic situated context of the interview and the co-construction of meaning. Furthermore, it allows interviewees to draw on familiar (emic) concepts and meanings and respond to questions "within their own frame of reference" (T. May, 2011, p. 136), providing more nuanced understanding of self (and other) positioning (Lillrank, 2012; T. May, 2011; Sunstein & Chiseri-Strater, 2007).

In approaching the interviews in my study, I prepared some general themes to cover in the first interview, based around the interviewee's personal, educational, and employment background, the impetus for their migration to New Zealand, their desired employment, steps taken in their search for desirable, appropriate employment, as well as their experiences in the New Zealand labour market. These were prepared with the intention that the interview would be conversational and arrive at these themes naturally in the course of the interaction. I piloted this thematic schedule with two non-refugee migrants to New Zealand; a native speaker of English from a Western country, and a second language speaker of English from a Middle Eastern country with high English proficiency. After having conducted these pilot interviews, I was satisfied that the thematic but conversational structure of the interview would be appropriate for interviews with my participants.

Conducting interviews

The first time I interviewed each participant the interviews quickly became very conversation-like and although I periodically came back to prepared topics, these frequently happened naturally in the flow of the conversation. Interviews thereafter were largely unstructured, predominantly focused upon the participant's experiences in either the labour market or their place of employment since the last time we had met. The interviews all took place in cafes, both within the university and the surrounding city, and continued for around an hour, on average. As I later listened to the recording of the interview, identified themes and transcribed relevant, interesting, and thematically representative sections, I identified any comments, themes or areas of misunderstanding for follow up in subsequent interviews (Sunstein & Chiseri-Strater, 2007). In total, the interviews resulted in almost 17 hours of interview data over the four participants of this study's interview phase. The frequency and total number of interviews with participants depended upon their availability, which was affected by employment status and family obligations, among other factors. Arwa had the most availability of these participants, which has allowed for nine interviews over a twenty-month period.

Interviewee	No. of interviews	Total interview time
Arwa	9	9 hours 14 minutes
Isaac	2	1 hour 20 minutes
Kelly	3	3 hours 39 minutes
Omar	3	2 hours 28 minutes
Total	17	**16 hours 41 minutes**

Figure 3.1 Interview data

Collecting workplace data

The workplace interaction recording component of my research closely follows the methodology developed by the Language in the Workplace Project (LWP). LWP began in 1996 at Victoria University of Wellington, studying spoken communication in New Zealand workplaces. Its aims are identifying characteristics of effective workplace communication, diagnosing possible miscommunication causes, and exploring potential applications of findings for New Zealand workplaces (Language in the Workplace, 2014). Data from LWP has had practical application including the development of materials for a Victoria University-run course focusing on teaching pragmatic work and language skills to skilled migrants (Language in the Workplace, 2014).

The LWP team aim to gather naturally occurring data from authentic settings, and accessing this kind of data requires "... positive and productive working relationships" (J. Holmes et al., 2011, p. 26) with participants. The methodology is designed to give participants control over what data is collected, and to reduce researchers' involvement in the actual data collection to a minimum. Control of data collection is handed over to participants, who wear unobtrusive recording devices during a normal work day, recording "a range of their talk as it occurs in their everyday working life" (J. Holmes et al., 2011, p. 26). They are asked to turn the recorders on and off as they deem appropriate, and provide some context for the recorded interaction (Stubbe & Ingle, 1999, p. 1). Participants are able to delete, or request later to have deleted, material which they subsequently decide they do not want analysed. This kind of control over the recording process allows the development of excellent research relationships based on trust (Stubbe & Ingle, 1999, p. 1).

Studies conducted within LWP have explored a wide range of elements of workplace talk, including small talk (J. Holmes, 2005b), narratives and storytelling (J. Holmes, 2005a; J. Holmes & Marra, 2005; Marra & Holmes, 2004), managing disagreements and impoliteness (J. Holmes & Schnurr, 2017; Marra, 2012), the intersection of leadership and ethnicity (J. Holmes & Marra, 2011; J. Holmes et al., 2011), gender (J. Holmes & Marra, 2004; Stubbe, Holmes, Vine, & Marra, 2000), humour (J. Holmes, 2000; J. Holmes & Marra, 2002a) and the navigation of unfamiliar local norms and pragmatics (J. Holmes, Marra, & Lazzaro-Salazar, 2017; J. Holmes & Riddiford, 2009, 2010). The studies have been based on data collected in a variety of workplace settings, from white collar offices (J. Holmes & Marra, 2002b), to blue collar factories (Daly, Holmes, Newton, & Stubbe, 2004), building sites (J. Holmes & Woodhams, 2013), hospitals (J. Holmes & Major, 2003; Major & Holmes, 2008), and eldercare facilities (Marsden & Holmes, 2014).

The work LWP has undertaken in intercultural contexts has led to the development of materials and tools for migrant jobseekers and employers of migrants aimed at improving communication between local employers or managers, and newcomers. This methodology, developed and implemented by LWP, is based on two important principles: Addressing issues that are of interest to both the researchers and the researched; and building strong relationships with volunteers in organisations (J. Holmes et al., 2011, p. 32). This approach helps create collaborative, mutually beneficial relationships with participants, and promotes the development and maintenance of trust (J. Holmes et al., 2011, p. 33).

Gaining access

I encountered several challenges in gaining access to participants' workplaces in my study. Unlike most studies undertaken by the LWP team, I was attempting to gain access to a workplace via one employee, rather than gaining access to employees via employers (cf. Stubbe, 2001).

Some of my participants were not in employment, and some were in part time employment, or had short periods of full-time, but temporary, employment. After discussing the possibility of workplace recording with a participant, and gaining their agreement in principle, I would ask them to mention my research to their managers, and to give them an information sheet about the study. Some managers refused at the participant's first mention of the research, and others emailed me for more information, and then replied refusing my request, citing concerns around time constraints and customer or client confidentiality. One manager stated that he was happy to be contacted by phone but was too busy to speak with me each time that I called, until such a time as the participant moved on to a new job. Had I been able to sit down with these managers in person, I believe that many of their concerns could have been assuaged by engaging in face-to-face dialogue about the research.

This, I believe, is a limitation of attempting to access workplaces from the bottom up, as it were (particularly as the participants asking their managers about the possibility of workplace recording were either in fairly junior positions, were new to the roles, or both, speaking to the limits of their recognised capital). Temporary placements presented another challenge, as in one instance where all parties were happy for the data collection to take place, but high workloads, conflicting schedules, and Christmas workplace close-down meant that we could not arrange all necessary elements before the contract came to an end. These challenges may be rooted in the well-documented challenges that former refugees encounter in their journeys towards appropriate, acceptable employment. Temporary positions, junior roles, and multiple changes of job that are often the experiences of former refugees (Feeney, 2000; Gans, 2009) do not lend themselves to gaining managerial approval for research. Thus, it is worth noting the methodological implications for any workplace research with former refugees going forward.

Salvation came with the assistance of one of the founding members of the LWP, who offered to liaise with a family member who worked at Pinewood, an eldercare workplace where the LWP team had collected workplace data some years earlier (*Pinewood* is a pseudonym). The family member put me in touch with Nina, a Colombian former refugee carer employed by Pinewood, who had been living in New Zealand for some years. Nina agreed to take part in the research, and the manager of the eldercare facility at the time was also very happy for me to collect data, having also given approval for the earlier LWP data collection. I attended a residents' meeting to explain the nature of the research and distribute information sheets, in anticipation of their potential involvement by nature of interaction with Nina in her workday. However, before I was able to get official consent, the manager moved to a different site and was replaced with a manager much more hesitant about the idea. The new (temporary) manager, who had never encountered the LWP or its research, was concerned about confidentiality and recording potentially vulnerable elderly residents, despite my assurances that I would not consider recording anyone who was not able to give informed, independent, and clear consent for participation in my project. However, once her permanent replacement arrived and was brought up to speed on the LWP and its history, aims, and methodology, he agreed to allow my data collection to proceed.

Consent and data collection

Nina identified two residents that she believed would be suitable for and willing to participate in my research, Charlie and Ava. After confirming with administrative staff at the eldercare facility that these residents were capable of giving informed consent, I asked Nina to provide them both with information and consent forms to read at their own leisure, and then visited them both (separately) at Pinewood a week later to discuss the research with them in person. I spoke with each of them for around an hour in their rooms of residence, about the research itself as well as topics that came up naturally, including their lives prior to living at Pinewood, their families, and Nina herself. I went through the information sheets and consent forms with them in the same manner as with my former refugee participants. As with this study's former refugee participants, Ava and Charlie said that they had already read the contents of both and were happy to sign.

Over the following months, Nina wore a small recording device on her arm on six separate days, recording her morning interactions with Charlie and Ava, which ranged between three and ten minutes. Nina turned the recorder on as she entered the room and turn it off when she left. I met with her regularly to debrief if she had time and change her recorder for a new one. Often Nina would be so busy that she only had time to make the exchange and then go back to work.

Resident	**No. of recordings**	**Total recording time**
Ava	5	21 minutes 31 minutes
Charlie	4	24 minutes 6 seconds
Total	**9**	**45 minutes 37 seconds**

Figure 3.2 Nina's workplace data

Outside of the workplace, I also interviewed Nina several times in the same manner as the other participants discussed earlier. These interviews provided contextually salient information and understanding of Nina's position in New Zealand, details of which are included in her bio in the following chapter. As I have focused upon Nina's identity navigation in the workplace, I have not included analysis of this interview data in this study. As with the other participants, we also spent time together socially, and continue to do so.

Transcription

I transcribed the data using modified conventions borrowed from the transcription conventions of the LWP and the Wellington Corpus of Spoken New Zealand English (Vine, Johnson, O'Brien, & Robertson, 2002) and aligned with Interactional Sociolinguistic attention to micro-level detail, including pauses, hesitation markers, false starts, intonation and prosody.

+	short pause up to one second e.g. so I told her + don't put it there
(1)	pause one second or longer, number of seconds of pause e.g. but she wasn't (2) she wasn't even listening
wha-	hyphen indicates cut off word, both self-interruption and other interruption e.g. I didn't know wha- + I couldn't tell what was going on
//[x]\ /[x] \\	indicates overlapping speech e.g. A: and if you want to come //you\ can ok B: /yep\\ + yep
^{1}// [x]\\$^{1}$ ^{1}/ [x]\\\\$^{1}$	indicates multiple overlaps in one section e.g. A: then after I came back ^{1}//I saw\\$^{1}$ that the other one ^{2}//was\\$^{2}$ gone B: ^{1}/yeah\\\\$^{1}$ + ^{2}/mm\\\\$^{2}$
[*laughs*]	square brackets with text in italics indicate paralinguistic and relevant non-verbal features e.g. yeah [*laughs*] but it wasn't until later that [*clears throat*] I realised
so::	colons following letter and words indicate that sound has been drawn out e.g. he was there for a re::ally long time
?	High rising terminal e.g. then he picked it up? and saw it was broken?
CAPITALS	Words spoken with emphasis; louder than surrounding speech e.g. but I had said the FIRST one

Figure 3.3 Transcription conventions

I have not accounted for any non-standard pronunciation of words in the transcription, except where it has resulted in meta-commentary on that pronunciation (see Excerpt 9.8, Chapter 9). After transcribing the interviews, I noted any important points where I was unclear on the participant's meaning, so I could follow up on these in subsequent interviews. The participants and I discussed at the start of the research that they would be able to view any of the transcripts or analysis of interactions they were a part of. Additionally, I offered each of the participants the opportunity to do so at several points during data collection. Interestingly, none of the participants took up this offer.

Analysis

This study's data set is comprised of the 17 interviews with Arwa, Isaac, Omar, and Kelly, conducted between March 2016 and January 2018, and the nine morning round workplace interactions between Nina and Pinewood residents Charlie and Ava, recorded between August and December 2017.

Data type	Collection dates	Recordings	Total recording time
Interviews	March 2016–January 2018	17	16 hours 41 minutes
Workplace interactions	August 2017–December 2017	9	45 minutes 37 seconds

Figure 3.4 Total data set

Impact of interview language choice

Before outlining the type of analysis that I undertook, it is important to acknowledge that all of the data – both the interviews and the workplace data – are entirely in my first language – English, which is an additional language for all of the participants. Language is both a form of symbolic capital (Bourdieu, 1986), and the site of multiple, dynamic, flexible identity construction (Pavlenko, 2001, p. 319). In countries where English is the dominant language, it is "understood as the language of power, status, and opportunity" (Seals & Peyton, 2017, p. 88). Thus, as the sole speaker of English as a native language in this study's interviews, I am in possession of valuable symbolic capital which has the potential to contribute to power imbalances. But power, as Lammers (2007, p. 74) notes, "springs from many sources," including (for example) physicality, personality, and intellect. Symbolic capital afforded by native speaker status is only one type of power which may be claimed within a given interview context. Second language speakers' "linguistic, social, cultural, gender, racial, and ethnic identities mediate their access to linguistic resources and interactional opportunities available" in the target language (Pavlenko, 2001, p. 319; also Pavlenko, 2000).

Leaving aside for the moment that I believe, after hours of interaction with them, that all of the participants in this study have sufficient linguistic competence to skilfully navigate multiple and dynamic identity positions in English, it is worth considering that any speakers of a non-native language are potentially in some way limited in their self-expression. Furthermore, perhaps, given the intercultural context, the range of identity positions available in English may be limited, disempowering, or incompatible with their extant senses of self (Miller & Kubota, 2013; Norton, 2000; Pavlenko, 2001). This kind of conflict, Pavlenko (2001, p. 319) notes, is not uncommon in migrant contexts where newcomers find themselves positioned (by others) as incompetent. However, to frame this another way, participating in new contexts may lead newcomers to develop or take up new identity positions in order to be heard and have their capital recognised (Norton, 2000; Pavlenko, 2001). Equally, speaking English may allow access to certain Discourses that are not available in their first (or subsequent) languages, providing access to new or different ways of self-representation (Pavlenko, 2001, p. 319).

Thus, it is clear that concerns that interacting in an additional language may affect identity negotiation are unfounded from an IS, social constructionist perspective, not because this will *not* affect the identity work, but because all contextual factors *do* impact upon identity work. The particular speakers, their linguistic repertoires, the physical context, the participants' intersectional identities, social distance (and so forth) – all impact upon the co-construction of the data, and it is the goal of an IS analysis to account for these contextual factors. Blackledge and Pavlenko (2001, p. 245) note that the significance of an individual's first language as their sole legitimate language is tied up in ideologies of language that are rooted in issues of social power dynamics, "as if only the language learned at the mother's knee could convey the true self of the speaker" (2001, p. 245; Miller & Kubota, 2013). Many studies (e.g. Blackledge & Pavlenko, 2001; De Fina, 2003; Giampapa, 2004; J. Holmes & Riddiford, 2009; Marra, 2012; Norton, 2001, 2013, 2017; Pavlenko, 2001) have shown that, from a position of marginality, second language speakers can find ways to "to re-articulate their identities within the multiple spaces of their multiple worlds" (Giampapa, 2004, p. 216). To discount non-native speakers' ability to do so may in itself be an instantiation of symbolic violence.

Approach to analysis

The rich data and contextual knowledge afforded by the ethnographic approach this study takes provides excellent grounds for an interactional sociolinguistic analysis of former refugees' identity navigation in discourse. Focusing primarily on this identity work in narrative (the strengths of which are discussed further in Chapter 5), I have explored how the stories people tell allow insight into the emergent nature of the self and identity (Bamberg, 2004b). Drawing on the extensive discursive narrative work of Michael Bamberg and colleagues (e.g. Bamberg, 2004b, 2004c, 2006, 2011a, 2011b; Bamberg et al., 2007; Bamberg & Georgakopoulou, 2008; De Fina & Georgakopoulou, 2008; Georgakopoulou, 2006a), in my analysis, identification of emergent themes in narratives leads to a closer analysis of story construction, and conversational devices employed by participants (Bamberg, 2004b; De Fina, 2006). Bamberg (2004b, p. 225) notes that analysing data in these two ways allows "differentiation of how speakers work up a position as complicit with… or countering dominant [D]iscourses" and shows how those speakers "position themselves in relation to [D]iscourses by which they are positioned" (I have capitalised *discourse* in quotations when it aligns with Gee's (2015) definition of capital-D *Discourses* which I am following in this study (see discussion in previous chapter)).

Following Bamberg and Georgakopoulou (2008, p. 84), I have analysed my data at three 'positioning levels' that consider the contextual emergence of identity and the "interrelated positioning processes at work." These three levels do not, at least in my analysis, suggest a linear, step-by-step method of data analysis. Rather, they point toward layers of analytical depth that deserve consideration in an iterative, reflexive analysis process, and not every element of these levels will necessarily be salient in any given piece of data.

The first level considers how individuals in the stories are positioned in relation to each other and in space and time. The second focuses on the ways that the narrator positions themselves and *is* positioned within the interactive situation. This level involves consideration of: what is being interactionally accomplished through the narration; the setting in which a question has been asked, how it was answered in the form of a narrative and what conclusions can be drawn from that; and the joint interactional engagement between all participants. The third positioning level involves reflection on how the participants construct each other and themselves in terms of teller roles and in doing so establish a sense of self/identity (Bamberg & Georgakopoulou, 2008, p. 84). This approach to narrative analysis is particularly appropriate for this research context. It allows examination of individuals' self and other positioning, the interactive nature of the data, and their relationship to an emergent identity, being explored for the first time, renegotiated in new settings, and recounted through narrative.

Bamberg's approach to narrative (2003, 2004b, 2004a, 2006, 2009, 2011a) is grounded in social constructionism and draws on both ethnography and discourse analysis. It is an approach which is "fully interested in the inconsistencies, contradictions, and ambiguities" (Bamberg, 2004b, p. 222) that arise interactionally, and the ways in which these inconsistencies can illuminate how narrators "[bring] off and [manage] their social identities in contexts" (2004b, p. 222). While Bamberg's narrative analysis focuses on identification of rhetorical and argumentative organisation (2004b, p. 221), within an interactional sociolinguistic framework, this approach to narrative analysis can be enhanced by the close examination of micro level discourse features.

A fine-grained, situated analysis which concentrates on features such as contextualisation cues and conversational inference (Gumperz, 1982, 2005); and micro level features and discourse/pragmatic markers (Schiffrin, 1987, 2001), in combination with the analyst's knowledge of the context provides deep insight into the ways that meaning and identity are negotiated moment to moment between all participants in an interaction. Drawing on IS resources and Bamberg and Georgakopoulou's (2008) three-level positioning analysis provides me with valuable tools to explore the co-construction of identity as emergent within narrative. Simultaneously, this approach illuminates the relationships between discourse and Discourses, between discursive agency and wider social structure, and between identity and the ideologically-shaped contexts in which it emerges. Situated within this study's social constructionist, anti-positivist approach, in the analysis to follow I offer an interpretation of the collected data grounded in well-established personal relationships with the study's participants, a sound understanding of the interactional context(s), and extensive sociolinguistic, sociological, pragmatic, and migration literature.

Analysis illustration

To illustrate briefly how I apply this analytic process to my data, I present here a brief excerpt taken from an interview with Isaac, after he had been working for some months as a union representative. Here he has been describing a particular industry with many sub-sectors, which has, overall, a very high rate of union membership. Isaac notes that there is one sub-sector of this industry which is more challenging for the union to work with than others:

Excerpt 3.1 2 December 2016; 4.41–4.46

```
1. Isaac:   we just need to maintain that + um + but this area is a little bit
2.          + you know the cafes + and the food the food stores?
3. Emily:   mm
4. Isaac:   that's a little bit like struggle they the employer jus::t (1)
5.          awful + or + it's like a + Donald Trump [laughs]
6. Emily:   [laughs]
```

In terms of Bamberg and Georgakopoulou's (2008) first positioning level – how individuals in the stories are positioned in relation to each other – Isaac can be seen here to position himself as a member of the union community, through use of inclusive pronoun *we* (line 1, cf. Íñigo-Mora, 2004). The employers of potential union members are positioned in opposition to this community of the union by virtue of the *struggle* between them (line 4). Isaac mitigates this *struggle*, however, through use of discourse marker *like* which is often used to signal "a certain psychological distance to the following lexical material" (G. Anderson, 2000, p. 18), and here has the discursive effect of signalling that *struggle* is not to be taken literally or afforded much weight.

The second positioning level unpacks how the narrator positions themselves and *is* positioned within the interactive situation. Isaac positions himself here as a professional by demonstrating his industry knowledge, and as being in an informed position to pass judgement based on his evaluation of some employers as *jus::t...awful* (lines 4, 5). Furthermore, he positions both himself and me (as interlocutor) as politically engaged and (at least somewhat) liberal by comparing these bad employers to the current President of the United States. It is possible that he is also drawing on our recent (at the time of the conversation) past of having watched together in horror the unfolding of the 2016 US election. His hyperbolic comparison is, as with *struggle*, above, somewhat attenuated through the metarepresentation marker *like* (G. Anderson, 2000, p. 19) and his following laughter (Billig, 2005). In mirroring his laughter, I discursively accept the positioning he has assigned me, and echo his evaluation of the absurdity of the comparison. Thus, the interactional accomplishment here is Isaac positioning himself as professional, politically liberal, and aligning himself with me through our established, shared opinions of Donald Trump.

Finally, Bamberg and Georgakopoulou's (2008) third positioning level involves reflection on teller roles and the emergence therein of identity. The teller roles Isaac takes up in this excerpt – ratified by my positive, solidarity-indexing responses, contribute to the co-construction of a competent, professional identity for Isaac. Furthermore, by drawing on our shared political repertoire Isaac orients to a liberal, political identity. These both feed into an employable identity appropriate for his role within a union, as an advocate and representative for employees.

Thus, analysis of this short excerpt illustrates well how attention to micro discursive features, in combination with Bamberg and Georgakopoulou's (2008) positioning levels and a broad ethnographically-informed understanding of situated interaction, allow rich analysis of the emergence of identity in interaction. As mentioned earlier, this type of analysis does not necessarily follow such a linear progression illustrated here, but I have outlined it here to display the ways in which the analysis in the chapters to come has been undertaken.

Conclusion

The theoretical approach in the previous chapter, and the methodological approach and tools that have been described in this chapter set the scene for a rich exploration of former refugees' negotiation of their employable identities in (narrative) discourse. In keeping with the ethnographic ethos and approach taken in this study, it is important to understand a little about the people whose stories will be examined here. This is the focus of the following chapter, in which I present a brief background of each of this study's participants informed by both interviews and my own observations. I also address the ethnographic approach's call for reflexivity by including a brief sketch of my own background to locate myself within this research as a contributor to the emergent narrative data collected.

CHAPTER 4

Participants

Introduction

The five participants who generously volunteered their time to take part in this study began their lives scattered across the globe, in South America, the Middle East, and North and East Africa. War, political conflict and instability, and oppression eventually led them all to take their destinies into their own hands and set out to forge new lives thousands of miles from home. In New Zealand they have taken on the multiple and ongoing challenges of resettlement with resilience and a fortitude of spirit. Here I introduce each of them to provide some context for the explorations of their narratives which are to follow. These descriptions are based upon their own presentations of self in interviews. I also provide background on myself, in keeping with my commitment to recognising my own contributions to the co-construction of interactional data.

Kelly

Kelly was born in Kuwait to fairly affluent Palestinian parents. After the Gulf War, Kelly, her parents and sister came to New Zealand as refugees. Kelly's arrival in New Zealand as a child, and number of years in the New Zealand education system, are reflected in her high level of English proficiency. When she was in her mid-teens, the family moved to Palestine – the first time she had visited her parents' homeland – and she and her sister completed school there. Kelly got married soon after finishing high school and had two children. She describes her marriage as having been characterised by a controlling husband who sabotaged her attempts to study and restricted their extra-familial activity. As a result of the escalation of the Palestine-Israel conflict, Kelly's parents decided to return to New Zealand, and did so quickly, followed by Kelly's sister six months later. For some time, Kelly was unable to follow them as her husband would not allow it, but he eventually agreed (as discussed in later chapters). Their marriage ended once Kelly was back in New Zealand, and she now raises their children on her own. After some years back in New Zealand, Kelly completed a Bachelor of Business Studies. She had been searching for employment matching her qualifications for some months, without success, when we met.

Omar

Omar grew up in a coastal city in Syria. He worked as an engineer on cargo ships that travelled the world, eventually becoming chief engineer. The small crews that worked on these ships used English as a lingua franca. When Omar was back in Syria in early 2013 after completing a contract, a massacre took place in his city. Situated within an already dangerously deteriorating political situation in the country, this event prompted Omar's decision to leave Syria with his wife and children. They flew to Egypt and applied for asylum through the United Nations, eventually resettling in New Zealand after about twenty months.

Though highly qualified and experienced, Omar was not able to find suitable employment in New Zealand. Eventually, with the help of a recruitment agency, he secured a job as an engineer, but well below his experience level. About a year later Omar made a lateral move to a different company, where his duties were much the same as the previous position. Omar feels that his skills are wasted, and that everything he has worked towards in his career has been lost. Though he continues to look for work more suitable to his experience, he says that he must accept how things are, and that he continues to work for his family, and do his job to the best of his abilities.

Isaac

Isaac was born in Eritrea and lived there until he was about 19. Eritrea is a one-party state with one of the worst human rights records in the world (Human Rights Watch, 2018), and indefinite national conscription. Afraid he would be arrested for his political views, Isaac convinced his family to let him leave Eritrea. After obtaining a counterfeit security pass to allow him to travel from his city to Eritrea's border with Sudan (several hundred kilometres away), Isaac paid a smuggler to get him into Sudan, where he made it to a UNHCR camp and was granted asylum. In Sudan, he worked as an interpreter for the UN for some years, and eventually was granted a place in New Zealand, a country he had never heard of. Initial settlement was very difficult for Isaac. He eventually took up two jobs cleaning, at a local university and at a hotel in the city.

While working as a cleaner Isaac became involved with an on-campus union. During a local election, a union delegate asked Isaac to speak at a mayoral candidate debate on campus, on the topic of raising the wages of cleaning staff. He received a huge, positive response from the crowd of students when talking about his experiences and hopes for his future. One spectator even tweeted – displayed on a large screen at the event – that they would rather see Isaac become mayor than any of the present candidates

Following this event Isaac was offered part time work at the university union, and later began studying International Relations at that same university. He was in his second year of study when I met him. Isaac uses English in both his educational and employment contexts and has high conversational proficiency.

Arwa

Arwa grew up in a Middle Eastern country with migrant parents, in a well-educated family (Arwa asked me not to specifically name her country of origin). At the age of 29 she moved to Malaysia to study towards her master's degree and then PhD in Computer Science, specialising in Security. Once she had completed her studies, Arwa did not wish to return to her country of origin, believing it to be a dangerous and restrictive place. She claimed asylum while in Malaysia and was granted refugee status by the UNHCR. She was resettled in New Zealand three and a half years ago.

Arwa threw herself into life in New Zealand, volunteering with local charities and involving herself with language learning communities. She makes use of local refugee support services and is very active in trying to create opportunities for herself but has had little success in the labour market despite her qualifications and networking skills, and her strong conviction in her own abilities and worth. Arwa reports that she had high English proficiency upon arrival in New Zealand, but that her pronunciation and speaking speed occasionally impeded communication. Since her arrival in New Zealand she has taken several English-language courses to address this, as well as for social reasons.

Nina

Nina was born in and grew up in Colombia. After her family received death threats, she fled to Ecuador with her young daughter to start a new life. She lived in Ecuador for ten years and had three more children there. Eventually Nina and her children were offered resettlement in New Zealand. In their first year after arrival, the family moved seven times, motivated variously by unwelcoming neighbours, high accommodation costs, and isolation.

Nina did not speak English when she arrived in New Zealand. She sporadically attended English language classes but frequent moving and working long hours made regular attendance difficult. After six months in New Zealand, Nina says she had picked up enough English incidentally to be able to engage in basic communication. When I met her, her grammatical proficiency was fairly non-standard. However, she displayed high pragmatic proficiency both in conversation with me and with others in this study's recordings, and is more than capable of achieving her communicative goals. She initially worked as a cleaner in schools and private homes. Eventually she was sent on a course for aged care workers run by a local charity, which led to an unpaid trial, and then full employment, as a carer in an eldercare facility, where she worked when I met her.

Situating the researcher in the research context

In keeping with my intentions to recognise the situated nature of this study's data collection, the co-constructed nature of interactive data, and the inescapable subjectivity of research generally, I will here provide some background on my own position as a contributor to this study's data.

I am a Pākehā woman in my mid-30s. I was born and raised in New Zealand in a middle-class, socially liberal family. The first six years of my life were spent living in a small, isolated community in the Whanganui region of New Zealand, on what was known as an *Ohu*, one of several intentional communities set up in rural areas under a government scheme in the 1970s. I attended primary school in a small town in south Taranaki, and then high school in Whanganui. After high school I completed a Bachelor of Arts in Sociology and Media Studies at Massey University, which included two elective papers in linguistics which piqued my interested in the discipline.

I spent some years away from New Zealand, travelling and working in France and the United Kingdom. Upon returning to New Zealand, I decided to act upon my latent enthusiasm for linguistics and returned to university to do so. After undertaking research into representation of refugees and asylum seekers in New Zealand print media as part of my BA (Hons) in linguistics, I was motivated to continue research in this area. My interests in linguistics, the connections between language and wider social issues, social justice, and the complexities of refugee resettlement have culminated in this book, which began life as my PhD thesis. I acknowledge that my position as a politically liberal, feminist, middle-class, Pākehā woman necessarily impact upon every step of this research, just as any researcher's own intersectional identities impact upon theirs. It is my aim that in situating myself within the research and making my position clear, I provide the reader with enough background knowledge to see my presence in the data to follow, which I have also attempted to make explicit where necessary.

Summary

Having introduced this study's participants and myself as researcher and co-contributor to this study's interactional data, I now turn to an exploration of the various and dynamic ways in which these former refugees take up and assign identity positions in narrative.

CHAPTER 5

Identity in narrative

Introduction

Narratives are stories we tell about ourselves and others, and through which we make sense of our experiences and our place in the social world, connecting past events to our contemporary senses of self, and imagining our possible futures (Pomerantz, 2012; Schiffrin, 1996b). They are thus important and rich sites within which to explore the co-constructed negotiation of identity generally, and an employable identity specifically. While the content of narratives can of course be illuminating, from an identity perspective, they are invaluable for examining the positioning of self (both as narrator and protagonist) and Other (both present interlocutor(s) and other characters within the storyworld), and thus the taking up or rejection of dynamic identity positions (Bamberg, 2011a; De Fina, 2003). Exploration of narrative allows us to consider how narrators position themselves relative to the wider Discourses that circulate socially, and which permeate all interaction, whether or not they are directly referenced in little-d discourse. This is particularly pertinent for my focus on the experiences of former refugees. We will see below that in order to take up desirable identity positions as they narrate the stories of their literal and figurative journeys to becoming refugees, Isaac, Kelly, and Omar variously align with and distance themselves from Discourses of Refugeehood, Gratitude, and the Middle East (that is, Western Discourses that involve an essentialised depiction of the Middle East as a 'region of risk' where women are oppressed, passive, and vulnerable (Bankoff, 2003; Mohanty, 1988; Sensoy & DiAngelo, 2006)). Isaac, telling a well-rehearsed story that orients to his audience's expectations of content and narrative moments of tension, aligns with Discourses of Refugeehood, as well as Discourses of Gratitude, wherein telling this type of story might be expected (Nayeri, 2017). Kelly and Omar, however, tell these stories in a different way, interactively positioning themselves in opposition to these Discourses, and rejecting my bids to align them with these Discourses or imagined communities. In telling their stories and positioning themselves vis-à-vis Discourses, they negotiate a sense of belonging and involvement in the local context, with flow-on effects for their ability to negotiate employable identities.

As a short introductory example of the presentation of self within narrative, consider the follow excerpt from Kelly. We had met at a video arcade where her children were attending a birthday party. Almost as soon as we sat down, Kelly casually asked me how I knew the woman who had put us in touch with one another (a refugee resettlement worker). I explained that in fact I did not know her well at all, but that we had mutual work and research associates. Satisfied with this information, Kelly then continued that she would have withdrawn from my research if I had been close to this intermediary, and went on to describe a confrontation with the woman which left her feeling humiliated and undervalued. Kelly told me that she was yelled at by this woman, and berated for using her as a reference on job applications without advising her each time:

Excerpt 5.1 21 May 2016; 10:27–11.03

```
1. Kelly:  there was there was other people + around me
2.         and they saw what she was + they overheard her talking? +
3.         and they're like + she's taking advantage of you because +
4.         you don't + to her + you're a foreigner +
5.         and you don't know what's your right and you don't know that +
6.         you know she thinks that I'm one of the other refugees
7.         that she can yell at? and they would think oh that's fine?
8. Emily:  mm
9. Kelly:  because they've been treated bad for that for all of their life
10.        that they think + yelling at + them + is less than being killed
11.        you know what I mean it's like (2) but I'm not that kind of person
```

The dynamic and emergent nature of identity is clearly evident in this excerpt. Kelly's narrative here, and the wider story that this except comes from which she told over ten minutes, describes an unjustified and public attack on Kelly's character which left her humiliated and led to her withdrawal from participation in a refugee support organisation. However, at an interactional level, Kelly is revealing how she wants to be understood. She is performing identity work and positioning herself as narrator within our interaction and as protagonist within the storyworld she is creating. Kelly uses the constructed dialogue (Marra & Holmes, 2016; Tannen, 1986) of storyworld witnesses to her humiliation (lines 3–5) to position the resettlement worker as exploitative and xenophobic, discursively providing credibility to this position by representing it as being the opinion of others (Bangerter, Mayor, & Doehler, 2011; Matoesian, 2000).

Kelly reassigns this initially-externalised evaluation to herself when she switches from second-person to first-person pronouns on line 6, aligning with me as her interlocutor with the discourse marker *you know* (Stubbe & Holmes, 1995). She firmly positions herself in opposition to the imagined community (B. Anderson, 1991) of refugees and thus Discourses of Refugeehood, distancing herself through third-person pronouns (lines 7, 9, and 10), and simultaneously pitying and belittling the imagined refugees for accepting such objectionable circumstances – perhaps an instantiation of Bourdieu's symbolic violence (Bourdieu & Wacquant, 1992). That is, by invoking Discourses of Refugeehood she contributes to the reproduction of these disempowering Discourses which also impact upon her own experiences in the social world, as a former refugee herself (cf. Bourdieu, 1991).

Kelly further orients herself towards me as interlocutor and away from an imagined community of refugees on line 11, inviting my inference through both *you know what I mean* and an assumed understanding of what *it's like*. Then, introduced by *but*, marking a contrast between these refugees and Kelly to drive home her disalignment with this imagined community, Kelly tells me that she is not *that kind of person*. In an interview situation directly related to her former refugee status, Kelly effectively negotiates a *non*-refugee identity. She does not challenge the storyworld resettlement worker's narrated characterisation of refugees, but rather implicitly supports the depiction (and reinforces Discourses of Refugeehood) while at the same time distancing herself from it.

I use Tannen's (1986) nomenclature of *constructed dialogue* here rather than *reported speech* to emphasise the narrative function of the act of assigning dialogue to storyworld characters. It is unlikely that utterances reported in the storyworld precisely match what was said in 'the real world,' or are necessarily even intended to be taken as such (Marra & Holmes, 2016; Tannen, 1986). Rather, they are reconstructions of dialogue (or even interpretations of actions or inner speech) which the narrator deems relevant to the discursive act being undertaken. Constructed dialogue is then *double-voiced* (Bakhtin, 1981), "the speech of both self and other" (Bucholtz, 1999, p. 447), reporting and evaluating the quoted material at the same time (Bucholtz, 1999; Goffman, 1981; Lanza, 2012; Trester, 2009).

We can see here the rich exploration of identity that narrative data can provide. In fact, narrative analysis, Lanza (2012, p. 303) claims, "is most fruitful when it takes into account the interactional dynamics involved in the emergence of, and performing of, identities." The worlds, characters, and events of narrative accounts are of course not "faithful representations of a past world" (Riessman, 2004, p. 6), but are subjective constructions of past (or ongoing) events that a narrator creates with contextually-specific goals. They are a way for storytellers to draw connections between the past, the present, and the future (Riessman, 2004), and in doing so, take up diverse and changing identity positions.

In narratives that unfold within interview contexts, De Fina (2003, p. 26) notes, "the level of explicit negotiation of identities is important because tellers are often invited to reflect on who they are and how they are defined by society, and therefore they use stories to accomplish socially acceptable self-presentations." That is, the act of narrating is a way for narrators to make sense of the world, their lived experiences, and indeed themselves (Haynes, 2006, p. 402; Pomerantz, 2012, p. 1; Schiffrin, 1996b, pp. 168–169). Through the telling itself, a storyteller may interpret, revise, and reconstruct the contradictory or confusing elements of a story into a "coherent, logical whole" (Pomerantz, 2012, p. 1) in a way that allows them to understand themselves and the role they play within the narrative interaction, in the story being told, and in relation to broader Discourses.

Origins of narrative research

Early narrative research was not focused on its potential to explore identity negotiation. After falling out of vogue in the early 20th century, postmodernism's examination of ideas of 'truth' and power lead to a revival of narrative research in the social sciences, as researchers returned to exploring the stories people tell as a source of data. Labov and Waletsky (1967), motivated to understand as much as possible about the structure of narratives and their use in everyday conversation, proposed a widely influential framework for analysing narratives, which view them as having a somewhat predictable structure, made up of a predictable set of components, following a fairly predictable order (Labov, 1997). Though Labov (2014, p. 204) noted that at a minimum, a narrative will contain "a sequence of two clauses which are temporally ordered," a 'fully formed' narrative may contain an abstract (a clause or two summarising the story), an orientation (identification of the setting, time, persons), one or more complicating actions, an evaluation (the point of the narrative), a resolution, and a coda (a signal that the narrative has finished, and possibly a connection between the end of the story and the present time) (Labov, 2014; Labov & Waletsky, 1967). This structural or functional approach looks at what was said and how it was said in a narrative (its structure), with a view to understanding why it was said (its meaning) (Bamberg, 1997b, p. 335).

While Labov's structural definition advanced narrative studies significantly, subsequent narrative scholars have argued that his approach has led to a tendency to recognise only well-organised, "largely monological" texts as narratives (De Fina & Georgakopoulou, 2008, p. 380). Later interactional approaches to narratives on the other hand, view narrative as both 'talk in interaction' and as social practice, and investigate links between interactive narrative and wider social practices (De Fina & Georgakopoulou, 2008). Thus, a wider range of texts have become recognised as narratives.

The idea of narrative as talk-in-interaction suggests that the structure of a given narrative cannot be separated from the context in which it was created – that is, narratives are emergent, and historically, socially, and politically situated (R. J. Berger & Quinney, 2005; De Fina & Georgakopoulou, 2008; Riessman, 2004). Stories that people tell exist within wider structures of power and inequality that impact upon the form the story takes (R. J. Berger & Quinney, 2005, p. 6; citing Rosenwald & Ochberg, 1992, p. 7). Thus, as noted by Brett Smith (2007, p. 391), "the context, setting, audience, the particular situated purpose of a story, tellability, and the narrative resources available to tellers frame *what* might be said and *how* it can be narrated" (emphasis original). Tellability, according to Ochs and Capps (2001, p. 34), relates to the significance of the narrated events to the interlocutors, and the "way in which events are rhetorically shaped" in the narrative. While storytelling allows storytellers opportunities to create a multitude of meanings and occupy a number of positions within the narrative, these opportunities are culturally and linguistically limited, as the resources for creating meaning "... are highly embedded in what is available and what is normative or dominant in immediate and/or broader cultural/ideological contexts" (Tanyas, 2016, p. 88). Thus, wider Discourses and other social structures play a role in shaping narratives and the identity positions available within them.

Many existing studies recognise this potential of narrative inquiry for exploring identity performance and negotiation. These come from a wide range of disciplines and cover a wide range of topics, including identity as negotiated through Discourses surrounding parenthood (e.g. Attanucci, 1993; V. May, 2004), childhood and adolescence (e.g. Bamberg, 2004c; Kyratzis, 1999), health (e.g. Mills, 1997; Riessman, 2003), crime and incarceration (e.g. McKendy, 2006; Ward & Marshall, 2007), as well as sexuality, race, and class (e.g. Hammack, Thompson, & Pilecki, 2009; C. Johnson, 2005; C. O'Connor, 1999). Studies within linguistics have focused on, among other topics, narrative and identity in workplaces (e.g. Baxter, 2008; J. Holmes, 2005a, 2006a; Marra & Holmes, 2004; Vásquez, 2007), migration and employment (Lanza, 2012), and second-language education (e.g. D. Block, 2006; Darvin & Norton, 2015; Morita, 2004; Norton, 2013; Pavlenko & Lantolf, 2000).

Narratives of flight

To preliminarily examine the ways in which my participants take up identity positions in narrative in this study, and how this relates to their employable identities specifically, we will first look at stories told by the participants about leaving their countries of origin, or a secondary country outside their country of origin (as told in each of their first interviews). These can be described as *narratives of flight*. As mentioned in Chapter 1, media representation frequently depicts refugees as traumatised victims, and thus socially-prevalent Discourses of what it means to be a refugee, including a tellable story of flight, invoke helplessness and victimhood. Discourses of Gratitude may mean that a story of flight might be something that is expected of anyone of refugee background (Nayeri, 2017).

Telling stories about difficult times or traumatic experiences in our lives is not something which is expected of people under ordinary conditions. Reticence to compel someone to relive difficult and potentially upsetting past events means that these kinds of stories are ones which, at least in the Western world, are to be approached with caution or left until the teller initiates such a telling (Nayeri, 2017; Puvimanasinghe, Denson, Augoustinos, & Somasundaram, 2014). This is not the case for (former) refugees however (cf. Hatoss, 2012; Nguyen, 2013). The very act of becoming officially recognised as a refugee by the UNHCR requires the telling and retelling of the conditions which led to a claim for asylum in order to prove a legitimate and well-founded fear of persecution (UNHCR, 2011). Eventual arrival in the ultimate country of resettlement with the status of refugee may require further retellings to support workers, new friends, media, strangers on the street, or, as here, researchers.

It is important to appreciate that, individually, most people of refugee background are people who, up until a certain point in their lives, had the same outsider's view of what it means to be a refugee as those who have not experienced flight. That is, up until the circumstances that necessitated their flight, those who eventually experience refugeehood may have had the same external view of the imagined community (B. Anderson, 1991) of refugees that perhaps the media plays the largest role in shaping, a view that may be informed by framing and images of trauma, dehumanisation, threat, fear, and pity (Gabrielatos & Baker, 2008; Greenbank, 2014; Martínez Lirola, 2014; Sulaiman-Hill et al., 2011).

A typical story of flight influenced by these Discourses might be expected to include elements of hardships, pitiable conditions, danger, resilience and eventual safety. For some former refugees, as Eastmond (2007, p. 252) discusses, telling their stories of struggle can be a "source of self-esteem and agency," and some felt that in *not* telling their stories, "suffering became meaningless as it became socially invisible" (Eastmond, 2007, p. 252). However, social and media Discourses might lead a non-refugee audience to expect a certain kind of story when former refugees describe the stimuli for and conditions surrounding their departure from their countries of origin. Although these Discourses may be benevolent in nature, such representation can hinder recognition of refugees' skills and ability to contribute to their host societies (Greenbank, 2014, p. 51), and can in fact be an "impediment to… standings as full members of society" (Fraser, 2003, p. 31; cited in Marlowe, 2010, p. 7). It may thus impact upon an individual's capacity to navigate the labour market successfully and enact a locally-useful employable identity. It is unsurprising, then, that in the telling (or avoiding the telling) of stories of flight, people of refugee background may not feel particularly inclined to orient towards Discourses of Refugeehood and Gratitude, or to enact victim-like, powerless identities.

I recognise the irony in, on the one hand, calling attention to the ways in which a perpetual expectation of retelling a story of flight contributes to othering Discourses of Gratitude, and on the other, asking my participants for their stories of flight. In a research context in which former refugee status is salient, I believe that examination of this aspect of participants' identity work can be helpful and illuminating. Nonetheless, it is clear to me as I reflect upon my research trajectory that I was influenced by these same Discourses of Refugeehood and Gratitude that I have come to problematise here in my analysis.

Narratives of flight are a rich data source for exploring people's senses of self, providing speakers with the opportunity to instead negotiate an empowered identity in discourse (Lanza, 2012, p. 289), as well as, for the researcher, "[providing] insight into how speakers position themselves to Discourse within the local discourse of interaction" (Lanza, 2012, p. 288). As we will see, my participants are aware of and position themselves relative to these Discourses, in some cases aligning with and sometimes distancing themselves from them.

Aligning with discourses

Isaac's narrative of flight from Eritrea follows a typical Labovian narrative structure. He has told this story many times, both privately and publicly, and this is reflected in the well-honed and skilful telling of it. The narrative's *abstract*, in this telling, was in fact provided by my question. Earlier, I had asked Isaac what age he had been when he left Eritrea, and the conversation had drifted towards his (beginnings of) university education there. I repeated his age at departure in an attempt to elicit his story of flight, which Isaac recognised as such and provided. As discussed in Chapter 4, Isaac travelled to the border with Sudan using a forged travel permit, was almost caught at the last checkpoint when his travel document was taken away to be checked by a soldier, re-boarded the bus and left before the soldier returned, paid a smuggler who took his money and disappeared, and paid another smuggler who finally got him across the border. Isaac began this story by replying to my abstract-providing question with the story's *orientation* of his city's distance from the Sudanese border, and the checkpoints along the way:

Excerpt 5.2 30 March 2016; 17.21–17.40

```
1. Emily: yeah (1) so you were about eighteen when you left
2.        and you went to Sudan did you say
3. Isaac: yeah so I I got some + money from so + from the capital city where I
4.        where I lived +to the border is around three hundred fifty + or + close
5.        four hundred rightso there is probably more than hundred check +
6.        + security check points
```

Isaac then provides four sets of *complicating actions* for his narrative of flight, beginning with a forged document:

Excerpt 5.3 30 March 2016; 17.48–17.55

```
1. Isaac:  my brother like faked (1) ah the (2) security pass for me?
```

An extra check at the last checkpoint:

Excerpt 5.4 30 March 2016; 18.19–18.26

```
1. Isaac:  I made it in the last check point in the last check point he said
2.         ok we're gonna + I'm gonna take this to my commander
```

His brother being called back to the capital:

Excerpt 5.5 30 March 2016; 19.29–19.44

```
1. Isaac:  so they have to take him back (1) to one like two hundred fifty k
2.         to + he they told him that we will investigate you you your document
3.         his document even though it was a + genuine (1) document
```

And finally, the disappearance of a smuggler whom Isaac had paid to get him across the border:

Excerpt 5.6 30 March 2016; 20.15–20.20

```
1. Isaac:  so this guy we gave him four hundred + in advance
2.         he took that four hundred and disappeared
```

Isaac then provides the *evaluation*, or the importance of this narrative, quickly followed by the resolution:

Excerpt 5.7 30 March 2016; 20.45–21.14

```
1. Isaac:  if you got caught and then (1) seven eight years with no caution
2.         you would be like languishing in undergrounds + because you are
           a traitor +
3.         you trait your country (1) so + either way it was was it was it
           was very
4.         (1) um important moment in my life + if I made it that day and then
5.         I would be free forever and if not + then I would be +
6. Emily:  //yeah\
7. Isaac:  /you know\\ my life would be like + dark forever
8.         I I did made it +luckily
```

Then after a short description of presenting himself to a refugee camp in Sudan, Isaac provides the *coda* to signal the narrative's conclusion and bring as both as interlocutors back to the present:

Excerpt 5.8 30 March 2016; 21.20–21.27

```
1. Isaac:  I + went through the interviews and +
2.         blah blah blah you know the all the (1) the the process
```

It is perhaps not surprising that Isaac's story is so Labovian in structure, given the number of opportunities he has had to publicly tell his story (cf. van de Mieroop,

2009), and thus refine the flow of the narrative steps, cut any unnecessary 'filler,' and focus on the details that he has become aware are most salient or interesting to his current interlocutors. He has considerable experience in discerning what kind of story it is that his various audiences are actually requesting. Isaac's use of *blah blah blah* as (part of) the story's coda speaks to the frequency with which he has – and does – tell this story, as well as the extent to which his story aligns with Discourses of Refugeehood and stories of flight. He displays a confidence that the information implied by *blah blah blah* can be inferred by me as his interlocutor.

In fact, I have witnessed Isaac tell his story of flight more than once outside of the interview from which this chapter's excerpts are taken, and it has never included precisely the same elements. Isaac adjusts what Labov (2014; Labov & Waletsky, 1967) would called the complicating actions in each telling, skilfully reworking the salient aspects of his story depending on his interactional context. However, the strongly Labovian structure of Isaac's story leaves little room for the micro, fleeting moments of identity negotiation found in less rehearsed stories (cf. van de Mieroop, 2009), and thus his story stands in contrast from the other participants' narratives of flight, as we will see below.

While structure and thematic content still contribute to an interactional analysis of narrative, attention turns to the co-construction of meaning where both the storyteller and the audience of the narrative are active participants in the creation of the story, and meaning is jointly created (Bamberg, 1997b; De Fina & Georgakopoulou, 2008; Riessman, 2004). Thus, the unit of analysis is the social practice, not the story in and of itself (Bamberg, 2011a, p. 107). This shift away from a focus on a narrative's structure and coherence has also meant that inconsistency and ambiguity rather than being "analytic nuisance[s]" can be the most valuable sources of data for analysis (Bamberg, 2004b, p. 222). Narratives are also a useful source of identity work because of the fact that, in the telling of stories, speakers "… rework and reimagine the past, reflect back upon [themselves], and entertain what [they] have become and could become," (R. J. Berger & Quinney, 2005, p. 5). The very act of narrating creates and maintains a sense of self or identity for the teller (Bamberg & Georgakopoulou, 2008), and highlights the dynamic nature of identity; "because we can tell different stories we can construct different versions of self" (Benwell & Stokoe, 2006, p. 138; cited in Lanza, 2012, p. 287). From this view, narratives do not so much reflect or reveal identity, but rather function as the vehicle through which identity emerges. Compared with Isaac's story, the seemingly less-rehearsed narratives of flight of Kelly and Omar allow greater exploration of this co-constructed and interactively negotiated identity in narrative, along with their rejection of wider Discourses and my attempted positioning relative to them.

Resisting discourses

In the data presented below, Omar and Kelly, in different ways, resist their positioning as what we might think of as a typical refugee as informed by Discourses of both Refugeehood and Gratitude. In answering my (direct or indirect) questions about how they came to be a refugee (i.e. to tell their stories of flight) both Omar and Kelly took the opportunity to tell me a different story about themselves – stories of strength, of competence, and of resilience.

Of course, there may be many reasons for rejecting the opportunity to tell a 'typical' story of flight. It may be a painful or difficult story to relive. It may have become tedious to relay after multiple retellings. Refusing to tell may be a rejection of the expectation that, by nature of being a refugee, this story must be told upon request. Or it may be that the retelling of the story, the reliving of it, and the continued orientation to this identity itself acts as a barrier to full participation in your new society, a constant reminder of your Otherness that sets you apart from the rest of your host society. For any migrant to truly be a part of the host society, as Chavez (1991, p. 259) points out, "depends not just on their own personal changes but also on the larger society's willingness to "imagine" them as members of the community." Continually orienting to an outsider identity may negatively impact on a former refugee's sense of self as well as act as a barrier to social inclusion. The impact for former refugee jobseekers, then, is clear: to continually be required to enact a grateful or vulnerable refugee identity is to continually be denied the opportunity to negotiate a desirable, competent employable identity (cf. J. Holmes, 2014; Marra, 2012).

Kelly

Kelly's ostensive narrative of flight is not the story of how she came to be a refugee, but rather her later flight as an adult, from Palestine in a state of war, and equally (or perhaps more so) from her husband. This narrative was prompted by my asking her why she had remained in Palestine after her parents and sister had returned to New Zealand. She begins her story by describing the rising tensions between the two main political parties, Hamas and Fatah, and in doing so interactionally positions herself vis-à-vis Middle Eastern Discourses, and her former husband:

Excerpt 5.9 8 April 2016; 28.27–28.53

```
1. Kelly:  so + we have nightclubs in Palestine (1)
2.         all those nightclubs were burned + um women that wear trousers:::
3.         were like + sh- + um (2) threatened a little bit? [one beat laugh]
4.         so um (1) I was locked up I didn't have to worry about anything
5.         I mean my whole marriage I was + basically locked up
6.         he wouldn't allow me to go anywhere
```

Opening her story with sequence-initial, other-attentive discourse marker *so* (Bolden, 2009), Kelly orients this utterance towards my assumed knowledge gap, indicating that she expects the information given on line 1 to be new, and perhaps surprising, to me. This is further indicated by the demonstrative tone of the utterance, and the pause following it, allowing me to react to this news (although I have not recorded my non-verbal minimal feedback, when not giving verbal feedback, I was typically nodding to acknowledge my participants' utterances). Here she positions me as a novice on the topic of Palestine and positions herself by contrast as an expert, a qualified narrator.

The framing of nightclubs in Palestine as newsworthy, and the imagery of their destruction (line 2), both assume a shared understanding of Discourses of the Middle East. Kelly had established her (negative) position on traditional Middle Eastern values earlier in our conversation, and her assumption of my understanding discursively aligns her with me (a Western woman) and distances her from those Discourses (as well as, perhaps, denying their power). This is further highlighted when Kelly refers to *women that wear trousers* seemingly as a metonymic surrogate for women who do not conform to conservative Middle Eastern expectations. She is able to further distance herself from the Discourses by interactively minimising the threat to the women, and thus trivialising it. She achieves this through her hesitating description of the intimidation of the women, with a false start, discourse filler *um* and a two second pause, and then underlined by explicitly following *threatened* with *a little bit* (said with a high-rising terminal (HRT) – see Warren (2016) for a discussion on the role of HRT, or 'uptalk,' in New Zealand English).

Kelly then laughs at this scene she has painted as a backdrop to her story. Kelly laughs frequently throughout all of our interactions, and rarely in response to humour. Although laughter in discourse frequently accompanies occurrences of humour, the two have been shown to be "discrete entities" which are "functionally distinct in interaction" (Warner-Garcia, 2014, p. 158). The strategic placement of laughter can be used to perform particular interactional functions and to manage social relationships (Billig, 2005, p. 190; Warner-Garcia, 2014, pp. 157–158). Strategic laughter (as opposed to involuntary laughter in response to humour) may be culturally-specific and thus depends on context for 'correct' interpretation (although Milford (1980) claims that such "symbolic laughter" is used similarly across cultural contexts). Nonetheless, in this particular interactive context, this instance of Kelly's laughter has the discursive effect of framing the preceding content as trivial, or foolish.

Having provided her story's (Labovian) orientation, Kelly then employs *so* again (line 4) to resume the personally-relevant orientation of her narrative (Bolden, 2009, p. 982), moving the focus from the outside battle and (re)setting the scene for the discursively salient battle (in which she can perform important identity work) within this narrative: her domestic battle. After stating that she was *locked up*, Kelly softens this premise on line 5, introduced by *I mean* which can mark an adjustment in positioning (Fox Tree & Schrock, 2002, p. 742), and rephrasing her imprisonment as *basically locked up*, with *basically* here seeming to function to indicate that the following material is not to be taken literally. Then explaining what she means by this on line 6, Kelly-as-narrator makes clear that Kelly-as-protagonist was subject to her husband's will.

The *content* of the scene that Kelly describes is at odds with the identity of strength and independence (not to mention a low tolerance for being treated badly) that Kelly so consistently orients to throughout her narrative. However, in fact Kelly spoke lines 4–6 in a tone which sounds as if she were on the verge of laughter the whole time. In doing so, she appears to discursively reframe the situation in a less serious light, as if it were almost comical, perhaps allowing Kelly-as-narrator to save face within the interaction (Warner-Garcia, 2014), and reconcile the experiences of Kelly-as-protagonist (and prisoner) with a current sense of self as a self-reliant and free woman.

It could be argued from the way that Kelly uses laughter and the specific points at which she uses it, that she is not seeking to indicate humorous content in her utterances, but rather to agentively interactionally position herself and other characters within her narratives, and thus take up various and dynamic identity positions. Similar use of laughter can be seen a little later in this narrative, when Kelly talks about how her parents, who had already experienced (and fled) war in Kuwait some fifteen years earlier, left Palestine at the first hint of war (i.e. Hamas winning the election):

Excerpt 5.10 8 April 2016; 29.52–30.05

```
1. Kelly:  as soon as they won my parents saw absolutely nothing [laughs]
2.         from all of that + um + they left straight away they knew like
3.         this is not good we're leaving bye bye [laughs] and they left
```

Kelly repeatedly describes her parents' rapid departure: they *saw absolutely nothing* (line 1), they *left straight away* (line 2), they said *we're leaving* (line 3), and finally, *they left* (line 3). This repetition alone would indicate that this incident is to be understood as significant, but Kelly's humourless laughter on lines 1 and 3 interactionally mitigate this somewhat. As Warner-Garcia (2014, pp. 159–160) notes, laughter can be used to conceal loss of face, and can shift a serious framing of an incident to a more non-serious one. If being left by one's parents in a war zone could be described so trivially as 'face-threatening,' it is easy to see how Kelly's laughter allows her to distance herself (as narrator) from herself as protagonist by interactionally brushing off the incident as non-serious. This is further emphasised on line 3 as she characterises her parents' farewell as a flippant *bye bye*, an extraordinarily casual depiction of a farewell from parents leaving their daughter in an unhappy, controlling marriage, not to mention a literal war zone.

Functionally mitigating laughter, as Billig (2005, pp. 190–191) notes, must be "precisely placed within utterances, in order to indicate exactly what is to be softened, mitigated, [or] marked as problematic," and Kelly is skilfully doing so here in a way that interactionally serves to distance herself from the narrated events as protagonist, and save face. Thus, she agentively counteracts the threat to her identity as an in-control woman which is posed by her narrated abandonment.

Kelly then went on to tell me her strategy for dealing with her unhappy marriage and the fact that her husband would not allow Kelly and their children to leave Palestine despite the war: to make her husband's home life as unpleasant as possible. While Kelly's parents were still in the country her husband would complain to them about Kelly's behaviour, and they would tell her to *behave* (Kelly's term), but once they had left he was unable to access this support:

Excerpt 5.11 8 April 2016; 30.50–31.03

```
1. I swear there was like two months (1) that I spoke absolutely nothing to him
2. (2) after my parents left and he just ran out of ideas
3. what to do with me [laughs][1]
```

Kelly introduces her act of rebellion on line 1 with *I swear*, which functions to add credibility to the claim she makes about not speaking to her husband for two months when this might otherwise be inferred as exaggeration (Opsahl, 2009). It also underscores its impact as a form of defiance, which is further emphasised by intensifier *absolutely* later on line 1 to highlight the magnitude of her 'disobedience.' Her two-second pause on line 2 may indicate an expectation of a verbal reaction from me as listener, which was not forthcoming (beyond non-verbal feedback), and Kelly continues to describe her husband's failure to redress the situation, in which Kelly is by implication the agent of his failure. Here her laughter (line 3) seems to play an interactionally ridiculing function (Billig, 2005), belittling her husband's failing, assigning a powerful position to both Kelly-as-protagonist and Kelly-as-narrator. Although Kelly has narrated a scenario in which she is essentially a prisoner, by creating a storyworld in which she is able to psychologically outwit her husband, she interactively negotiates an identity of resilience and resourcefulness, and as powerful relational to her husband who physically controlled her body but was unable to control her spirit (I use physical here to describe Kelly's

1. I should note here that although from my own perspective as a Western woman, Kelly seems to position both her husband and herself as children here (him telling on her, her being reprimanded by her parents), it is not unusual in Muslim families for children to be expected to obey their parents even as adults (Binghalib, 2011, p. 14). I thus hesitate to label this as 'childlike' positioning in Kelly's narrative. Nonetheless, Kelly is narrating this in a New Zealand context as a woman who generally orients away from Middle Eastern norms. She would be well aware that this situation is not 'normal' to me, and thus her choices of positioning vis-à-vis me as interlocutor may be meaningful.

husband's restrictions on her whereabouts and activities rather than to suggest he used violence to do so. Whether he used physical force or power imbued by social structure (or both) is unknown to me).

Kelly then continued to orient to her identity of victor (over her husband) telling me how, when stuck between 'a rock and hard place,' her husband relented and allowed her to return to New Zealand:

Excerpt 5.12 8 April 2016; 32.17–32.44

```
1. Kelly: he just gave up and he thought + that's it go + to + ah New Zealand
2.        but (1) so I had a bit of money? + he took my money
3.        and he said this money is my insurance that you will send me a visa
4.        (1) I sent him a visa + and I told him you can shove the money up
          your ass
5.        if I don't want no money I don't want anything to do with you
6.        and + that's it [laughs] yeah
```

Kelly uses the same adverbial *just* phrasing described above (Excerpt 5.11) to describe her husband's surrender on line 1. While frequently used as a minimiser, *just* here has the effect of emphasising his failure to control Kelly (Lindemann & Mauranen, 2001; Vine, 2017), positioning him as weak, and as the loser of their battle of wills. Kelly narrates from a powerful position as she constructs her husband's inner dialogue (line 1), *that's it*, wording she repeats in her own constructed dialogue (directed towards her husband) on line 6 to indicate the end of their relationship.

These two instances of *that's it* bookend her husband's final attempt to control her in the storyworld, and Kelly-as-protagonist's repetition of her husband's words discursively reassigns the power of declaring 'the end' from the husband to herself. Kelly's reclamation of this final power play by both sending him the visa *and* rejecting the money he had withheld seems to construct her husband as pathetic and desperate, and herself by contrast as in control, and on the moral high ground (having sent him the visa because it was the right thing to do for her children, and not because he was wielding any financial power over her).

Her violent (reported) language directed toward her husband (*you can shove the money up your ass*, line 4) underscores her highly agentive position as protagonist and the force of her rejection of his power play. In addition, I would argue that Kelly's use of double negative *I don't want no money* on line 5 is a kind of double-voiced (Bakhtin, 1981) performance of a resolute or 'tough' position, indexing the covert prestige of non-standard English varieties (Trudgill, 1974). Finally, Kelly's laughter following this description of the end of the relationship on *her* terms has the interactional effect of both ridiculing her husband's narrated actions and mitigating Kelly's strongly-worded rejection (Billig, 2005; Chafe, 2003).

In this story of flight, Kelly's actual return to New Zealand is passed over entirely. The literal war that was (at least in part) Kelly's motivation for leaving

Palestine is also backgrounded as she focuses the narrative on her victory over her husband. This omission is meaningful as, by implication, what Kelly presumably gained in her return to New Zealand – independence and distance from her husband and the war – is less important in the context of this interaction than Kelly's self-positioning as the battle's winner.

Kelly describes here some objectively terrible circumstances – war, abandonment, imprisonment, blackmail – but never once portrays the storyworld conditions as pitiable, or traumatic, nor positions herself as vulnerable, or a victim. Instead, the telling of this story creates an opportunity to negotiate an identity of independence, resilience, and strength. Portraying the fight for her freedom as a sort of battle of wills within her household mirroring the actual conflict outside her household, Kelly describes her struggle against her husband, and her eventual emergence from the ruins of her marriage as the victor. She consistently and variously distances herself from Discourses of the Middle East and Refugeehood, both explicitly and by omission, choosing instead to focus on her own resilience and resourcefulness in orchestrating her escape. Kelly's story is one of a personal battle with the backdrop of an actual war, and her self-positioning within it, as we will see (Chapters 6 and 7, to follow), is reflected in the way she negotiates her employable identity in her job search.

Omar

Like Kelly, Omar, in telling his story of flight, continually orients away from Discourses of Refugeehood. Making clear the substantial danger that prompted his family's flight, he nonetheless interactionally distinguishes his family from media Discourses of Refugeehood, and orients to an identity of capability and competence in the face of danger. Here, Omar had been describing returning home after finishing what turned out to be his final contract as a ship engineer:

Excerpt 5.13 4 June 2016; 9.05–9.31

```
1. Omar:  I came back to Syria + and a massacre happened place in my city
2. Emily: mm
3. Omar:  (1) you know several thousand people been slaughtered
4.        have been killed (1) in my city
5. Emily: [quietly] oh my god
6. Omar:  after that I: tell myself I have to + take my family
7. Emily: mm=
8. Omar:  =my children my wife and my children + and went + directly
9.        from Syria to Egypt + legally + not illegally legally by airplane
```

Interestingly, Omar assigns no agent to the massacre which was the impetus for his family's departure (line 1); portraying it simply as something which *happened*. By not narratively engaging with the perpetrators of this act, he assigns them no role in his narrative, and keeps the focus firmly on his (and his family's) journey. My minimal feedback to this information (line 2) seems to be insufficient to Omar, as (after a pause in which he perhaps was allowing me room for comment) he invites my further inference with *you know* (line 3) (Fox Tree & Schrock, 2002) and rewords and expands his description of the scenario. This reiteration draws a response from me which is more appreciative of the gravity of his words (line 5). My initial (underwhelming) reaction may have implied to Omar that I had not fully understood, or that I had not yet heard sufficient motivation for his family becoming refugees. Through his reiteration and my revised response, Omar and I discursively co-construct an agreement of the significance of the narrated event, which may stand in opposition to negative media Discourses of the validity of flight, and voluntary vs. involuntary migration.

Positioning himself as a competent and rational man with respect to his relationship and responsibility to his family (lines 6 and 8), Omar then dialogically disaligns with an imagined community (B. Anderson, 1991) of Other refugees and asylum seekers by emphasising that his family travelled *directly* to Egypt, and by repeating that they travelled *legally*, not *illegally* and that their trip was by *airplane* (line 9), dialogically responding to an absent challenge to their legal status. This description indexes by implication, and distances him from, the unmentioned (and at the time, very prevalent in the media) image of hundreds of thousands of refugees – Syrians and others – travelling on foot and by sea to an ambivalent and often hostile Europe. Omar here orients away from Discourses of what it is to be a refugee (particularly media Discourses), and instead orients to an identity of independence and competence in a crisis, as he looked after his family.

A little later, after describing his family's time in Egypt, Omar came to the point in his story at which his family came to New Zealand, wherein we see Omar discursively reject my implicit invitation for him to align with refugeehood.

Excerpt 5.14 4 June 2016; 10.17–10.49

```
1.  Omar:  an::d they sent us to + New Zealand
2.  Emily: ok (1) so that would have been sort of just before + I guess maybe
3.  Omar:  I spent about twenty months in Egypt + //after I\ came here
4.  Emily: /did you\\ (2) so tha- so you must have come here
5.         just as the kind of the whol:e + refugee crisis //was\
6.         was starting (1) that must have been quite a
7.         (2) strange thing to witness on the media
8.  Omar:  /yeah\\
9.  Omar:  for me see + ah to go outside of Syria is not a big issue
10. Emily: mm
11. Omar:  because I used to
12. Emily: yeah
13. Omar:  travelling but this is the first time I take my family with me
```

Beginning with *so* to mark an inferential connection (Bolden, 2009) between Omar's narrative and the following material (line 2), I begin a highly mitigated attempt to ask a question (evidenced through a quick succession of markers of uncertainty *sort of, I guess* and *maybe*), before being cut off by Omar either redirecting the conversation, or misinterpreting my aborted question as pertaining to his time spent in Egypt (line 3). Following a two-second pause which would have allowed Omar to continue narrating, had he wished to, I then relaunched my question, with the expectation that Omar would pick up on my cue and discuss his relationship to the wider exodus of Syrians from Syria. Initially, I attempted to be delicate in my approach lest discussing the topic be distressing for him, and then as my long-winded circuitous question continued and I saw no uptake in Omar's body language and a one syllable acknowledgement of the times matching up (line 8), I began to feel uncomfortable about what I was asking.

My discomfort is evident in the false start, pauses, and mitigating *kind of*. I began, on line 6, to respond to my own question by suggestion how Omar might have experienced media coverage of the event, but in fact by line 7 had changed tack once more part way through my utterance (unwilling to project hardship when I was receiving no uptake) to arrive at a much-diluted conclusion that it must have been a *strange* experience. Through Omar's lack of visual or verbal uptake and my own backing away from the question even as I asked it, we co-constructed distance between Omar (and his family) and the (media coverage of the) so-called Syrian refugee crisis, and thus Discourses of Refugeehood. Omar then reinforced this rejection of my position by redirecting the conversation toward issues of resettlement (lines 9, 11, 13), positioning himself as a worldly and experienced traveller whose only challenge was the company of his less well-travelled family. Although discursively encouraged to do so through my convoluted line of questioning, Omar seems to reject the invitation to orient to a refugee identity, and agentively reorients to an identity of competence.

While Omar's narrative includes the expected elements of danger, flight, dealing with the UNHCR, and eventual arrival in New Zealand, he uses his narrative of flight to negotiate a competent, worldly identity, and in doing so perhaps establishes a sense of self that is resilient and equipped to deal with the challenges of resettlement (and the labour market). As we will see in the chapters to come, this identity performance plays a large role in the way that Omar attempts to navigate his employable identity in New Zealand, as he struggles with the personal challenges of underemployment and his attempts to ameliorate his circumstances.

Discussion

Exploring identity through storytelling can be particularly useful in studies of forced migrants, where narratives are sometimes "the only means we have of knowing something about life in times and places to which we have little other access" (Eastmond, 2007, p. 249), and provide opportunities "to [grasp] the interplay between self and society" (Eastmond, 2007, p. 249). Narratives can help displaced persons "make sense of [their] displacement... [and] re-establish identity in ruptured life courses" (Eastmond, 2007, p. 248). A narrative approach can reveal the complex nature of acutely challenging resettlement situations, and the specific social and economic implications therein.

Studies exploring forced migration and its ongoing ramifications through narratives have covered a wide range of areas, including Mexican migrants in the United States (De Fina, 2006), Jewish-American mothers (Schiffrin, 1996b), New Zealand workplaces (J. Holmes, 2006b), LGBT asylum claimants (Berg & Millbank, 2009), (former) refugee youth (Hoffman Clark, 2007; Oikonomidoy, 2010), and both media and individual narratives surrounding refugees in Australia (Hatoss, 2012; Leudar et al., 2008). These studies examine the ways in which former refugees position themselves (and others within their narratives) and are positioned in relation to wider Discourses, recognising that "the self is social in origin and narratively structured" (Leudar et al., 2008, p. 190), as well as exploring experiences of Othering where it becomes clear that identities "are in a dynamic relationship with the identities ascribed by outsiders" (Hatoss, 2012, p. 65).

These studies recognise that in the telling of stories about ourselves we reveal how we wish our interlocutors to understand us. By positioning self and other both within the interaction itself and within the narrated storyworld, we take up or resist dynamic identity positions, co-constructed with our interlocutors who may in turn accept or reject our positioning. Within narrative we also draw upon and position ourselves relative to wider social Discourses. We have seen here how exploration of the navigation of identity in the narratives of flight of these former refugee participants is particularly useful for exploring the interactional strategies they employ to align with, distance themselves from, or draw upon Discourses of Refugeehood, the Middle East, and Gratitude. These Discourses can serve to Other those associated with them, and being Othered can present a threat to one's sense of sense as employable, especially if it is tied up with a sense of belonging.

For Isaac at least, alignment with Discourses of Refugeehood did not seem to pose an identity threat. His narrative of flight closely followed a Labovian narrative structure and, evident in the way it was delivered, was a well-rehearsed story designed to hit all the points expected of a narrative of flight without discursively mitigating any aspect of it. In telling this story in this manner Isaac drew upon Discourse of Refugeehood and discursively oriented to a refugee identity. It is worth noting, of course, that the very telling of his story, publicly, is what Isaac believes initially opened doors to him in terms of his current educational and employment situation (see Chapter 4). Thus, the telling of a typical refugee story for him is not a face-threatening act or one which risks him ceding any power; it is not an identity which is at odds with his employable identity, but rather one which had augmented it.

Kelly's narrative of flight, on the other hand, while containing descriptions of what might ordinarily be considered terrible or trying circumstances, is presented as a darkly comical marital battle. Even as she describes war, abandonment, imprisonment, and blackmail experienced by Kelly-as-protagonist, Kelly-as-narrator continually mitigates the seriousness of the storyworld – and saves face both as protagonist and narrator – through laughter (and laugher-like tone). Presenting her escape as a battle against her former husband from which she emerges the eventual victor, omitting the details of the actual war, and interactionally belittling and dismissing her husband, Kelly agentively distances herself from Discourses indexing vulnerability and helplessness that are associated with former refugees. She negotiates instead an identity of strength, determination, and resilience.

Like Kelly, Omar rejects Discourses of Refugeehood in the telling of his narrative of flight. He employs agency to dialogically pre-empt an unmentioned challenge to the legality of his family's journey to Egypt, making a contrast between his family and 'other' refugees (I refer here to Discourses of 'illegal asylum seekers,' which is a nonsensical term, as seeking asylum is never illegal). Furthermore, a later discursive attempt in my hesitant questions to align Omar and his family with the Syrian refugee crisis was agentively and decisively rejected by Omar. Instead of orienting towards media Discourses surrounding Syrian refugees at the time, even when explicitly invited to do so, Omar skilfully controlled the conversation and navigated an identity of personal capability, worldliness and responsibility to his family.

Kelly and Omar employ agency as narrators to tell the stories they want to tell, and to assign their protagonist selves agency in the storyworld, as they describe circumstances which might otherwise assume low agency. Here all of these participants are able to retain or reclaim power in the telling of a potentially disenfranchising story, by, when necessary, orienting to other aspects of their identity, and not allowing themselves to be positioned in undesirable ways relative to social Discourses. Lanza (2012, p. 303) notes that narratives are "without doubt an important resource for… identity construction in interaction, especially in regards to issues of agency and power in multilingual contexts," allowing these storytellers the interactive space in which to navigate desirable and powerful identities. We can see the importance of agency in granting narrators the ability to reframe themselves within their stories, and view themselves as competent, capable, resilient – and (directly or indirectly) employable.

They face a 'dilemma' however, in presenting themselves as employable and resisting Discourses of Refugeehood and vulnerability, while at the same time not entirely rejecting Discourse of Gratitude which may be salient in the co-constructed negotiation of an employable identity in a New Zealand context. This capacity to reframe themselves in narrative and to resist undesirable positioning is important in the negotiation of an employable identity, where disempowering Discourses may undermine attempts to orient to competent, capable identities. It is this agency dilemma (Bamberg, 2011a, 2011b), and the strategic discursive employment of agency in identity navigation, which I explore in the following chapter.

CHAPTER 6

Navigating structure and agency

Introduction

Telling stories about ourselves and our past experiences plays an important role in the negotiation of identity. In doing so, narrators make choices about the way they position themselves relative to social Discourses and past (protagonist) selves. This becomes particularly salient when attempting to interactively negotiate a locally-useful employable identity. We saw in the previous chapter that when asked to tell me their stories of flight (explicitly, or implicitly through the interview context), Kelly and Omar chose to tell me stories that deviated from what might be expected to be a typical refugee narrative of flight, by variously taking up and rejecting higher and lower agency discursive positions. For Isaac, the retelling of his story of flight as a typical or expected narrative did not present any threat to his sense of self as agentive, as the very telling of it had opened doors to him. But Kelly reframed her story as a battle with her husband from which she emerged victorious, and Omar interactively avoided or rejected any positioning – by either himself as narrator or me as interlocutor – that might align him with an imagined community of pitiable refugees, or with Discourses of Refugeehood. Through agentive narration the participants were able to position themselves in ways that allowed them to retain a sense of themselves as powerful and capable.

Discursive agency plays an important role in negotiating an employable identity. Speakers navigate agentive self- and other-positioning as narrators and protagonists in narrative to explain the challenges they face, retain a sense of self as being able to act upon the world, and navigate expectations of refugeehood. Narrating events in which the teller is a participant requires choices about how the self is positioned in relation to others and in relation to dominant social structures including Discourses and ideologies. Examining these choices and how agency is navigated allows observation of the emergent identities that are performed and co-constructed through that narrative (Bamberg, 2011a, p. 106). To illustrate the discursive enactment of agency as it relates to the negotiation of an employable identity, let us briefly examine the following excerpt from Omar, in which he discusses having given up his dream of studying towards a master's degree upon arriving in New Zealand in favour of engaging in what Piller (2016) calls 'survival employment,' that is, working below one's skill and education level:

Excerpt 6.1 18 January 2018; 19.15–19.33

```
1. Omar:  here I've been in between two choices
2.        + to continue studying or to ah:: go back to work
3. Emily: mm
4. Omar:  for that (1) because I'm family man + I tell myself
5.        that it's better for me to go to work
6. Emily: mm
7. Omar:  instead of continue my study
```

Omar discursively takes up an agentive position as he describes giving up his dream (as well as perhaps the opportunity to improve his chances of gaining employment more commensurate with his experience and existing qualifications). Omar-as-protagonist is depicted at being at a crossroads, faced with a difficult choice, but a choice nonetheless. Orienting to his identity as a *family man* (line 4), Omar portrays two narrative selves (Bamberg, 2017) where the first narrative self (*I*) tells the second narrative self (*myself*) to choose work (and family) over study (and self) (line 5). Omar takes up an agentive position in the storyworld, portraying the choice as his to make, despite the structural constraints.

In the here-and-now interview context, speaking from a position of underemployment, Omar also positions himself agentively with regards to his earlier choice, in which he made a sensible, family-oriented, and perhaps sacrificial decision (Bamberg's (2011b) agentive hero positioning; see agency dilemma, below). This may allow Omar to retain his sense of self as agentive and in control, which are important elements in performing an employable identity. Thus, he reconciles his past, protagonist self – who was between a rock and a hard place – and his present self – employed, but considerably more employable.

The exploration of agency plays a significant role in narrative research. In telling stories, speakers frame and reframe events and characters, creating meaning and shaping interpretation of the storyworld. That is, the narrator (consciously or unconsciously) arranges, selects, and neglects information to guide inference, and in doing so can claim or cede agency through both the role of a character within the narrative, and through the act of narrating itself (Bucholtz & Hall, 2005; Schiffrin, 1996b; Tanyas, 2016).

It is in this manipulation of discursive meaning that identity emerges. Exploring the ways in which speakers construct their narratives can shed light on how the narrators represent the self and position themselves as agentive or otherwise (De Fina, 2003, p. 220). Of course, the possibilities for narrators to use agency to create meaning and take up various positions are not limitless. Due to the mutually-constitutive nature of structure and agency, both are "intertwined as components of micro as well as macro articulations of identity" (Bucholtz & Hall, 2005, p. 607). While an employable identity is, for anyone, negotiated against a backdrop of existent social structure, former refugees have consistently been shown to come up against greater structural challenges than the average job seeker (e.g. Bloch, 2000; Colic-Peisker, 2009; Feeney, 2000; Koyama, 2013; Lamba, 2003). Alongside possible challenges such as language barriers, lingering trauma, changing family roles, and non-recognition of qualifications and experience, as discussed in Chapter 2, former refugees face discursive hurdles such as local cultural (linguistic) norms, and the socially-appropriate navigation of social Discourses.

From an interactional sociolinguistic perspective, the performance of identity is "one kind of action that agency can accomplish" (Bucholtz & Hall, 2005, p. 606). However, storytellers do not have equal access to linguistic and wider social discursive resources with which to take up and assign various positionings. Discourses which index helplessness and vulnerability, alongside Discourses of Gratitude, may impact upon former refugees' ability to maintain a sense of self as agentive, or have agentive self-positioning ratified by interlocutors, and to perform a locally-appropriate employable identity. We will see in the data to follow the ways in which former periods of low agency can be narratively reframed to reclaim agency in the present. A 'dilemma' (Bamberg, 2011b, see further details below) of navigating agency vis-à-vis structural and Discursive obstacles will be shown to present further challenges.

Agency in discourse

Agency in narrative has been explored to greater or lesser extents by a number of scholars investigating a number of different settings, including classrooms (e.g. Davies, 1990; White, 2016), and workplaces (e.g. J. Holmes & Schnurr, 2017; Sotirin, 2000). Bamberg (2011a) explores agency in diachronic identity navigation through the interview transcripts of a man accused of kidnapping his own child and living under a false name, who claimed to have very little memory of his own past. This presented challenges to interviewers, as his apparent dearth of memories made reconciliation of his past actions and present self difficult. Bamberg, De Fina, and Schiffrin (2011, p. 178) note that, in navigating identity, speakers attempt to "weave past and present into some more or less coherent whole." Thus, drawing on 'problem zones' of low agency and vulnerability in one's past can allow reclamation of agency in the here-and-now by presenting those earlier times as having been successfully "reflected and mastered by a newly claimed agentive self" (Bamberg, 2011a, p. 120). For Bamberg's (2011a) case study, his apparent lack of access to early life memories made such reconciliation impossible. However, it can perhaps be seen in the narratives of Isaac in this study, both in the previous chapter when he appears more than happy to tell his narrative of flight, and below in this chapter, where he can be seen to draw on his refugee identity to act agentively in his storyworlds (Excerpt 6.5, below).

Strategies for reconciling past and present selves were also investigated by McKendy (2006) in paradoxical discourses of responsibility and victimhood in the narratives of men incarcerated for violent crimes. He specifically examined how the men construct agency as narrators and as protagonists. Institutional expectations compel prisoners to continually claim agency and take responsibility for the actions that have resulted in their imprisonment – following an axiomatic belief that claiming responsibility is a first step towards rehabilitation and reduction of recidivism (in fact, as McKendy (following Maruna, 2004) notes, recognising external causes for criminal behaviour has actually been linked to *decreased* recidivism). For many of the prisoners, however, lifetimes of poverty, instability, and abuse have not provided great opportunity for learning "self-regulation, empathy [and] reflectivity" (McKendy, 2006, p. 477). McKendy observed that the prisoners, as narrators, employed agency to periodically 'paste in' statements of personal responsibility throughout narratives that otherwise seem to construct low agency and victimhood (for the protagonist). In doing so they were able to externalise the causes of their past criminal activity. Thus, the narrators were highly agentive in their storytelling, by portraying generally lower-agency selves as protagonists, all the while complying with institutional expectations of personal responsibility.

Challenges involved in negotiating agency for migrants and refugees has been explored, both in the telling of migration stories and in the practicalities of integration. Tanyas (2016) explored the stories told by young Turkish migrants to the UK, and, despite similar migration experiences, found gendered differences in the ways that the young women and men construct personal agency, and position themselves with regards to vulnerabilities. The young men's narratives appeared to distance their protagonists from vulnerabilities and allowed them to claim personal agency in overcoming their migration challenges. The young women's narratives, on the other hand, detailed challenges and vulnerabilities that the protagonists had encountered, and linked them to their current identities. This suggests that the "experiences of vulnerability and suffering are within the bounds of acceptability for young women" (2016, p. 98), but less so for young men. This is important for discussion of migration, as Tanyas (p. 88) notes that while narratives allow narrators/protagonists to exercise agency through taking different positions and making different meanings, the extent of this flexibility is limited by both language and culture, and the subject positions available in their immediate cultural contexts.

Eternal expectations and Discourses of what it means to be a refugee inform the work of O'Higgins (2012), who explores the stories of young, unaccompanied former refugees in the UK. She discovered that social service providers' expectations of how a young refugee might behave – as a vulnerable victim – was leading to denial of social services to young people who displayed adaptability, resilience, and the ability to cope. These young people were often deemed to be either adults or economic migrants, because they could articulate their own needs or, in one case, being "... assertive, well spoken, and able to use the underground train system in London" (O'Higgins, 2012, p. 86). Here, the young people's ability to agentively and meaningfully direct their own lives was negatively affecting their access to support. Thus, citing Utas (2005), O'Higgins (2012, p. 82) observes that these young refugees might engage in 'victimcy,' itself a "manifestation of agency" wherein they play the role of a helpless victim in order to benefit from institutional support.

De Fina (2003) observed similar strategies in the narratives of Mexican immigrants describing their border crossings into the United States. She describes how these narrators discursively construct non-agentive selves in their stories, stressing "their dependence on the actions of authorities and on the help of strangers" (De Fina, 2003, p. 136). However, De Fina notes that while downplaying their own individualism within a collective group, these migrants were able to keep a sense of themselves as strong and resourceful, maintaining agency through their sense of community.

The turn-by-turn enactment of agency in discourse has been explored in more micro detail by relatively few scholars. Taking a Critical Discourse Analysis approach, Kettle (2005) investigated agency navigation in interviews with a Thai English teacher undertaking a master's degree in Australia. Counter to the reported Discourse of ESL student's low-agency conduct, Kettle's participant was aware of his situation (silenced and marginalised by second language and culturally unfamiliar classroom practices) and agentively undertook steps to transform it. Agentive transformation also becomes relevant in Tainio's (2002) study in which she examined the negotiation and co-construction of both gender identity and sexual agency in interviews with elderly heterosexual couples in Finland. She investigated the ways that the men and women variously orient to and distance themselves from both available identity categories in naturally occurring interaction, noting that while identity negotiations can contribute to the reproduction of political discourses, they are also "necessary for the purposes of the politics of emancipation" (2002, p. 200). Brian King (2014), too, explored the moment-by-moment enactment of (hetero) sexual agency, in the classroom discourses of female teenagers in a New Zealand high school. The study aimed to explore how young women were able to enact a sexual agency that did not emerge secondarily to the sexual agency of men. King

(2014, p. 323) observed that while the course material of the sexuality lessons positioned the young women as non-sexual or as sexually non-agentive, they applied these subject positions "to sexually agentive ends," and he concludes that capacities for sexual action in classroom conversation must be viewed as intertwined with the "agentive sexual practices of young people beyond the classroom's walls" (2014, p. 310), pointing to the importance of context in the negotiation of agency.

The discursive co-constructed nature of agency becomes evident in Al Zidjaly's (2009) moment-by-moment exploration of the negotiation of agency in the joint writing of a letter by herself, a paraplegic friend, and the friend's sister. Observing "constant shifting of participants' footings and alignments" in this agency navigation (2009, p. 180), Al Zidjaly (following Tannen, 1987) notes the interconnectivity of agency and power, and advises considering power as "co-constructed moment to moment, with all participants involved in the process of claiming and/or ratifying or rejecting it" (Al Zidjaly, 2009, p. 179). I draw upon the moment-by-moment exploration of agency in discourse of these studies in my own analysis of my participants' narratives. We have seen that contexts of migration – particularly for former refugees – create both opportunities and challenges for the discursive navigation of agency in discourse. Similar themes can be observed in the narratives of my participants.

Agency in former refugees' narratives

Agency becomes relevant in my participants' narratives in two ways: in their role as narrator (the way they claim or reject agency through the process of telling) and in their role as protagonist (the way they present themselves as characters within their own narratives or storyworlds) (McKendy, 2006; Schiffrin, 1996b; Tanyas, 2016). Narrators have the ability to guide the vantage points from which the narrated events can be viewed: "that of the omniscient narrator, that of the witnessing narrator, and that of the character" (De Fina, 2003, p. 95) Each of these vantage points can be dynamically taken up by narrators to negotiate agentive or non-agentive identity positions, as well as simultaneously contradictory ones (e.g. low agency as protagonist but higher agency as narrator, or vice versa).

As shown in the previous chapter, as people of refugee background, this study's participants must reconcile their present selves with the selves that are characters in their narratives; former selves, who may have found themselves in positions of low agency in their past, but with whom the present-day narrator may not wish to align themselves. Alternatively, as noted above, past, low agency 'problem zones' can be discursively drawn upon to reclaim agency in the present (Bamberg, 2011a). Either way, this reconciliation impacts upon the present-day negotiation of employable identities. This is especially the case for former refugees who are already impacted upon by Discourses of Refugeehood that assume vulnerability and victimhood.

In the following excerpt, in the face of a storyworld challenge to her agentivity, Kelly reconciles her protagonist and present selves by taking up agentive positions both as narrator and as protagonist within her story. She discursively rejects both attempted positioning by other characters in her story (as aligned with refugees, generally) and Discourses of Gratitude. In this narrative excerpt Kelly describes an event that a refugee support organisation (which she had already decided was not actually in the business of helping refugees) had invited her to. This expo-type event was intended to make connections between refugee-background job seekers, and recruitment agencies and employers.

Excerpt 6.2 21 May 2017; 7.01–7.57

1. Kelly: they invited me to um a function? +
2. and the way they were talking about refugees as if they are (2)
3. slaves basically? you bought yourself a slave? (1)
4. and yes other people would sit there and think + oh yeah +
5. they're talking + they're s- they're saying good stuff about me
6. but because I grew up here I know what they're saying?
7. they're literally telling people + employ this person because
8. you'll have a slave for the rest of your life? (1) if you treat them bad
9. they'll come back the next day happy + dressed up well + on time
10. they will do + twice as much as + any kiwi
11. Emily: mm
12. Kelly: and um + they don't care if you treat them bad basically (1) and then
13. they'll be grateful for whatEVER you do to them that + they'll still have a job
14. Emily: mm
15. Kelly: that's what they [*high tone*] said + in the + presentation
16. and I was like + oh barf what the hell

Kelly positions the function organisers as malevolent in their intentions in this excerpt, almost as if they have planned the whole event in order to exploit refugees. This is achieved on lines 3 and 8 with repeated use of the metaphor of a *slave* – a highly emotive word, particularly when used in proximity to refugee, and one which expresses "diminished humanity or agency" (Tracy, Lutgen-Sandvik, & Alberts, 2006, p. 158). The imagery of enslavement is heightened on line 3 when Kelly explicitly references buying a slave, and on line 8 when she links it with the phrase *for the rest of your life*, seemingly indexing indefinite indentured servitude.

It is worth noting that Kelly pauses for two seconds before the first instance of *slave* which may indicate that she was searching for a word strong enough to express her indignation. Alternatively, it is possible that she was weighing up whether *slave* was the word she wanted. Even if this is the case, however, once she decided upon it she enthusiastically elaborated upon it. Kelly employs uptalk (Warren, 2016) on all three of the phrases in which *slave* is found (twice on line 3 and once on line 8, accounting for all but one of the HRTs in this excerpt), perhaps both signalling important information (slavery or general poor treatment as the underlying theme of this narrative) (Warren, 2016, p. 55), and eliciting and checking my reaction to this strongly emotive metaphor (Britain, 1992, p. 79; cited in Warren, 2016, p. 57).

Kelly further highlights the organisers' constructed malevolence by attributing dialogue to them on lines 7–10 and 12–13 which read like hyperbole but are bookended by *they're literally telling people* (line 7) and *that's what they said* (line 15). When she first introduced the *slave* metaphor (line 3) it was framed in a way that suggested that Kelly-as-narrator was summarising and paraphrasing the storyworld speakers' sentiments, but here now she presents the storyworld speakers as both Goffman's (1981) *authors* and *principals*, that is, discursively indicating that the storyworld speaker both verbalised the utterance, and had their beliefs accurately depicted by the utterance. As De Fina (2003, p. 95) observes, all constructed dialogue in narrative discourse functions specifically to convey evaluation, as "narrators use their own voices or the voices of others to implicitly highlight elements of the story." Constructing this dialogue, and framing it as an accurate recounting, helps to firmly position these storyworld characters as unreasonable and bigoted villains, against which a reasonable narrator can position herself.

Within the storyworld, the event organisers are seen to attempt to position former refugee jobseekers – and thus Kelly – as disenfranchised and metaphorically enslavable, a very low agency position. While Kelly-as-protagonist has attended this employment event in the hopes of improving her employment prospects, as narrator she is highly agentive in rejecting this diminished other-positioning (Davies & Harré, 1990). In doing so, she orients to an employable identity which seems to be tied to her sense of self as competent and enfranchised, and not linked to her refugeehood.

In fact, as in Excerpt 5.1 in the previous chapter, Kelly distances herself from refugees as a group in this excerpt, by both employing the third person plural pronoun throughout when referring to this imagined community (B. Anderson, 1991), and by positioning herself as, unlike *them*, being savvy enough to understand what she believes to be the true meanings behind the function organisers' words. She begins this on line 4 when, in an instance of Bakhtinian answerability (Bakhtin, 1981, 1990), Kelly responds to the organisers' actions, and attributes words (or thoughts) to, presumably, any former refugees at the event, saying *yes other people would sit there and think + oh yeah… they're saying good stuff about me*. By virtue of having spent a large portion of her life in New Zealand, however, Kelly draws on her embodied cultural capital and positions herself as culturally competent in local discourse norms and orients away from this particular framing of a refugee identity.

Despite distancing herself from former refugees and arguably positioning herself as superior to them, in this extract Kelly does in fact 'stick up' for this group. Indexing Discourses of Gratitude in the constructed dialogue (Tannen, 1986) of the function's organisers (lines 12–13), Kelly, in her own way, defends refugee-background jobseekers against this attempted positioning by providing her own evaluation on line 16. Both *BE + like* and *oh* signal that she is about to provide an attitudinal or evaluative statement (G. Anderson, 2000; Trester, 2009). North American slang for 'vomit,' *barf* has the effect of mocking and denying power to her storyworld characters, and this is emphasised by the following, stronger expression of negative evaluation, *what the hell*. Thus, in this excerpt Kelly appears to display her awareness of Discourses of Gratitude but strongly reject them, through exaggeration via metaphors of slavery.

By attending the event Kelly is engaging with the 'refugee label,' arguably a strategic identification in order to access refugee support services. She does not, however, engage in what O'Higgens (2012), above, terms 'victimcy,' downplaying her competence and strength in order to comply with expectations of refugeehood. She refuses to let her former refugee identity be her master status (Marlowe, 2010). However, she does not do so from a standpoint of solidarity with others of refugee background, but rather from a standpoint that she is different from an imagined 'average refugee.' Kelly is clearly aware of the Discourses and low agency positions she might be expected to align herself with, but she refuses to play this expected role, taking up a higher agency position of rejecting the event organisers. In the storyworld context in which refugee employability is being discussed explicitly, we see that Kelly's sense of herself as employable seems to be incompatible with what she perceives to be expectations of former refugee jobseekers, and the expectations being created for potential future employers. This mismatch may help her to *retain* her sense of employability and competence: a discriminatory structural roadblock with which Kelly is unwilling to engage as an educated and well-informed woman.

Thus, in Kelly's narrated storyworld, she has positioned the refugee resettlement organisation as the antagonists to her protagonist. She does not, it should be noted, position herself as a hero relative to these adversaries. Although she provides a lukewarm defence of the imagined community of refugees, she distances herself from all other storyworld characters. Positioning herself as superior to both the organisers on account of their unpalatable metaphors of slavery, and to the other former refugees present at the storyworld expo because of their inability to accurately interpret their context, Kelly orients to an outsider identity. Outside of what, exactly, is not clear, but perhaps the 'game' of the labour market: the negotiated dance that job seekers and potential employers engage in. Kelly may here be orienting to traditional ideas of employability in which gathering and displaying pre-ordained skills and attributes is the fundamental, and individually-constructed, route to employment (Hinchliffe & Jolly, 2011; L. Holmes, 2001; LaPointe, 2010). It seems that the co-constructed and interactively achieved nature of an employable identity is not evident to her, at least in this excerpt.

Agency dilemma

A co-constructed negotiation of identity in narrative, Bamberg (2011b) argues, involves three dilemmatic challenges. These are: "(i) sameness of a sense of self across time in the face of constant change; (ii) uniqueness of the person vis-à-vis others in the face of being the same as everyone else," (cf. Bucholtz & Hall's (2005) discussion of adequation and distinction) and "(iii) the construction of agency as constituted by self… and world" (2011b, p. 6). Bamberg notes that the first two dilemmas have been considered central to identity formation for some time. However, the third, the agency dilemma, has, at least until recently, received less analytic attention (Bamberg, 2011b, p. 9). Bamberg (2011a, p. 106) observes that speaking subjects, although agentively engaging in narrative practices (and indexing positions in relation to dominant Discourses), must either employ narrative devices "that lean toward a person-to-world direction of fit, or they pick devices that construe the direction of fit from world-to-person," or somewhere between the two.

A person-to-world fit depicts high agency, portraying a 'heroic self' who is strong, in control and determined. At the other end of the continuum, a world-to-person fit presenting low agency portrays the speaker in a victim role, not only less influential and powerful but also less blame-worthy, should any blame need to be assigned as a result of the narrative or real-world outcomes. That is, a person-to-world position depicts the speaker (or storyworld character) as being capable of acting upon the world and transforming their own circumstances. A world-to-person position depicts that speaker or character as being acted *upon* by the world; as a recipient of action rather than as the architect of it.

This agency dilemma is particularly pertinent to exploration of former refugees' negotiation of employable identities. My participants must discursively navigate the structural challenges that they face, at the same time as presenting themselves as capable, competent, agentive – and employable. This may be a dilemma facing any job seeker, but, as previously discussed, the structural barriers faced by former refugees are greater. This includes having to navigate expectations and Discourses surrounding what it is to be a refugee. For example, treading a perhaps fine line between presenting a highly agentive, proactive, and independent self which counteracts Discourses of Gratitude and may jeopardise access to support, and presenting a low agency, vulnerable self that invites sympathy but may undermine negotiation of an employable identity and acceptable sense of self.

Navigation of this agency dilemma can be seen in Omar's discussion of his frustration regarding the limitation of his role in both his previous and current jobs. In the conversation from which the following excerpts are taken, he told me how he had attempted to implement what he saw as a more efficient schedule for maintenance of the machines in the factory, which was ultimately rejected by his superiors. This was very disheartening for Omar, who saw his suggestions as both self-evidently more efficient, and as an opportunity for him to exhibit his wealth of experience in the field – his embodied cultural capital. He also spoke about his fruitless attempts to have his qualifications fully recognised by his employers and mentioned that to regain these qualifications from a New Zealand institute he would be required to start from the most basic engineering courses. Throughout these excerpts Omar employs metaphors of death, violence, and sacrifice, where death equates to defeat (Lakoff, 1993).

Excerpt 6.3 22 March 2017; 24:55–25:16

```
1. Omar:  yeah this is crazy this is killing for the:: + proficiency
2.        my competence + my dream my everything (2)
3.        can you imagine yourself as you are going to
4.        study English from ABC
5. Emily: mm
6. Omar:  from the beginning (1) this is same + for me (3)
```

Throughout this excerpt and the following one (Excerpt 6.4, see below) Omar uses metaphors of death and violence, initially here portraying himself in a low-agency victim role (Bamberg, 2011a) saying that the idea of studying engineering from the beginning *is killing for the:: + proficiency* (line 1). His low agency in the face of structural obstacles is highlighted through his use of *crazy* (line 1), which seems to discursively index his frustration at his inability to change the circumstances or act upon the world. His self-positioning as victim is emphasised on line 2 as he represents the projected loss of his skills and hopes as deeply personal through repeated use of possessive pronoun *my*. This is discursively linked to his employable identity by indexing Discourses of Employability (that is, socially-circulated and widely-accepted ideas around what it means to be employable, as discussed in Chapter 1) through naming employment-related attributes (Moreau & Leathwood, 2006; Reissner-Roubicek, 2017) *proficiency* and *competence* (lines 1 and 2).

Then, following a two-second pause (line 2) in which Omar receives no verbal feedback from me, he invites my inference and solidarity (lines 3–4) by framing his predicament in terms I can relate to, asking me to imagine myself in a comparable situation. In doing so he positions me as interlocutor within the ongoing narrative and, aided by my verbal acknowledgement (line 5), we co-construct his low agency position (as protagonist) together. Within the interactive context, Omar regains some discursive agency as narrator by guiding my inference and aligning himself with me, by providing me with a relatable lens through which to view his predicament. It is clear, however, that Omar presents this structural obstacle as a challenge to his agentivity, and equally a challenge to his ability to perform a personally acceptable employable identity.

Further dynamic negotiation of the agency dilemma can be seen in the next excerpt, which follows Omar having discussed how the responsibilities of his job are well below his qualification and experience level. He initially orients to a world-to-person (Bamberg, 2011a), low agency position of surrender to his circumstances, then abruptly reframes his battle as unfinished, and reorients to a person-to-world (Bamberg, 2011a), high agency position:

Excerpt 6.4 22 March 2017; 27:03–27:44

1.	Omar:	but I have to accept what + is existed (1) it's not for me
2.		this is (1) to be a good example for my children (2)
3.	Emily:	[*quietly*] yeah (1) it's tough though
4.	Omar:	it's tough but what can I do (2) this is my situation
5.	Emily:	mm (2) [*tut*] (2)
6.	Omar:	I tried my best (2) tried hard I fight (2) and
7.		I will not surrender + I will continue fighting + fighting
8.	Emily:	mm
9.	Omar:	until maybe in the future I fi- can find something
10.	Emily:	mm
11.	Omar:	can prove myself as (4)

Omar orients to a low-agency position of resignation on line 1 using modal of obligation *have (to)*. I am always conscious that my participants are second language speakers of English, and thus it is risky to rely too heavily on individual word choice in making discourse arguments. However, in this case, and other cases where I do so, I am confident that the Omar's choice of word is meaningful, when viewed in light of the surrounding discursive context. It could be argued that he in fact orients to a higher agency position in the face of structural barriers, however, by framing his acceptance of his lot in sacrificial terms (*it's not for me*, line 1) and thus taking up something of Bamberg's (2011b) hero role, which is tied to his identity as a father (or *family man*, Excerpt 6.1, above) as we see on line 2. My reactions and input early in this excerpt (lines 3, 5) tend towards sympathy, and I believe also reflect my discomfort at being unable to provide any kind of useful feedback or solutions to Omar's circumstances. After offering my commentary that *it's tough though* (line 3), intended to recognise the extent of what Omar had given up despite his self-positioning of acceptance, Omar agrees by repeating me (line 4), remaining in a low-agency, world-to-person position of powerlessness.

My nominal feedback (and long pauses) following this (line 5), again motivated by my feelings of inadequacy, may have had the discursive effect of implying that surrender to the circumstances was not an interactively desirable position, because at this point Omar begins to take up a higher agency, person-to-world position. While he introduces a battle metaphor to describe his struggle on line 6, in the past and present tenses (*(I) tried hard I fight*) that suggests defeat (Lakoff & Johnsen, 2003), he then, on line 7, takes up a higher agency position as he switches to the future tense and reframes himself as undefeated, stating that he will continue to fight for what he wants. This turnaround in positioning, in addition to Omar's conditional reference to potential success in the future on line 9, appears to index his imagined future identity (Darvin & Norton, 2015).

Imagined identities, drawing on Benedict Anderson's (1991) concept of imagined communities, refers to not only our ideas of who we are now, but also who we are hoping to become in the future (Darvin & Norton, 2015; Norton, 2001). By taking up an agentive position in narrative Omar seems to be able to maintain a personally acceptable employable identity, negotiated concurrently with myself as interlocutor. Additionally, he points to the co-constructed, and dynamic nature of identity on line 11 when he suggests that he may be able to *prove* himself at some point in the future (although he trails off before actually stating what he hopes to prove himself *as*, I believe that it is contextually clear that he refers to his embodied capital of experience). That is, he indicates that he is already employable (at a higher level than that at which he is currently working) in his own eyes, but that he will have to continue to work towards getting others to recognise his employability. Omar's positioning seems to relate to Bakhtin's (1984) *unfinalisability*: "As long as a person is alive he lives by the fact that he is not yet finalised, that he has not yet uttered his ultimate word" (Bakhtin, 1984, p. 59). Omar remains in dialogue with his future and his ongoing battle for recognition and success.

Thus, we can see in these two excerpts Omar's dynamic negotiation of discursive agency with regards to his employable identity. He balances low agency positions vis-à-vis the structural obstacles preventing him from achieving his full potential with higher agency positions in the taking up of hero positions in metaphors of battle and sacrifice, and his engagement with his imagined identity. In this way, he is perhaps able to retain a sense of self as agentive and employable while at the same time justifying his underemployment.

Isaac, too, can be seen to dynamically navigate agency in his narratives. Unlike Kelly and Omar, however, he appears more willing to engage with past positions of low agency, particularly as they relate to his present-day achievements. The last time we spoke (in a research context), he had graduated university and had been working full-time since then at a union. Reflecting upon his university experience, he recounted times in which he strategically found himself acting in a low-agency, in some ways vulnerable, position, in order to access the help he required.

Excerpt 6.5 2 December 2016; 40.41–41.05

```
1. Isaac: I have lecturer when I did [policy course xxx] (1) um Jacob Boswell
2.        he's a professor in (1) um so I did (1) I asked to have a look on
          my draft +
3.        told him my story hey man + I'm not um + like you know
4.        English is not my first (1) this is a struggle for me + but I'm +
          you know
5.        I'm working hard and I need + do you have anyone + do you know
6.        to have a look yeah I can think of people
```

Isaac's navigation of agency in this excerpt is very dynamic, flitting swiftly between high and low agency positions as he narrates. As a narrator he locates his lecturer as holding a high-status position from the outset, clarifying that he is not simply a lecturer but a *professor* (line 2). As protagonist, Isaac appears to orient to Discourses of Refugeehood by 'telling his story' to the professor (line 3); perhaps engaging in Utas' 'victimcy' (2005, cited in O'Higgins, 2012) – displaying vulnerability and deficiency to access support. Unlike O'Higgins' (2012) observations of young refugees, however, Isaac (as protagonist) seems not to be *playing out* vulnerability, but rather discursively indexing it as a backdrop for his request for help within the storyworld. Thus Isaac-as-protagonist here is simultaneously occupying low and high agency positions. The discursive indexing of vulnerability suggests a low-agency, world-to-person position for Isaac, but the strategic employment of that indexicality suggests a higher agency position.

He then begins to construct his own dialogue (Tannen, 1986) with the professor, momentarily orienting to a higher agency position as protagonist, through a reported casual opener – *hey man* (line 3). According to Giles-Mitson (2016, p. 91), the address term *man* in New Zealand English "seems to be widespread enough in usage that it is typically unmarked not only for gender, but for ethnicity and class." This suggests a certain comfort with his storyworld interlocutor and the (potentially face threatening) act he is undertaking, and thus a familiarity with and confidence in acting upon the world. Isaac then lays out his apparent shortcomings (in the form of constructed dialogue directed at his professor, line 4), noting his status as a second language speaker and that writing is a *struggle* for him, taking up a low agency position in that he is unable to overcome these shortcomings alone. This is underscored by him saying that he is *working hard* and yet *needs* help (line 5). That his work ethic is introduced on line 4 with adversative relation marker *but* (Schiffrin, 2001, p. 56) on the one hand seems to emphasise his low agency by highlighting his inability to overcome his struggle alone, and on the other hand suggests agency in his dedication to continue trying.

So as a protagonist Isaac orients to low agency positions of vulnerability and deficiency, as well as toward a refugee identity. At the same time, by discursively employing a low agency backdrop (as protagonist), and the narrative recounting thereof as narrator, he takes a higher agency role, revealing how agentively 'leaning in' to his refugee identity allowed him to access the additional support he required to do well.

Moments later Isaac reveals the outcome of his actions and his (Labovian) evaluation of the narrative:

Excerpt 6.6 2 December 2016; 41.30–41.37

```
1. Isaac:  I got I think a B plus at the end of the day so (1)
2.         you have to have that courage to speak to people
```

Isaac narrates that his earlier actions have resulted in his attaining a respectable mark for the essay in question. This attribution of cause and effect is indicated by linking the result to this evaluation on line 1 with a causative *so* (Schiffrin, 1987), as well as the phrasing *at the end of the day* which has the discursive effect of indicating that the grade he received results from his earlier agency in going to his professor with his *story* (a canonical Labovian resolution). The evaluation itself, that *you have to have that courage to speak to people* (line 2) positions Isaac as speaking from a position of authority on scholastic success and highlights his agency in his own success. Speaking from the discursive position of a graduated, gainfully-employed person, Isaac reconciles his past and present selves. His past periods of low agency present little challenge to his present employable and competent identity, as he was able to skilfully – and successfully – discursively utilise them in order to achieve his goals. He presents his past, low-agency 'problem zone,' as having been conquered by his present, agentive self (Bamberg, 2011b).

Isaac's present-day employable identity does not appear to be challenged by past vulnerability. Kelly, on the other hand, appears less comfortable with past periods of low agency. In discursively recounting such periods, she externalises accountability to other storyworld characters. As such, she navigates the agency dilemma by consistently presenting her own recounted actions (and reactions) as contextually appropriate, while continuing to enact an employable identity with me in the interview context, seemingly unburdened by any discursively enacted past missteps.

In the excerpt that follows, Kelly uses her agency as a narrator to reconcile her past and present selves, unfolding in an explanation and discursive reframing of a humiliating experience. This excerpt relates to the same incident that Kelly was discussing in Excerpt 5.1 (previous chapter) in which she was berated by a refugee resettlement worker. The excerpt comes some minutes before Excerpt 5.1. At this point I was feeling slightly taken aback by hearing about such an acrimonious encounter between these two people, neither of whom I knew very well at the time. Reluctant to provide an evaluation to match Kelly's, I asked why the woman had yelled at her. This request required Kelly to reveal herself in a position of low agency as she described not having sufficient social capital (Bourdieu, 1977c, 1986) to provide referees for her CV, a revelation which has the potential to threaten her employable identity enactment. Her storyworld adversary had offered to act as a reference on her CV, but had been dismayed to have been called by a potential employer without verbal warning from Kelly:

Excerpt 6.7 21 May 2016; 2.47–3.30

```
1.  Kelly   she said oh I'll be your reference + so I'm like
2.          s:preading my CV everywhere (1) applying for so many jobs
3.          so I'm not gonna ask her every time I apply for a job
4.  Emily:  yeah yeah
5.  Kelly:  or hey by the way I put this application and I put your name on it
6.          she knows that I'm applying for [high tone] jobs
7.  Emily:  mm
8.  Kelly:  cause this is what it is [laughs]
9.  Emily:  mm
10. Kelly:  and she got upset that she got called by one of the people? (2)
11.         she said + they told you notify me and I'm like (1) [laughs] (1)
12.         they didn't like + I shouldn't really be telling you
13.         hey by the way they gonna ring you up about me because
14.         you already know that I'm applying and you're on my CV
```

On line 1 Kelly introduces the resettlement worker's constructed dialogue (Tannen, 1986) with *oh*, an indexical feature which not only marks the transition from animating her own words to animating her storyworld interlocutor's but is also perhaps employed as "an identity resource in interaction" (Trester, 2009, p. 148), indicating to me her retrospectively negative evaluation of that constructed dialogue (Tannen, 1986). Trester (2009) notes that *oh* can serve to 'double-voice' dialogue (Bakhtin, 1984), providing additional information about the speaker's stance. That is, Kelly paints her storyworld interlocutor's words in a negative light, potentially in readiness for the negative narrated outcome that is to follow.

Twice (lines 5, 13) Kelly uses the same phrasing – *hey by the way* – to introduce constructed dialogue, hypothetically attributed to herself but discursively implied to be understood as never having actually been said in the storyworld. Dubois (1989, p. 346) claims that *hey* is often used to introduce what she calls a 'pseudoquotation,' which "has the form of a direct quotation but which is entirely constructed by the quoter." Furthermore, pseudoquotation can point to the "dramatisation of an idea... that [serves] to emphasise an important point" (Dubois, 1989, p. 355). Here, Kelly uses this phrasing with the discursive effect of emphasising the unlikelihood of her actually notifying, or the unreasonableness of an expectation that she should notify, her referee every time she applied for a job. Kelly takes up a discursively high agency position by resisting – and ridiculing – the absent Other (Vitanova, 2005).

This is further underlined on line 8 when Kelly aligns herself with me as interlocutor in the here-and-now, through phrasing that suggests a shared assumption of 'how things are,' combined with dismissive laughter, positioning herself as superior to and distancing herself from her storyworld interlocutor (Ladegaard, 2013, p. 402). As Partington (2006, p. 232) notes, this kind of laughter can be used to express superiority, as well as attempting to create it. Similarly, Vitanova (2005, p. 164) notes that laughter can be an act of resistance and thus an act of agency, and one that does not "necessarily require a direct confrontation with the Other." Laughter can be very socially significant as it is "directed toward something higher – toward a shift of authorities and truths, a shift of world orders" (Bakhtin, 1984, p. 126; as cited in Vitanova, 2005, p. 154). Indeed, it seems that Kelly here, as she does elsewhere, uses laughter to resist the absent Other indirectly, and to reclaim discursive agency – and a sense of authority – in the process. She takes up a high agency position as narrator, evaluating the incident from a distance and finally judging the woman's expectations to be absurd or silly rather than hurtful and humiliating.

After having firmly positioned herself as holding the moral high ground throughout this excerpt, Kelly appears to unintentionally position herself as being in the wrong on line 10 when she constructs the woman's dialogue: *she said they told you notify me*, implying that Kelly's potential employers had told Kelly to notify her referees. A number of discursive features point to this reversal in positioning being unintentional: Kelly's hesitation and laughter, and false start (*they didn't like +*) directly following this (lines 11 and 12). She then swiftly reframes the situation as one of obligation – or rather, lack thereof – using the modal *should*(n't) to make her stance clear with respect to her duties as job seeker (line 12). On lines 13–14, while all the time addressing her absent storyworld adversary directly, Kelly changes from pseudoquoting herself (saying what she is not going to say) to responding to the woman's admonishment in a way that perhaps she was unable to do at the time of the actual incident. Kelly-as-narrator appears to temporarily lose control over the narrative by inadvertently providing information that puts her in the wrong but regains control quickly through a skilful reframing.

Thus, as a *protagonist* she avoids a high agency, blameworthy position in the narrated incident, but as a *narrator*, takes up an agentive position by framing herself as having acted appropriately and rationally, despite her storyworld adversary's constructed words to the contrary. In this way Kelly is able to dynamically maintain her negotiation of an employable identity in the here-and-now interaction with me, and discursively reclaim agency that Kelly-as-protagonist was denied in the (wider) humiliating incident that she describes. She was able to do this through positioning the resettlement worker as irrational and unreasonable, and by reframing the event in terms of obligation. As discussed, continuing to align oneself with a past, low-agency protagonist-self may not be desirable. Regarding oneself as having low agency, or being powerless, is not only face-threatening, but also potentially damaging to one's sense of self as an individual capable of controlling one's own path (Marlowe, 2010; Moulin, 2012).

Kelly can be seen to use a similar strategy of assigning her protagonist self low agency in the face of structural challenges or obstacles in the following excerpt. Having secured a job interview with the help of her social capital – her sister who already worked there – Kelly positions her potential employers' expectations of her as unreasonable, in the face of her inability to meet them. It should be noted that this excerpt is taken from a point at which Kelly had been unsuccessfully job seeking for over a year and had expressed to me that she was at her wits' end in terms of rejection and failure.

Excerpt 6.8 14 September 2016; 24.17–24.46

```
1. Kelly: the receptionist took my CV and gave it to the human resources and
2.        (1) so I got an interview through that? +
3.        um but they're being really really difficult like they're still
          asking for
4.        so much things that I don't have + I mean + you're looking for a +
5.        someone + as an entry level and then you're telling them give me
6.        I don't know how many refe- referees and
7. Emily: mm
8. Kelly: and I told them I can't provide what you're asking me for (1)
9.        [laughs] so + yeah
```

After stating that she had been granted an interview (line 2), Kelly immediately mitigates the possibility that this will lead to employment with *but* (line 3) to describe the interviewers or recruitment staff as *being really really difficult* by nature of their request for *so much things* that Kelly cannot provide, in this case once again, multiple referees. She then says *I mean* (line 4), a forward-looking indexical feature frequently used to introduce justification or commentary (Fox Tree & Schrock, 2002, p. 741) to defend this negative characterisation of the staff's expectations. Using second person pronouns she seeks my alignment with her positions, which is implied through the apparent contrast of *entry level* (line 5) and *I don't know how many... referees* (line 6) (which has the discursive effect of implying an unreasonably large number of required referees). Kelly-as-protagonist's response to this request, *I can't provide what you're asking me for*, (line 8) serves to accentuate that it is unwarranted through her formal register, indexing professionalism (and employability) and avoiding framing herself as deficient (i.e. avoiding a statement such as *I don't have any other referees*).

This is followed by a short laugh on line 9, which may function to mitigate any inferred loss of face at her inability to meet the potential employers' demands (Warner-Garcia, 2014), and finally *so + yeah*, which discursively suggests – and assumes my inference that – Kelly's prospects for getting this job are not good (in fact, happily, Kelly did end up getting this temporary position). Her discursive face-saving strategies are also relevant to her negotiation of an employable identity in the interview context with me. Framing her potential employers' demands as unreasonable has the discursive effect of neutralising the potential threat of my awareness of her long-term unemployment to her sense of self as capable and employable.

Here once again, Kelly-as-protagonist is in a low-agency position in the storyworld, up against structural barriers that she is unable to surmount through no fault of her own. By presenting this narrated obstacle as unreasonable, however, Kelly-as-narrator takes a higher agency role. By framing what she has provided to the employers as perfectly adequate for the job in question, and the employer's request for more as excessive, Kelly seems to be able to retain a sense of self as employable, and agentive. She appears to be anticipating failure and protects herself against this by blaming unfair structural expectations, perhaps pre-emptively saving face. Thus, Kelly's dynamic navigation of Bamberg's (2011b) agency dilemma means that her employable identity, though not successfully negotiated with her potential employers (in Kelly's narrated storyworld here), remains negotiable with me in the interview context.

Discussion

Agency plays a significant role in negotiating an employable identity (or, for that matter, negotiating any identity). Co-constructing an enactment of employability with interlocutors, recruitment gatekeepers, interviewers, employers, and colleagues requires skilful navigation of more and less agentive roles within discourse. The narrative taking up, ceding, and other-assignment (or -denial) of agentivity, both as narrator and storyworld protagonist, allow speakers to locate themselves within the social world, relative to social structure and wider Discourses, thus orienting to dynamic and various identity positions (Duranti, 2004; Schiffrin, 1996b; Tanyas, 2016). This is true of any jobseeker, interviewee, or employee. Former refugees, however, encounter different, additional hurdles. Facing greater structural obstacles from the outset, which themselves require agentive behaviour to overcome, refugee-background jobseekers must discursively – and appropriately (for the sociocultural context) – navigate agency as storytellers and protagonists relative to Discourses of Refugeehood and Gratitude (see also Moulin, 2012).

These Discourses suggesting vulnerability, victimhood, and trauma, and supposing perpetual demonstrations of indebtedness, may restrict the range of identity – and particularly, agentive – discursive positions available for a refugee-background speaker in a given context (Tanyas, 2016). Furthermore, the social structure former refugees come up against may necessitate the dynamic navigation of agentive positions. That is, in negotiating an employable identity, former refugees may need to discursively navigate past periods of low agentivity and reconcile those times with a present, interactively negotiated, competent, highly agentive self, capable of acting upon the world and directing their own paths through life. This is Bamberg's (2011b) agency dilemma, which provides a useful entry through which to explore narrator's dynamic taking up and ceding or more and less agentive roles. This dilemmatic lens allows insight into how agency in narrative may be employed to reconcile past and present selves, to enact a contemporary employable identity which has conquered past 'problem zones' (Bamberg, 2011b).

For Kelly, narrating past occasions in which her sense of agentivity was challenged, such as being publicly berated, compared to a slave, or asked for proof of employability that she was unable to provide, appear to present threats to her enactment of an employable identity in the interview context with me. She responds to these challenges by exercising agency as a narrator, creating storyworlds in which her adversaries are unreasonable, or in some cases, seemingly ill-intentioned. In doing so she positions her protagonist self as agentive as well, actively rejecting the other storyworld characters' unconscionable behaviour or expectations. She is thus able to take up sensible or defensible identity positions with regards to her employability. Positioning herself as something of an outsider and employing indexical features which have the discursive effect of suggesting superiority, Kelly appears unacquainted with an understanding of an employable identity being something which is co-constructed in negotiation with others. Or perhaps she is, and her narratives of her past low agency times reflect an attempt to save face for a failed attempt to interactionally negotiate an acceptable employable identity.

Omar's narrative excerpts in this chapter reflect a similar incidence of low-agency, when he attempted to create an opportunity to prove himself as overqualified for his current responsibility level and make use of his embodied cultural capital at work, and was rebuffed. At first, he takes up low agency positions, indexing despair and resignation at his failure and the suggestion that he re-train in New Zealand from an entry level. He presents this as too great a challenge to his sense of self as a qualified and competent engineer. As a narrator he discursively employs agency to justify his low agency storyworld position: by framing it in terms of sacrifice for his family, that is, taking up a hero role within the storyworld.

After previously suggesting acquiescence to his circumstances, he repositions himself as a fighter in an unfinished battle, and discursively indexes a future identity in which he might have had the chance to negotiate the type of employable identity he desires. This dynamic navigation of Bamberg's (2011b) agency dilemma demonstrates Omar's negotiation of a personally-acceptable identity in the present. His struggles with low agency in the face of structural barriers are narratively mitigated through an ongoing battle metaphor and an eye on his possible future success.

Isaac's past periods of low agency, as evidenced in the excerpts in this chapter and in his story of flight in the previous chapter seem to present little threat to his present-day sense of self. Reflecting upon his university experiences after graduating and promptly securing a full-time job, he constructs a storyworld in which, despite his shortcomings, he is the master of his own destiny. He recounts a time when he was discursively agentive in strategically orienting to a low-agency position, as well as to his refugee identity. While not engaging in victimcy (Utas, 2005) in either the storyworld or the interview context, he is willing, and able, to index his 'problem zones' from a position of high agency in the here-and-now.

He has successfully negotiated an employable identity in the New Zealand workforce, and reflecting upon his former low agency times does not compromise his present-day success. Omar and Kelly have not successfully negotiated their desired employable identities in the New Zealand workforce at the point at which these stories were told, and thus their ability to act upon the world is questioned in a way that it is not for Isaac. Thus, the challenge of discursively reconciling their past and present selves, and enacting a present, employable self, may be greater. In terms of the structural obstacles they face it is important to take intersectionality into account (Beck at al., 2001; Davis, 2008) and note that Kelly and Omar also may face further obstacles additional to that of being of refugee background. Both Omar and Kelly are parents, and thus the opportunities available to them, and any decisions they make, are impacted upon by their familial obligations (cf. Z. Long, King, & Buzzanell, 2018). Kelly, unlike Omar, is a single parent, which adds further constraints upon opportunities and freedom of choice. Furthermore, her gender may impact upon her successful negotiation of an employable identity, given that "most workplaces are predominantly masculine domains with masculine norms for behaving" and thus women are frequently at a disadvantage in this arena (J. Holmes, 2006a, p. 1).

Agentive behaviour may be necessary to counteract any lack of locally-useful capital, as social and cultural capital are often significantly diminished by the process of migration (Ricento, 2015). An example can be seen in Excerpt 6.2 where Kelly draws on her embodied cultural capital to justify her reported ability to read the real meaning behind the event organisers' constructed words. We also saw an unsuccessful attempt by Omar to have his embodied capital recognised by his employers in Excerpt 6.4. Highly agentive behaviour is required on the part of newcomers to regain or transform their capital to useful forms within the bounds of the new social structures in which they find themselves. This agentive negotiation of various forms of capital in the pursuit of a sanctioned employable identity is the focus of the following chapter.

CHAPTER 7

Social and cultural capital

Introduction

As the data in the previous chapter demonstrated, dynamic discursive agency positioning can be an effective means of navigating disempowering Discourses and other-positioning in narrative. This becomes critical when we recognise that an unequal distribution of power occurs in almost every society. The basis of that power may be grounded in violence, some form of locally-recognised mana, or access to economic resources. When the structures or processes that created the power structure are no longer visible, oppressor and oppressed alike can unthinkingly reproduce the conditions for the imbalance. The game of gaining access to power is not played upon an even field, as players enter the game with disparate amounts of resources and knowledge of the 'rules' that will provide an advantage. In the social world, our skills, competencies, knowledge of behavioural norms and so forth, along with the kinds of people and networks we have access to, impact upon the ways in which we interact with social institutions such as education and the labour market (Reissner-Roubicek, 2017; V. Smith, 2010). This, as discussed in Chapter 2, is captured in Bourdieu's (1977a, 1986) notion of cultural and social capital, which can be exchanged for further benefits in the social world. Capital is thus a powerful conceptual tool with which to discuss the negotiation of employable identities in narrative for refugee-background jobseekers, for capital amassed across a lifetime may become worthless in a new social setting (Colic-Peisker & Walker, 2003; Darvin & Norton, 2015; Ricento, 2015).

Capital is dependent upon its bearer's ability to make use of it, and its recognition as legitimate capital by others. To explore how the recognition (or lack thereof) of one's capital contributes to identity negotiation (and in particular, employable identity negotiation), I begin with an excerpt in which Isaac describes a *turning point* in his life. When Isaac was working as a cleaner, his social and cultural capital, while recognised by his colleagues, was largely invisible to his desired imagined community, namely the students around and for whom he cleaned. In the speech that Isaac was asked to give at the mayoral debate that was discussed in Chapter 4, he was provided with a rare opportunity to showcase his capital in a public forum of his (desired) peers. Isaac describes transcending his low-status role as a cleaner and displaying his embodied cultural capital in the form of his competencies as a speaker, an advocate, and an activist, to an audience who willingly took up and ratified his claims to capital. Isaac explains that this validation and recognition of his capital marked a *turning point* in his life in New Zealand:

Excerpt 7.1 30 March 2016; 50.02–50.33

```
1. Isaac:  I think that that was a turning point for me
2.         if I didn't do that that day + probably things wouldn't go (1)
3.         the way they are now and I + I think everything happens for
           a reason +
4.         and that day that speech came for a reason and changed
           everything + for me
5.         changed the way that people look at you + because
6.         sometimes if you are just cleaning and you are just a cleaner
7.         you don't have any + any potential ah you can't do anything
```

Isaac, in a manner which recalls his moment of truth at the point of crossing the Eritrean border to Sudan (Excerpt 5.1), depicts this moment like a fork in the road. On one path, unspoken by Isaac but clear by its comparison, is his continuation as a cleaner with unrealised potential. The other, happily the one upon which he finds himself, is the path towards higher education and recognised potential. Isaac discursively frames this as fate: *everything happens for a reason* (line 3). In doing so he takes up a low agency, world-to-person (Bamberg, 2011b) position, attributing his speech to destiny, and giving the speech, and not himself as speech-giver, the agentive position: *that speech came for a reason* (line 4). This kind of narrative structure, as discussed in the previous chapter, positions a narrator as "the central character who is… at the mercy of outside… forces or who is rewarded by luck, fate, or personal qualities" (Bamberg, 1997b, p. 337).

Isaac alludes to the importance of recognition of capital by others when he says that giving the speech *changed the way that people look at [him]* (line 5). That is, in his storyworld, it is not Isaac-as-protagonist that has undergone a change – he already 'possessed' this capital – but rather the world that has changed its view of Isaac – his capital has been recognised. He also discursively indexes a structural barrier to recognition of capital: employment as a cleaner may preclude appreciation of the various types of capital those individuals might possess. Here he constructs the internal dialogue of the aforementioned general *people: you are just a cleaner you don't have any… potential… you can't do anything* (lines 6–7). The indexing of capital in order to make identity claims depends upon the speaker's ability to have that capital acknowledged even in the face of structural limitations, with consequences for the successful co-construction of an employable identity. Isaac's opportunity to exhibit his capital to a large, captive, and public audience of his imagined community members is an extraordinary one, and by his own account, a successful one.

Capital and identity

From a poststructuralist perspective, the value of capital can be seen to be negotiated in interaction and intrinsically tied to the performance and negotiation of identity (Meadows, 2009; Norton & Toohey, 2011). The capital one has at one's disposal will impact upon the enactment of identity: a person's understanding of their relationship to the world will be shaped by their social and cultural capital, which of course is variably valuable across time and space. Furthermore, access to capital affects how one might imagine one's future and the possibilities therein. The ways in which an individual employs and indexes their capital in discourse allows them to take up positions vis-à-vis that capital and make discursive claims about their identity.

Moreau and Leathwood (2006, p. 308) note that social and cultural capital's influence on employment recruitment and promotion processes is well established. Furthermore, labour markets, as Bauder (2008, p. 316) notes, are "important sites for the reproduction of social order: They operate at the intersection of economic, political, social, and cultural processes, and they are politically, socially and culturally regulated." Accordingly, part of the enactment of an employable identity involves "being able to present one's experiences, character and accomplishments in ways that conform to the competence profiles scrutinised by employers" (Brown et al., 2016, p. 194), which are locally- and contextually-dependent.

In order to appropriately perform this 'narrative of employability' (Brown & Hesketh, 2004, p. 145), an individual must have access to the 'right' kinds of cultural capital to recognise how a given practice is enacted, as well as to "be able to construct for [themselves] a *legitimate* identity" (Hinchliffe & Jolly, 2011, p. 566, emphasis mine). The structures of power that govern access to resources (here, job interviews and employment), "[do] so by presenting [the established] normative categories as being universal, necessary and obligatory principles to which all practices must conform" (Kerekes, Chow, Lemak, & Perhan, 2013, p. 272). Thus, a 'legitimate identity,' is contextually-bound, within and across workplaces, industries, and nations.

Capital in research

Recent research examining the effects of social and cultural capital – or lack thereof – comes from a wide range of disciplines and explores a wide variety of contexts. These range from the LGBTQ community (e.g. Cronin & King, 2014), to family leisure activities (e.g. Gracia, 2015), and the social network benefits of communities such as sports clubs (e.g. Coalter, 2007) and community gardeners (e.g. Glover, 2004). Studies have also considered capital in explorations of physical health (e.g. Mohnen, Völker, Flap, Subramanian, & Groenewegen, 2015; Schori, Hofmann, & Abel, 2014), mental health (e.g. Pinxten & Lievens, 2014), and disability (e.g. Holt, 2008, 2010; Mithen, Aitken, Ziersch, & Kavanagh, 2015). Recent work has incorporated the impact of the internet upon capital, exploring the effect of online communities and social capital upon an individual's offline wellbeing (e.g. Julien, 2015; Lambert, 2016) as well as the ways in which online cultural capital is built (Colburn, 2015; Nissenbaum & Shifman, 2017).

Fittingly for Bourdieu's original motivations, cultural and social capital have often been employed to explore scholastic achievement or barriers thereto (e.g. Cemalcilar & Gökşen, 2014; C. Fuller, 2014; Pérez & McDonough, 2008), including the effects of parents' (e.g. De Graaf, De Graaf, & Kraaykamp, 2000) and grandparents' (Møllegaard & Jæger, 2015) cultural capital upon their children's and grandchildren's education success. Phillip Brown et al. (2016) compared students at British and French elite universities and discovered that although the students were frequently conscious of their privilege, they were often unwilling to attribute their own success to anything other than personal dedication and diligence. This unwillingness to acknowledge the profitability of one's capital is a form of symbolic violence, in that it is the reproduction of an ideology that legitimates existing inequality – the ideology of hard work alone being sufficient to guarantee success.

The intersection of (non-white) ethnicity and cultural capital and the ramifications for both educational and employment success has been investigated as it pertains to Black youth in the United States (P. L. Carter, 2003; Lareau & Horvat, 1999) and the United Kingdom (Wallace, 2017), as well as Latinx communities in the United States (Monkman, Ronald, & Théramène, 2005; Trueba, 2002). These studies aim to explain the ways that certain privileged groups' cultural capital has rendered them better equipped to succeed in education, and thus to then succeed in a labour market set up to reward the institutional capital they have earnt. However, as discussed in Chapter 1, the advantages provided by institutional capital are less assured than they once were, and the returns that university graduates can expect are influenced by the intersection of social categories such as gender, ethnicity, and class (Beck at al., 2001; Moreau & Leathwood, 2006).

Fewer studies have focused upon the discursive employment of capital in interaction as it pertains to identity performance. Meadows (2009) explores how the cultural capital of a young Asian woman (in a Western context) who was not a native speaker of English was variously taken up and rejected by others in a group task, and the consequences for her investment in the activity. This study demonstrates that the discursive engagement of symbolic capital must be negotiated in conjunction with others and is inevitably linked to identity positions. Any discursive positioning, as touched upon briefly in Excerpt 7.1, must be ratified. That is, the employment of capital in discourse must be taken up by an interlocutor for the capital to have value in the given context (Darvin & Norton, 2015; Meadows, 2009; Seals, 2010). Competing ideologies at either an individual or societal level may mean that the capital an individual possesses "may not be accorded symbolic value by structures of power, or the capital they desire [may become] difficult to attain because of systematic patterns of control" (Darvin & Norton, 2015, p. 46). The effects of gender and the order of topic introduction upon symbolic capital uptake were further explored by Seals (2010), examining instances of men being given credit for ideas that were initially volunteered by women. In this study she concludes that *how* a topic is introduced (or any utterance for that matter) has an effect on how that information is remembered – specifically the type of symbolic capital that is first used. In particular, there was an effect of (capital-indexing) ordering shown upon the other participants' uptake. Successful negotiation of capital is important, as to have ones' capital valued is to have one's identity affirmed (Darvin & Norton, 2015, p. 49).

Researchers in Applied Linguistics, too, have incorporated conceptualisations of social and cultural capital into their discussions of second language learning and identity (e.g. D. Block, 2010, 2013; Bull, 2013; Darvin & Norton, 2015; Duff, 2015; Norton, 2000). Norton and others (Darvin & Norton, 2015; Norton, 2013, 2017; Norton & Toohey, 2011) have discussed at length the intersection of identity, capital, and ideology in learner investment (as distinct from motivation) in second language classrooms. Investment in a second language (though this can be extended to non-classroom environments), Norton (2013, p. 45) claims, is so done "with the understanding that [the learners] will acquire a wider range of symbolic and material resources, which will in turn increase the value of their cultural capital." This is important for those of refugee background who, "through the process of forced migration, [may have lost] aspects of their identities that were embedded in their former communities, jobs, skills, language, and culture" (Colic-Peisker & Walker, 2003). Investment in local educational, social, or cultural communities and practices can be undertaken with the assumption that this investment will lead to the development of locally-useful cultural and social capital, as we will see regarding Kelly's investment in the labour market, Excerpt 7.7 below.

Access to, and the successful display of, capital becomes more acute in the case of migrants. Bauder (2008) discusses the idea of citizenship as cultural capital, and the related consequences for migrant job seekers (discussed further below). Studies specifically focusing on the experiences of refugee resettlement and employability have explored the impacts of institutional support (Morrice, 2007) and social sports (Spaaij, 2012) on the creation of useful social capital, as well as the effects of gender (R. Allen, 2009; L. J. Goodson & Phillimore, 2008). It is important to note that while voluntary migrants may possess capital that provides opportunities, as well as the ability to move on should the local context prove unsatisfactory, such possibilities may not be available to refugee populations. As Duff (2015, p. 68) points out, for forced migrants, "transnational associations and identities associated with their former homelands and languages may be traumatic, tenuous, and politically risky."

Alongside reduced options to 'move on,' research in the Canadian context has discussed how former refugees' social capital and social status is often erased upon migration, and has explored the personal effects upon individuals as well as the ways in which this loss may be mitigated (e.g. Lamba, 2003; Lamba & Krahn, 2003; Ricento, 2015). In addition, former refugees encounter further barriers to potential employment due to discrimination by employers. As Ricento (2015, p. 138) notes, being labelled as a refugee alone may act as an employment barrier, and for 'visible minorities,' that barrier is even higher (*visible minorities*, according to Hatoss (2012, p. 53) can be defined as those who are "visually different" from a given context's dominant population, based (typically) upon ethnic background). This may be manifested in the way that job candidates may not be granted "the advantage of presumptive trust" if interviewers or gatekeepers perceive them to be in some way culturally or linguistically divergent from the local majority (Kerekes et al., 2013, p. 271). Thus, the cultural capital brought by former refugees, for example, may be squandered if it is not recognised, as they find themselves forced to find employment that does not reflect their competencies.

The acknowledgement of one's capital is validation of one's sense of self, and of worth. It also allows the possibility of positive imagined identities (Darvin & Norton, 2015), where capital can act as both "a tool of… social reproduction and transformation." A person's hopes for their future (or, as we will see in Omar's case (Excerpt 7.9, below), for their children's future (cf. Norton & Toohey, 2011, p. 415)) will depend at least in part upon the kinds of capital they have at their disposal and are expecting to have in future, as well as their ability to successfully negotiate that capital in discourse.

Capital and employable identity

The earning of institutional cultural capital has conventionally been thought of as the best route to gain admission to desired occupations or careers (Boden & Nedeva, 2010; Hinchliffe & Jolly, 2011; Moreau & Leathwood, 2006). It is not surprising, therefore, to find that this study's participants place a lot of value upon their institutional capital, as well as their embodied capital of skills and experience. As will be illustrated in this chapter, when their capital is not recognised, they face great challenges, both to their employable identities, and to their ability to access appropriate employment. Additional capital that may permit access to such employment, such as the capital of citizenship as we will see in Omar's case, is sometimes out of reach, or used as a gatekeeping device (Kerekes, 2007; Kerekes et al., 2013).

Recognising social capital as an essential element of labour market success, the participants variously celebrate their own social networks and extol their worth to others (in Isaac's case) or lament their inability to make and maintain connections that are locally useful (in Kelly's case). Kelly also stresses the discouraging consequences of a lack of emotional support that accompanies low social capital. Access to and recognition of capital, on other hand, allows the imagining of brighter futures (as we see in Isaac's narratives), and these imagined identities (Norton, 2000) have consequences for labour market resilience, confidence, and morale, as well as the navigation of locally-appropriate employable identities (L. J. Goodson & Phillimore, 2008; Lamba & Krahn, 2003; Ricento, 2015).

Cultural capital

Omar's embodied cultural capital in the form of his extensive experience seems to be closely tied to his sense of self as employable. In the excerpt that follows he both indexes and discursively employs this embodied capital in interaction with me. He and I had been discussing his journey toward securing his first job in New Zealand. He had told me that, after attempting to apply for jobs on his own, he had signed up with a recruitment agency, and got his first job within one month of doing so:

Excerpt 7.2 4 June 2016, 24.54–52.23

```
1.  Emily:  did you have many um interviews along the way or
2.  Omar:   you see it's not + kind of interview because you see
3.          if you are a skilled high skilled person (1)
4.          who will make you an interview what they will ask you
5.  Emily:  mm ok yeah [laughs]
6.  Omar:   I'm telling I told you that I work +
7.          as a chief engineer for more than eight years
8.  Emily:  mm
9.  Omar:   and who will interview me what will he ask me +
10.         and who would interview me
```

Omar begins his response to my question with *you see* (and repeats it a moment later, both line 2), frequently used in discourse to signal topics or explanations that a speaker assumes that their listener is unfamiliar with (R. Carter & McCarthy, 1997), as he explains that to speak of a job interview for his type of job is inappropriate due to the specialised nature of his embodied capital (I believe that Omar was rejecting the idea of a traditional job interview performed by someone who is not necessarily an expert in the field themselves, rather than the idea of a pre-job-offer discussion generally). In doing so he positions himself as the more knowledgeable party in our interaction, thus discursively putting his embodied capital to use.

He then begins to index his embodied cultural capital without explicitly connecting it to himself (lines 3–4), through use of second-person pronoun *you* (presumably in the third-person sense of *one*) and using conditional or hypothetical phrasing when he sets the scene: *if you are a highly skilled person*. Soon thereafter, however, he definitively assigns the discursively-indexed capital to himself, and names it (lines 6–7). By introducing his explanation as something assumed to be unknown, and quickly thereafter reminding me of relevant information that I already know (and could have, presumably, used to infer the information given in the explanation), Omar strengthens his high status and knowledgeable position within this interaction.

The value that Omar places upon his embodied cultural capital is evident in his use of rhetorical questions here. Three times, he asks me rhetorically *who*, given his capital, would be equipped to interview him (lines 4, 9 and 10), and what kind of questions, given the nature of his capital, could an interviewer possibly ask him (lines 4 and 9)? In fact, when Omar asked the first rhetorical question, I was momentarily unsure as to whether a response was expected of me or not. If this question was intended to be a literal request for an answer, I would have inferred it to be a slightly aggressive demand for recognition of Omar's highly-skilled status. My laughter on line 5 was an attempt to mitigate this possibility. Once he repeated the question of who would interview him, along with the additional question of what sorts of questions they might ask (lines 9 and 10), I revaluated the questions as an interactional strategy.

Rhetorical questions can perform multiple roles. As an indirect speech act, rhetorical questions "imply more than is said" (Frank, 1990, p. 737). This might mean strengthening the force or credibility of what is being said by encouraging the listener to follow the speaker's train of thought (Frank, 1990, p. 726). Alternately, they may be used as a politeness strategy to soften what might otherwise be taken as impolite or face-threatening remarks (Frank, 1990, p. 726). In Omar's case, his rhetorical questions could be seen to be serving both purposes. Firstly, by not only making his point in the form of a rhetorical question, but by repeating it several times, he seems to indicate that, on account of the quality of his cultural capital, the kind of person who would usually conduct job interviews would not be qualified to do so in his case. Furthermore, because of the embodied nature of his capital, he stresses through a repeated rhetorical question (lines 4 and 9) that interview questions are pointless, and he perhaps implies that his capital should speak for itself.

In terms of the second suggested function of rhetorical questions as a politeness strategy, Omar avoids the potentially face-threatening act of explicitly stating that he is too qualified to be interviewed. Thus, Omar here both indexes his embodied cultural capital, speaking explicitly about his experience, and employs it discursively.

In this excerpt, it seems that Omar's enactment of an employable identity depends upon his embodied cultural capital being recognised as such, and that to negotiate with a less (industry) experienced interviewer would present a challenge to that. Further, he employs rhetorical questions in the interaction with me, leading to a co-construction of his competent and qualified employable identity in the here-and-now of the research interview, aided by my accommodating feedback.

Like Omar, Kelly's sense of herself as competent and employable seems to be strongly connected to her institutional cultural capital, on which I observed her place great value throughout our discussions. Below we can see how her conceptualisation of her institutional capital and thus her employable identity is threatened by perceived credential inflation (Brown et al., 2016). Kelly had told me that at the time she was studying, stories of job shortages were making the news:

Excerpt 7.3 8 April 2016; 1.05.15–1.05.39

1. Kelly: I was like (1) [*high tone*] why am I doing this there is no jobs
2. and people are going back to study um (1) master's and ah (1) um P H-
3. (1) and (1) [*laughing tone*] so why am I bothered so that was like +
4. never + look too much up otherwise your neck will hurt you
5. Emily: [*small laugh*]
6. Kelly: so just look at the steps in front of you

Norton's (2000, 2013, 2017) concept of investment, though formulated originally for a second-language classroom, can be applied here. Kelly invested in her university courses with the understanding that she would gain "symbolic and material resources… [and] increase the value of [her] cultural capital" (Norton, 2013, p. 45). Although highly motivated, her perceptions of the job market and the higher qualifications of others could have threatened Kelly's investment in her own education. However, we see here that she maintained her investment by concentrating on one step at a time, not concerning herself with future problems she was not at the time able to address.

She begins her reaction to the reporting of labour market news stories using BE + *like* (line 1), used here to "mark off the following linguistic material as a thought, and attitude, or a feeling which is metarepresented" (G. Anderson, 2000, p. 34), that is, to describe a previous mental state which was not necessarily verbalised at the time. For the remainder of line 1, Kelly (as protagonist) questions the rationale of her decision to study, but the use of a high, almost laughing, tone, has the discursive effect of mitigating the potentially face-threatening situation of having heavily invested in a low-value qualification (Warner-Garcia, 2014). This tone may also be a mitigating device to counter any offense on my part that she is attributing her degree's apparent worthlessness to those who have gone on to undertake PhDs (abandoned part way through on line 2).

Following arguments from the previous chapter, Kelly takes up a low agency position as protagonist on line 2 and characterises her efforts to gain institutional capital as a futile endeavour by an implicit comparison of her undergraduate degree to others' postgraduate qualifications. She then takes up a higher agency position by describing how she managed her situation. This begins on line 3 when she switches from questioning the point of study to describing her coping strategy. She provides advice to herself (in an assertive tone) in the form of a metaphor that suggests embodiment: *never + look too much up otherwise your neck will hurt you* (line 4). Through agentively orienting to an identity of resilience and drawing on her experience of dealing with demoralising conditions, Kelly-as-protagonist can be seen here to maintain her investment in her institutional cultural capital, and not comprise her student – and future employable – identity.

Institutional capital, as discussed in Chapters 1 and 2, is rarely sufficient to secure desired employment. Embodied cultural capital becomes necessary to successfully perform 'soft' skills in both interviews and the workplace, as well as appropriately enacting local interaction norms (Brown et al., 2016). However, the combination of both institutional (qualifications) and embodied (many years' experience) capital is not necessarily enough to even secure an interview in which to attempt to negotiate or perform one's employable identity, as Omar came to realise in the excerpt that follows. Here, he describes feedback he received after being rejected (without an interview) for a job that he applied for online, despite the advertised job matching his experience and competencies well, and his resulting frustration at his powerlessness to display his employable identity:

Excerpt 7.4 22 March 2017; 29.22–30.13

```
1.  Omar:  I (1) just ask them (1) ah:: + can I know the reasons + why
2.         I'm not matching because I have the all + what you need
3.  Emily: yep
4.  Omar:  experience certificate degrees anything you want (1)
5.         and (1) give me a chance + make me interview or
6.         make me a meeting or anything after that you can
7.  Emily: yeah
8.  Omar:  say sorry or you can check me (1) he say no +
9.         it's not because of + your ah:: certificates or experience
10.        or whatever + but because my client he wanted (1) ah::
11.        a New Zealand + American + Australian + Canadian (1)
12.        it's ah:: or England (1) citiz- ah: yeah + citizen
13.        for that ah: + for that position
```

Omar positions himself here as highly – and wholly – qualified for this job, evidenced on line 2 when he constructs his storyworld dialogue (Tannen, 1986) to the recruiter, saying that he has *the all + what you need*. He underscores this on line 4 when he presents his cultural capital, both embodied and institutional, in list form, stressing that this is *anything you want*. Omar's sense of himself as employable here appears strongly linked to others' recognition of his considerable capital. This can be seen in the way that Omar-as-protagonist implores the recruiter, portrayed here as a gatekeeper to Omar's desired employment (Kerekes, 2007; Kerekes et al., 2013), to allow him the opportunity to prove his worth in an interview (lines 5–6), and implying that he would accept a rejection post-interview if only his capital would be recognised for its value (lines 6 and 8). His ability to interactively negotiate an employable identity appears here to be precluded by a lack of access to the appropriate context (a job interview) in which to attempt to co-construct such an identity.

Omar then constructs the dialogue of the recruiter matter-of-factly (lines 8–13). It is made clear that no amount of experience or qualifications would render him eligible for this job: the employer requires a citizen of a developed, Western, English-speaking, largely Caucasian nation, in what seems like a clear (yet plausibly deniable) instance of discrimination. Bauder (2008, p. 316) argues that "citizenship functions as a key mechanism of distinction that renders migrants vulnerable and exploitable," and is in itself a form of (cultural) capital. It can manifest itself in both institutional (legal) forms and embodied (practiced) forms. Bauder describes citizenship as a "historically and politically constructed concept" (2008, p. 317) that has real world (labour market) effects in that, while the national labour market is usually fully accessible to citizens, it may not be for migrants, for both legal and social reasons (2008, p. 321). Citizenship can be employed to "express identities of belonging" (2008, p. 324), and by extension, exclude or marginalise migrants who might be unable to enact the cultural performances expected from members of the imagined community of a given nation (2008, p. 325).

Thus, as could be the case in Omar's recounted experience, citizenship as a form of cultural capital may be exercised in the labour market as a proxy for other attributes (e.g. ethnicity, accent, and so forth) to the (racist) exclusion of recent migrants and former refugees (cf. Piller, 2016). In fact, as Omar went on to say, citizenship alone was not sufficient according to the recruiter; to have been a citizen for a minimum of ten years was required for consideration for the job. So we can see here the fluid and dynamic nature of capital and the ways in which it is "subject to… the dominant ideologies of specific groups or fields" (Darvin & Norton, 2015, p. 45). The devaluing or erasure of capital that refugees may experience upon migration can have consequences for resilience and identity. Being denied the opportunity to prove his embodied capital – and the institutional capital that preceded it – has ramifications for Omar's sense of his own employable identity in the New Zealand workforce.

Social capital

We have seen that the participants place great importance upon their cultural capital, both embodied and institutional. However, they all also seem keenly aware of the importance of *social* capital to their ability to enact an employable identity. Below, Isaac illustrates this sentiment, discussing a friend of his who had a PhD, rarely socialised outside of his family and a few friends, and was having little luck in the labour market:

Excerpt 7.5 30 March 2016; 55.33–55.46

```
1. Isaac: I I always tell him that you know if you don't have a a
2.        if you don't know the right people
3.        this job that I do + is a good example I always use it as example
4.        look at this job (1) if I came as stranger and applied for this job
5.        I wouldn't get it
```

Isaac-as-protagonist seems to take up a position of authority within the storyworld here, as an example of the fruitful outcomes of taking the advice he is here providing. As narrator, it seems that he aligns himself with me, assuming my agreement with his advice with discourse marker *you know* on line 1 (Jucker & Smith, 1998; Stubbe & Holmes, 1995) (although it is unclear if he is aligning with me as narrator or aligning with his storyworld interlocutor as protagonist). Stressing that he *always* has this type of conversation (lines 1 and 3), Isaac highlights the importance that he places on the creation and maintenance of social capital, at the same time as implying that he is frequently asked, or offers, to give advice. He then discursively backs this up with evidence in the form of his own labour market success on lines 4–5: *if I came as a stranger… I wouldn't get [the job]*. Isaac indexes the co-construction necessary in the enactment of employable identities. Even with the institutional capital of a PhD, his friend cannot negotiate employability alone; it requires social capital – networks of the *right people* (line 2) with whom to do the negotiating (perhaps particularly so in the New Zealand labour market (cf. Spellerberg, 2001).

While recognising the importance of social capital with regards to institutional capital, the inability to access such social capital may lead individuals to hold a rather dim view of the out-of-reach benefits of useful social networks, as Kelly demonstrates. This excerpt follows Kelly outlining her perception of other university students *just drinking and having fun* and then being given extensions and pass marks by overly lenient staff. She believes that this has led to a situation where degree-holders are not recognised as skilful or employable, which impacts upon her own sense of employability:

Excerpt 7.6 8 April 2016; 1.09.10–1.10.02

```
1.  Kelly: I've heard that rumours um (1) that that's how they look at people
2.         + people right now that have degrees that they just + you know
3.         party all time and + they never really learned anything
4.         and they gonna le- teach them + everything + from the start
5.  Emily: mm
6.  Kelly: it's not that they n- yeah so (1) um [tut] unless you have experience
7.         and you know someone that can + actually get you + into + your field
8.         you can't really get into your field
9.  Emily: mm
10. Kelly: [tut] yeah
11. Emily: //so\
12. Kelly: /most\\ of the girls that were studying with me + um (2)
13.        her father is a:: CEO of this her father is C- there and
14.        + that's how they graduate and get into business: +
15.        in the field that they want
```

Kelly's discussion of the salience of networks begins almost conspiratorially with reference to *rumours* she has heard (line 1) about how potential employers view graduates' capital. She invites my inference, or expresses her "confidence in [my] sharing of [this] relevant knowledge" (Stubbe & Holmes, 1995, p. 69) on line 2 with discourse marker *you know*. She goes on to describe the partying students and their lack of embodied capital (despite possessing institutional capital), but does so from the constructed position of potential employers, lending validity to a position which may in fact be her own (cf. Bangerter et al., 2011; Hodges, 2015; Matoesian, 2000). This also discursively positions her in opposition to the storyworld students, as well as in a low-agency role laying the blame for the apparent diminished value of her institutional capital at the feet of those who *party all time*.

In line 6 Kelly continues her evaluation before cutting herself off, using *yeah so* to create a causal relationship between partying students and the content to follow (Blakemore, 1988; Schiffrin, 1987). She changes her focus to the importance of social capital (and the embodied cultural capital of *experience* that social capital also permits access to). Kelly backs up this claim with evidence in lines 12–15, where she talks about the women she studied with getting into their desired fields on the strength of their fathers' positions as CEOs. So, while Kelly sees social capital as important to the enactment of an employable identity, she seems to be viewing it through a negative lens of nepotism. Kelly positions these fellow (female) students as uniformly privileged, and by describing them as *girls* and attributing their supposed success to their fathers' roles, she positions them as spoilt children and dismisses the credibility of their employment success. Her narrative attribution of success to nepotism allows the taking up of a low-agency role and may serve to discursively justify the apparent low value of her institutional capital in the labour market.

While Kelly might view the social capital inherent in family networks – or at least the kind of social capital she was unable to access – in a negative light, another side of social capital is clearly very important to her for navigating and maintaining an employable identity: emotional support. The search for employment, as anyone who has ever done so knows, can be disheartening and affronting to the ego. The importance of social support to manage and persevere in difficult times such as this cannot be understated (Gans, 2009; Hek, 2005; Ricento, 2015). As Kelly herself says: *you need someone to believe in you*. Below, Kelly describes the dispiriting effects that the closing of a job search and training centre had on her. She had applied for several jobs while the centre was open, and after its closure she says that she received all of the rejection letters on her own at home:

Excerpt 7.7 14 September 2016; 30.53–31.16

1.	Kelly:	so I don't have support and the only thing I'm hearing
2.		+ from + phone calls and emails +
3.		[*aggressively*] you don't have experience you don't have experience
4.		you don't have experience you don't have experience
5.		I had like th- (1) how many + jobs at least + like (1) fifteen jobs that you know
6.		got to me through that period and I thought (2) why am I applying [*laughs*]

Kelly narrates a storyworld in which she is alone, and bombarded, via phone and email, with rejections. The vital importance to her of the emotional support of her former (job centre) network is made clear in the way that she repeats four times, in an emotionally-charged tone, the feedback that every phone call and email contained: *you don't have experience* (lines 3 and 4). Through this repetition Kelly discursively embodies her re-enactment of the bombardment and emphasises the draining effect of the constant reminder of her lack of embodied capital. This is then reemphasised by an estimate of fifteen rejections that she received without social support to help her process them; this led to Kelly-as-protagonist questioning her resolve to continue applying for jobs (line 6). Here, as often, Kelly-as-narrator laughs in a non-humorous context, suggesting an attempt to save face in a demoralising storyworld situation (cf. Ladegaard, 2013; Warner-Garcia, 2014).

Kelly told me that this was the point at which she decided to stop applying for jobs, after a year of doing so, and direct her energies towards volunteer work where, although not receiving financial compensation, she felt that her skills were being put to use. Without a social network to provide emotional support, Kelly indicates that her investment in, and resolve to, continue attempting to successfully negotiate an employable identity in the labour market were severely impacted. Receiving only negative feedback, she appears to have been unable to maintain belief in her own capital and employability.

Kelly's lack of social capital seems to have restricted her ability to project success in the future. Access to social capital can have the opposite effect. We have seen that (non)recognition of cultural capital can affect former refugees' sense of self (Excerpt 7.4, above). Social capital, too, is important for both resilience and the ways in which former refugee jobseekers can envisage their futures, that is, their imagined identities (Norton, 2001). The significance of Isaac's social capital to his imagined identity can be seen in the excerpt below. While Isaac was still studying, he and I discussed what careers he might like to pursue after graduating. He floated the ideas of continuing to work for the union he had part-time employment with at the time, and returning to Africa to help others as he had been helped in the past, before arriving at the idea of entering local politics:

Excerpt 7.8 30 March 2016; 47.19–47.44

```
1. Isaac:  also I don't know the local politics kind of + looks fun [laughs]
2. Emily:  yeah
3. Isaac:  ah people cause I always associated myself with the Labour Party +
4.         and + I do a lot of campaigning when whenever I have the time
5.         for local politicians starting from my our MP [local MP name] and
6. Emily:  mmhm
7. Isaac:  councillors like [local councillor name] + so I don't know in
           the long term
8.         that could be maybe + local + yeah + council
```

Isaac heavily hedges his suggestion that he would like to enter local politics, on line 1. He precedes his first mention of politics with *I don't know*, which as Baumgarten and House (2010, p. 1194) note, is often used to signal "avoidance of the expression of an overt, unequivocal stance towards the subject matter." Here it seems to indicate that the following suggestion is to be taken as a casual thought, which may have just occurred to him. It should be noted that this is likely an interactional strategy and not a direct index of a cognitive state or a psychological process (Bolden, 2006, 2009), when viewed alongside the hedging and mitigation that follows.

Then after introducing the topic of local politics, he suggests that following this path *kind of + looks fun*, where *kind of*, often used to make a topic "vague and less well-defined" (Aijrner, 1984, p. 118), may be interactionally exercised to imply a lack of real investment in the idea. This is underscored by *looks fun*, which paints his potential career choice in a trivial and playful light. Furthermore, Isaac follows all of this with laughter, which he does not commonly do in non-humorous contexts (either in the recorded data or my unrecorded interactions with him), and here may serve to mitigate the potentially face-threatening act (in a New Zealand context) of imagining a high-status (on account of its public visibility) job for oneself (Billig, 2005; Warner-Garcia, 2014). He may be orienting to the *Tall Poppy Syndrome*, an Australasian social norm which encourages humility, discourages the overt success of any one individual, and "discourages grandstanding [and] boasting" about one's own achievements (Peeters, 2004, p. 86). All of this hedging and mitigation together indicates that Isaac is cautious to reveal this imagined identity of local politician, and displays orientation to local humility norms (J. Holmes at al., 2017).

To ratify this imagined identity, Isaac then draws upon his high-status social capital (lines 3–5 and 7 in the form of *the Labour party* and *local politicians*, including a central government MP and a local government councillor (and future mayor), both of who he knows personally. He positions himself agentively in the invocation of this capital, making himself the subject of *associating* (line 3) and *campaigning* (line 4), suggesting a more than casual involvement with politics. After having provided justification for allowing himself to dream big he reiterates his imagined identity, though still carefully hedging this hope through the use of *I don't know* (line 7), and the conditional modal *could*, the conditional adverb *maybe*, and several pauses (line 8). Thus, despite his apparent hesitance to claim a high-status imagined future, Isaac is able to dynamically do so by discursively drawing upon his social capital. This capital appears to be allowing him the discursive space to aim high in our interactional co-construction of his employable identity.

The imagining of such future identities may be difficult when one's capital is not recognised and valued. Omar, as we have seen, expresses frustration and despair at his inability to display his capital and have it acknowledged, both in job interviews and in the workplace (Excerpts 6.3, 6.4, 7.2, 7.4). Without recognition of his capital, Omar cannot regain his pre-migration status, and encounters great challenges in attempting to do so. It is unsurprising, then, that in some cases, former refugees may imagine a better future for their children instead of themselves, perhaps as a way to justify the pain of loss of status, self-worth and opportunity that may accompany this loss (Norton & Toohey, 2011). Omar orients to this position after discussing with me his despair at the idea of having to retrain from the lowest level of engineering if he wanted to obtain qualifications in New Zealand (as seen in Excerpt 6.3 in the previous chapter), contrasting this humiliating idea with his embodied capital: *but all information + still in my head (1) I'm able to do any test now.* While emphasising his disheartening situation, Omar, can be seen to orient to his children's, in lieu of his own, imagined identities, seemingly drawing on Discourses of Refugeehood related to hopes for better lives for children (cf. UNHCR, 2017):

Excerpt 7.9 22 March 2017; 26.05–26.11

```
1. Omar:  maybe this country is good for my children +
2.        but for me I find myself just (1)
3.        I'm dying here
```

Discussion

Changing labour market models and increasing numbers of graduates have destabilised the once-reliable rate of exchange between institutional capital in the form of tertiary qualifications and ostensibly guaranteed employment (for a certain rate of economic capital). In fact, in Bourdieu's own view, education systems are far better at "validating and augmenting" cultural capital acquired in the home than they are at engendering it in those who enter the system without the expected dispositions (Weininger & Lareau, 2007). Thus, people are directed by those educational systems into "class destinations that largely… mirror their class origins" (Weininger & Lareau, 2007), and the social order is reproduced. More often than in the past, a tertiary qualification is simply a pre-requisite for a job (Moreau & Leathwood, 2006, p. 306), and distinguishing oneself from other, equally-qualified candidates requires successful discursive negotiation of a range of competencies and aptitudes; that is, being able to display one's "experiences, character, and accomplishments in ways that conform to the competence profiles scrutinised by employers" (Brown et al., 2016, p. 194).

Thus, as Brown et al. (2016, p. 194, following Rose, 1999, and Skeggs, 2004) argue, employability involves narratively packaging the self "in ways that make it difficult to hide one's 'self' and cultural inheritance (embodied capital) behind the veil of technical expertise." What this means is that locally-valued embodied cultural capital becomes necessary to accompany institutional capital, as well as embodied capital gained elsewhere, in order to perform a locally-appropriate identity. We have seen in the narratives of Isaac, Omar, and Kelly how complex it is to negotiate appropriate and useful capital in the labour market.

Omar appears to place high value on his own institutional capital, and embodied cultural capital of eight years' experience as an engineer. Indexing this capital, he discursively orients to a highly employable identity (Excerpt 7.2); so highly employable he is, he implies, that he is essentially un-interviewable. Kelly, in Excerpt 7.3, describes a challenge to the value of her institutional capital in the form of credential inflation (Brown et al., 2016), but is able to maintain her investment in that capital by concentrating only on what is in front of her – what she can control. In a refugee context the concept of institutional and embodied cultural capital becomes complicated, in that, as we have seen, the crossing of international borders can erase or diminish the value of capital, as the possessor of that capital enters a new field where the rules are different (Bourdieu, 1991). While Isaac and Kelly gained their institutional capital in New Zealand, Omar gained his in Syria (and internationally on cargo ships). It appears from his narratives that migration has indeed diminished his ability to actualise his capital (Excerpt 7.4).

Additionally, in modern labour markets where focus has shifted from institutional capital to (often imprecisely-defined) *employability* (L. Holmes, 1999, 2001; Moreau & Leathwood, 2006), embodied cultural capital plays a larger role in employment success. In Omar's case, he does not even get the opportunity to attempt to discursively 'package himself' appropriately face-to-face, as he lacks the cultural capital of *citizenship* to even grant him an interview. Citizenship as capital here, and the requirement of ten years of it, may be standing in for other attributes less acceptable as job requirements. As Williams (2009, p. 24) notes, for refugees, constraints on employability may be "rooted in the politics of discrimination and racism," and requirements for longstanding citizenship may be a proxy for 'new racism.' *New racism* (M. Barker, 1981) describes a more recent form of racism (than explicitly race-based, hostile, violent, and biologically-justified racism) which "wants to be democratic and respectable, and hence first off denies that it is racism" (van Dijk, 2000, p. 34). It is a more subtle, 'value'-based racism which avoids mention of race, but instead focuses on cultural difference, sometimes framed as deficiency or pathology (Augoustinos et al., 2005; M. Barker, 1981; van Dijk, 2000). Highly educated refugees such as Omar, having escaped deplorable conditions, often find that there is a "hidden price to be paid for living in a secure environment… [where their] non-transferable professional credentials severely curtail their ability to enjoy the 'full blessings of liberty'" (Ricento, 2015, p. 142), and this impacts upon their opportunities to perform or prove employable identities.

Often, as we have seen, the "economic and social yield" (Bourdieu, 1986, p. 48) of *cultural* capital depends upon access to *social* capital, particularly as it pertains to the co-constructed nature of employability. Isaac expresses awareness of this in Excerpt 7.5, claiming that no matter how prestigious your institutional and embodied capital, knowing *the right people* is essential to getting a job. Creating and maintaining useful social capital, however, can be complicated by the process of migration, and forced migration particularly so. Displacement and resettlement are likely to "abruptly disrupt, if not sever, [former refugees'] social, economic and cultural networks" (Koyama, 2013, p. 948). Arrival in a new country with little or no local language proficiency or cultural capital, as is often the case for former refugees, only exacerbates this.

For Kelly, inability to access the kinds of social capital she perceives to be useful have led to a rejection of this capital as nepotism, as shown in Excerpt 7.6. Once again positioning herself as an outsider (as previously discussed in Chapter 6), with no way to get 'in' to the jobs she wants, she depicts her storyworld former classmates who have gained employment as having *unfairly* benefitted from their social capital. Through the narrating of an unjust system, Kelly's own institutional capital, as it pertains to her employable identity, is not threatened in the interaction context with me. As well as providing access to desired jobs, social capital may be important for navigating the inevitable rejections and setbacks that accompany a job search (Gans, 2009; Hunt, 2008). This seems to be the case for Kelly in Excerpt 7.7 when she recounts her support network disappearing, and weathering 15 rejection letters with no one to support her or maintain her employable identity in the face of constant rejection. Kelly discursively links this with her withdrawal from engagement with the labour market, and so the lack of social capital has clear implications for employment and employability.

When locally-valuable capital is accessible and recognised, it appears to allow the warranting of imagined identities and imagined communities. In Isaac's case, this allows him to envisage the realisation of his aspirations. In Excerpt 7.8 he cautiously floats the idea of entering local politics in the future, mitigating this potentially face-threatening act with ample hedging devices. He is able to warrant his imagined identity by discursively making use of his social capital (and imagined community) of local politicians whom he knows personally. Then in Omar's case, we can see in Excerpt 7.9 that when one's capital is not recognised or valued, imagined identities are more difficult to warrant. Hoping that their life in New Zealand will allow his children to achieve their dreams, Omar narrates his situation as desperate and hopeless as he struggles to have his extensive institutional and cultural capital valued. Although he has secured permanent employment, the effects of non-recognition of his competence on his identity are substantial.

The intertwined and self-perpetuating nature of the types of capital means that their successful use in narrative and the negotiation of their uptake is a complex, challenging, and continuous task for anyone navigating the labour market, and especially so in the case of refugee-background job-seekers. The negotiation and co-construction of an employable identity appropriate for the local context can be a long and bumpy road for those whose lifetimes' accumulations of capital have been diminished or erased through forced migration, requiring strategic and dynamic use of discursive agency in the various taking up and rejection of diverse and changing narrative positions. It is this longitudinal journey of complex and dynamic negotiation that is the focus of the following chapter, in which I explore in depth Arwa's navigation of a year of life and (largely fruitless) job-hunting in New Zealand.

CHAPTER 8

A longitudinal exploration of employable identity negotiation

Introduction

It is clear from the preceding chapters, supported by abundant existing research, that migration, and particularly forced migration, brings with it myriad challenges. The good work undertaken by those working and volunteering in refugee settlement organisations is invaluable in providing immediate and pressing resettlement services, such as housing, schooling, financial support, language assessment and training, CV and interview preparation, and so forth. However, obstacles to full involvement in a society can be less immediately visible, more challenging, and take longer to overcome than the support provided by governments and support agencies allows for. Socially acceptable ways of interacting across a range of diverse contexts and navigating unfamiliar and opaque social norms are among these. This is as true of low-stakes interactional contexts as of higher-stakes contexts such as employment preparation, interviews, and placement.

The concept of *employability*, as the literature has shown, is imprecise even to those 'native' to a given context, let alone newcomers. As well as being defined in conflicting ways by different sources, by universities and governments, and by job-seekers and employers, employability as a concept fails to take in the co-constructed nature of social life and interaction. Power differentials and discursive navigation of agency and capital are important in the negotiation of unfamiliar appropriate ways of being in a new environment. As explored in the previous chapters, I approach the navigation of the labour market via the concept of an employable *identity*, emergent from and negotiated within discourse. Successfully (co)constructing a locally-useful employable identity is no small feat for newcomers, and the journey towards doing so may be a long and challenging one. In this chapter I explore these challenges via a case study of Arwa, following her identity struggles as she navigates her own agency and capital in narrative over a year of job-seeking.

A year after we first met, Arwa expressed to me her realisation that her institutional cultural capital alone was not sufficient to secure a job:

Excerpt 8.1 7 April 2017; 0.20–0.37

```
1. Arwa:   so people just only need to know + what you can do actually +
2.         when I give you a job + could you do this one + could you do this one
3. Emily:  yeah
4. Arwa:   if you say no + I'm I'm very educated + I have PhD
5. Emily:  yeah
6. Arwa:   but you cannot do these things then?
7. Emily:  (1) yeah
8. Arwa:   there is not any point (1) to employ you
```

Arwa's framing of her institutional capital here is in stark contrast to that of a year prior. When I first met her, her PhD was a source of great pride and seemed to make up a large part of how she interactively positioned herself within the world. A year later, she portrays her PhD as useless without different kinds of embodied cultural capital and seems to allude to awareness of the co-constructed nature of employability. Arwa's negotiation of her identity in narrative, in interaction with me over around twenty months of largely fruitless job seeking in New Zealand, encompassed a considerable trajectory. A strong-willed and proud woman, she seemed to struggle with challenges to her sense of self and her place in the world, and adapting to locally sanctioned cultural and, importantly, interactional norms took some time. In particular, the development of recognition that her employability was something which required negotiation in any given context and was not something which resided purely in her own hands, can be seen in the longitudinal data to follow. Through an examination of Arwa's self- and other-positioning over an extended data collection period, it becomes clear that learning to negotiate a locally-valuable employable identity may take time and involves much 'trial and error' for newcomers unfamiliar with local communicative practices.

Arwa

When Arwa and I first met in person (after previous email communication), she had been in New Zealand for ten months. Although her unemployment was already frustrating her, she was confident in her own potential for employment, which was built strongly on the assumed value of her institutional cultural capital. After we had introduced ourselves to one another and sat down, the first thing Arwa wanted to discuss with me was a job application she had made at a local university, and within one minute she had indicated her expectation that she would be working as a lecturer within two or three years. Of course, her knowledge of my research area must have prompted this, but it demonstrated a clear orientation to her academic and employable identities.

In fact, Arwa showed me, in this first meeting, a diagram she had drawn outlining her imagined path to her dream job:

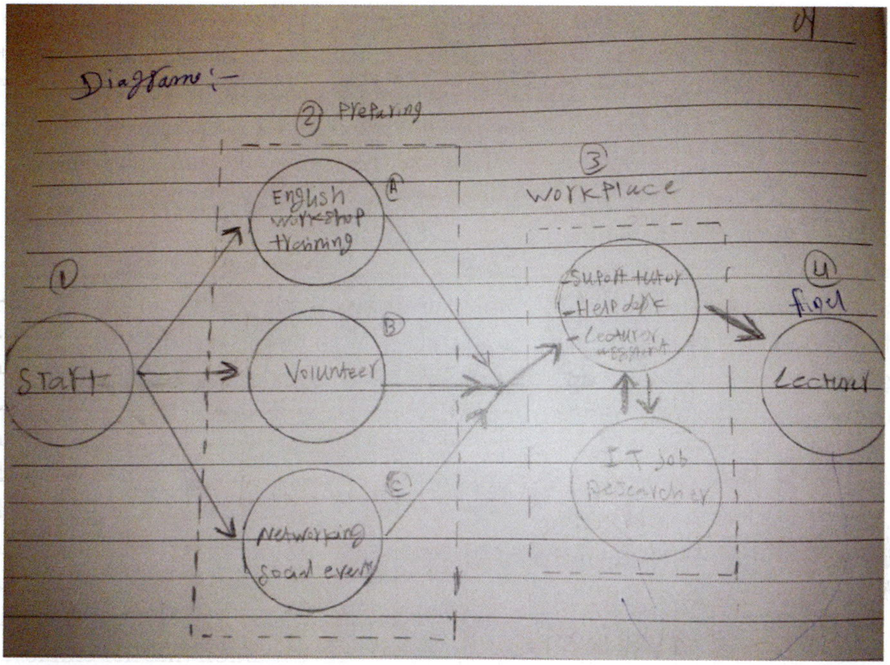

Figure 8.1 Arwa's employment plan

This diagram shows that her plan involves many aspects that might, in theory, contribute to employability: improving her English competency, volunteering, social networking, a willingness to start at the bottom of the ladder, so to speak. Her journey is laid out along a straightforward path, one step following the last as she logically works her way to her imagined future career. This aligns well with a 'skills and attributes' conceptualisation of employability as an individual and internalised quality, as discussed in Chapter 1 (Hinchliffe & Jolly, 2011; L. Holmes, 2001). So confident was Arwa in the realisation of this plan that she spoke of creating a resource based on it for other former refugees to aid their own trajectories into employment, despite not yet having accomplished her own goals.

Arwa's journey over the following year did not follow the trajectory laid out in her plan. She encountered many challenges and setbacks to her sense of self as employable, and eventually to her entire conceptualisation of what employability means. I explore here her development and negotiation of a locally-useful employable identity, as she navigates employability narratives, agency, and her own capital in nine research interviews over a 20-month period.

I begin with her ostensive narrative of flight, or rather the narrative of flight which I attempted to elicit from her. Arwa resisted my pursuit of this narrative and repeatedly redirected our conversation towards her education and capabilities. This early discursive manoeuvring provides insight into Arwa's self-positioning with regards to her sense of her own employability in the initial stages of our relationship, her agentive rejection of other-positioning, and the extent to which her employable identity was intertwined with the perceived value of her institutional cultural capital. From here I explore excerpts from interviews over the following months, as Arwa encountered labour market and interpersonal challenges, in particular how she struggled with her changing views on the value of her cultural capital, and the ramifications of this. The importance of co-construction in her development can be seen as she repeatedly narrates coming up against challenges to her expectations of behaviour and outcomes. I explore the ways in which she gradually, and largely outside of an employment context, gains opportunities to learn, practice, and gain locally-valuable capital, and the impacts of these gains on her navigation of an employable identity.

Arwa's avoidance of a narrative of flight

Arwa, like Isaac, Kelly, and Omar, used the opportunity of telling her story of flight to orient away from refugee-related Discourses which index vulnerability and powerlessness, and to position herself as capable and academic. This agentive reframing was immediately evident the first time I asked Arwa why she decided to leave her country of origin:

Excerpt 8.2 16 May 2016; 14:13–14:57

```
1. Emily: what made you decide to leave
2. Arwa:  actually:: (1) I want just to find other country + social- les-
3.        to have freedom + because I'm intellectual person +
4.        and I have like + good things to + I mean just have good idea
5.        I want to dev- developed country + to ah reflect my skills + ah
6. Emily: do you=
7. Arwa:  =and just yeah that's why I left + to go Malaysia
8.        to st- study my + Master + um + PhD
```

Implicit in my question on line 1 is the assumption that it was a 'push' factor that led Arwa to leave her country of origin, which is fairly reasonable given the salience of refugeehood to the circumstances under which Arwa and I were meeting (According to Kunz (1973, p. 131), migration is traditionally thought of as being motivated by 'push' or 'pull' factors: "(t)he 'push' factor of the old home environment provides the future migrant with causal motivations to leave the old country, and the 'pull' factor of the country of choice provides [them] with a purpose and a wish to migrate"). However, Arwa's response, beginning on line 2, begins with *actually*, in order to make a 'counterclaim' about this assumption (S. W. Smith &

Jucker, 2000; Vine, 2017). That is, she reframes her motivation for leaving to a pull factor (Kunz, 1973). This reorientation is highlighted by her use of *just* as a neutral limiter (Lindemann & Mauranen, 2001), indicating that what is to follow is the *only* reason she left.

Arwa indexes refugee-related topics of both physical and intellectual freedom, and developing vs. developed countries (lines 2–5), but these indices are building towards her academic identity, as she references Discourses of Academia (institutional Discourses, often used in marketing, surrounding the benefits of tertiary study, including increased employability, acquisition of transferable skills, and general self-betterment (Boden & Nedeva, 2010; Moreau & Leathwood, 2006; O'Shea, Stone, Delahunty, & May, 2018)) or Employability on line 5 stating she wanted to be somewhere that would *reflect [her] skills*. The orientation away from Discourses of Refugeehood (i.e. a narrative of flight) and towards Discourses of Academia is strengthened from line 7 when she cuts off my attempt to probe further by confirming where she is headed with this narrative (*yeah*, seemingly functioning as a coherence marker, augmenting her alignment with the claim she had made on line 5 (J. M. Fuller, 2003; Jucker & Smith, 1998)). She then introduces her institutional cultural capital, highlighting a strong orientation to her academic identity over her refugee identity.

A little later in this same interview I ask Arwa for clarification on why she felt that her intellectual freedom was limited in her country of origin, and she speaks briefly of restrictions on clothing and criticising authority. She alludes to danger with some levity, saying that *anyone just can take gun and* [2 × gunshot noise] *bye bye + finish*, employing cartoonish gunshot sounds and the playful, child-like expression *bye bye* to illustrate death, reminiscent of Kelly's use of *bye bye* used to a similar distancing effect when describing her parents' departure from Palestine (in Chapter 5). However, while Arwa appears to be drawing on notions of danger associated with Discourses of Refugeehood perhaps to legitimise her motivations for leaving her country of origin (while simultaneously distancing herself from that danger and any effect it may have had on her), moments later she reorients swiftly to her academic identity when I draw on Discourses of Refugeehood and flight asking Arwa if she left on her own or with family (lines 1–2, below):

Excerpt 8.3 16 May 2016, 16:15–16:21

```
1. Emily:   so when you left did you leave on your own or
2.          with any of your family or
3. Arwa:    no no I'm- + m- I mean basically I leave to study Master
4. Emily:   yeah
5. Arwa:    I get scholarship
```

Although I do not mention flight or refugees explicitly, the Discourses of Refugeehood implied by reference to leaving with her family seem to be evident to Arwa, evidenced by her rejection of the implication on line 3, repeating *no*, and drawing my attention back to her institutional capital with discourse marker *basically* marking the fundamental reason for leaving (Watts, 1988). She underlines her competence and academic identity on line 5 by telling me she received a scholarship.

Arwa then continues to tell me the story of her education in Malaysia until she arrives at the point at which she finished her PhD, and only then proceeding, without prompting, to describe her decision to apply for refugee status with the UNHCR and her eventual placement in New Zealand, never using the words *refugee* or *asylum*. One last time I attempt to explore the reasons Arwa did not feel safe in her country of origin further, which Arwa brushes off:

Excerpt 8.4 16 May 2016, 18:03–18:22

```
1. Emily: ok + so why did you say it wasn't safe for you to go back to [country]
2. Arwa:  because I told you the situation now is dangerous
3. Emily: ok=
4. Arwa:  =anyone just can kill anyone and then now + it's it's it's long
          long story
5. Emily: ok
6. Arwa:  it's really long story
```

On line 1 I make my final attempt to gather more details about why Arwa did not wish to return to her country of origin, which could be taken to imply that the narrative evidence she has provided is not sufficient for her to fill the image of refugee I have in mind. However, this positioning is rejected by Arwa, as she repeats – and tells me she is repeating – that the country is dangerous (line 1). She shuts down further questions by telling me twice that it is a *long story* (lines 4 and 6), a Labovian coda firmly bringing us away from her narrative-world departure from her country of origin and back to the present (Labov & Waletsky, 1967; see also Puvimanasinghe et al., 2014). At this point, it is clear that this is not a topic Arwa wishes to unpack any further, and I abandon the attempt to gain a clearer picture of Arwa's motivations for leaving.

Spector-Mersel (2011, p. 174) claims that in telling stories we aim for a 'valued end point,' i.e. the point of the story being told, which "may refer to the core of the identity to be claimed through the story." The telling of narratives requires (often unconscious) selection 'mechanisms' (Spector-Mersel, 2011, p. 174, following Sarbin, 1986). *Omission* and *silencing* are two of these, in which periods of life and events are not reported because they are irrelevant to the story's end point or because they contradict it, respectively (the other 'mechanisms' are *inclusion*, the reporting of events and periods of life that are compatible with the story's end point; and *flattening*, or the minimising of reported events and life periods in the life history, allowing the speaker to mention a 'fact' but simultaneously note it's narrative insignificance (Spector-Mersel, 2011, p. 174)). Arwa's choice to repeatedly avoid or redirect my questioning about her reasons for leaving her country of origin could thus be rooted in a mismatch between the identity positions this telling would oblige her to take up, and the identity 'end point' she is trying to achieve within our interaction.

Of course, Arwa's experiences may be painful for her to retell, and certainly necessarily involved "separation from family and friends, and the loss of home, community, and country" (Puvimanasinghe et al., 2014, p. 192). When retelling periods of a life story that have a negative impact upon sense of self, narrative avoidance or the construction of 'counternarratives' can assist former refugees to orient to new or more acceptable identities that are not defined by trauma and refugeehood (Bamberg, 2004a; Puvimanasinghe et al., 2014). Therefore, it is possible that Arwa's repositioning may have been a simple rejection of the role of refugee. Alternatively, she may have been rejecting the (perhaps disempowering) other-positioning as refugee coming from someone who was less educated than herself. As a PhD holder, she may have been resisting what she perceived as an attempt by someone with less status – a PhD candidate not yet graduated – to relegate her to a lower status role within the interaction. Positioning herself as my academic superior may have allowed her to take up a powerful discursive position as an accomplished woman and maintain her academic identity and sense of self as agentive. Research interviews, as Talmy (2010, p. 137) notes, are "constituted by complex relations of power, which can be differentially realised in many ways." That is, although all my interactions with Arwa were guided to a certain extent by my questions, Arwa could – and did – agentively take up discursively powerful positions by avoiding, redirecting or refusing to answer, and guiding my focus to the stories she wanted to tell (Finlay, 2012; Lammers, 2007; Talmy, 2010).

Given the circumstances under which we were meeting, I believe it likely that Arwa's foregrounding of her academic, intellectual identity here is linked to conceptualisation of herself as (highly) employable. That is, the employment-related (rather than the (former) refugee-related) angle of my research was seemingly most salient to Arwa in our conversation that first day (as evidenced by her 'cold open,' discussed above). Thus, her strong discursive guidance away from Discourses of Refugeehood and towards Discourses of Academia suggests that she views her institutional cultural capital as integral to her ability to successfully enact an employable identity.

Towards an employable identity

My interviews with Arwa between May 2016 and December 2017 demonstrate a moving conceptualisation of her employable identity. The content of these excerpts covers three main areas: securing employment, dealing with face-threatening feedback, and the navigation of the role of former refugee in New Zealand. In these excerpts Arwa navigates challenges to her sense of self and her capital, and to her management of agency in narrative, as both narrator and protagonist in the storyworlds. In these excerpts, which cover a 20-month period, Arwa's developing appreciation of the two-sided nature of employability becomes evident. That is, as she attempts to negotiate her employable identity over this period, both within her recounted storyworlds and in interaction with me, Arwa can be seen to observe and willingly participate in *co-constructing* her employable identity for the local context.

Interview 1 (May 2016)

Arwa made her academic identity (and institutional cultural capital), rather than her (former) refugee identity, salient in our discussion of her journey from her country of origin to New Zealand, as discussed above. Later in this same interview, it became evident that the *recognition* of Arwa's institutional cultural capital played an important role in her sense of self. As discussed in Chapters 2 and 7, for capital to be useful in a given field, it must be acknowledged as such according to the 'rules' of that field (Bourdieu, 1991; Hesmondhalgh, 2006). When erstwhile valuable capital is *not* recognised in a new field, the capital-holder may face challenges to their sense of self and of their position in the world (Colic-Peisker & Walker, 2003; Gans, 2009; Ricento, 2015). This seems to be the case in Arwa's recounting of an incident in which she perceived the worth of that capital as being challenged, or diminished, by a language teacher. Arwa had been asked to speak on a given topic in class, and then the teacher had indicated to her that she was speaking too fast: *she + said... you speak like dadadadada*. This shocked Arwa, who said nothing at the time but decided to bring her concerns to the teacher once the class was finished:

Excerpt 8.5 16 May 2016, 48.02–48.29

```
1. Arwa: I said can I can I speak to you please (1) she say ok
2.       + and then I said why are you doing this with me + she said ah
         because +
3.       I said why + first I am a doctor (1) second I am thirty seven +
         I'm oldest one
4.       so you don't respect my + age + and you don't respect my certificate +
5.       you don't respect anything here I'm of- I'm just trying +
6.       to do my best to speak I'm trying to do my best to +
7.       enhance my pronunciation + so now you destroy me
```

In the storyworld that Arwa is narrating here, her linguistic capital (as a form of embodied cultural capital) is being evaluated, and she takes the evaluation as an insult, at least in the setting in which it is delivered. For Arwa, this perceived attack on her linguistic capital seems to be an affront to her sense of self, her identity as a senior or high-status member of the classroom by virtue of her age and education. She employs her institutional capital explicitly in her constructed dialogue (Tannen, 1986) with her teacher on lines 3–4 (*I am a doctor; you don't respect my certificate*). Arwa uses her own constructed dialogue to position her protagonist self here as having been humiliated by the encounter, as the recipient or victim of a kind of attack, when she says that this *destroy*ed her (line 7). Similarly, repetition of the phrase *trying to do my best* (lines 5 and 6) invokes a low-agency position in which the 'tryer' is unable to successfully act upon the world despite their best efforts.

However, aside from this momentary low agency self-positioning, Arwa-as-narrator otherwise assigns Arwa-as-protagonist a high agency position throughout this narrative, strongly reprimanding her storyworld teacher from the moral high ground (cf. Lagenhove & Harré, 1999). As she recounts this storyworld conversation, Arwa-as-narrator assigns her teacher little voice, while assigning Arwa-as-protagonist considerably more. Reporting the words of others via narrative "allows narrators to… express stances and interpretations often through theatrical manipulation of the voices of others" (De Fina, 2003, p. 96). This can be seen in Arwa's discursive shaping of the storyworld interaction (line 2) when she begins to report her teacher's response to Arwa's question (*ah because*) but then returns to her own reported speech immediately on line 3, a repetition of her earlier question *why*. Here, Arwa's focus on her own words (as protagonist) over those of her storyworld interlocutor has the interactional effect of positioning Arwa as justifiably aggrieved and underappreciated. Arwa's institutional cultural capital, as discussed above, plays an important role in her sense of her own employability. Thus, perceived threats to that capital appear to threaten her ability to enact an employable identity in New Zealand.

Interview 2 (August 2016)

The second time I met with Arwa she had recently encountered another challenge to her institutional and embodied cultural capital. In her efforts to improve her chances in the labour market, she had applied for a course designed to teach skilled migrants pragmatic communication competence in a New Zealand environment. Arwa told me that thirteen people had applied for the twelve-place course, and despite being absolutely certain that she would be successful, she was the only applicant who was not accepted after the placement interview. In the excerpt below, she recounts to me the feedback she received from the course coordinator: that Arwa is confident and competent but comes off as angry. In the opening lines (1–3) she is (re)constructing the dialogue of her interlocutor, i.e. she is relaying the interlocutor's feedback to me. From line 4 Arwa is speaking in her own voice.

Excerpt 8.6 3 August 2016, 16:35–17:41

```
1. Arwa:  you are very confidence + you are strong + y- you answer all
          the question
2.        you listen very well + your answer is very perf- I cannot
          say anything (1)
3.        but she said + you look like angry (1) I said what + angry
[Some transcript omitted; 16:58–17:09]
4. Arwa:  angry is mean I'm crazy I can't do anything now I can [points
          to cup]
5.        broke this one that's angry + why you don't say sad
6.        + I'm very sad really I have like (1) I mean + I have like painful
7.        because of my situation I feel really painful + because I
          have a good skills
8.        I have a good qualification I have a lot of things but nobody
          appreciate (1)
9.        nobody appreciate these skills nobody appreciate that I have +
10.       just always + you w- I mean + you focus on the negative things
11.       and never + look at the positive things
```

Arwa-as-narrator interactively positions herself as competent, and suitable for this course on lines 1–2, which is both mitigated and warranted by the fact that she does so using the words of the storyworld course coordinator (Bangerter et al., 2011; Georgakopoulou, 1995; Matoesian, 2000). It should be noted also that the reported feedback aligns with the kinds of employability-enhancing skills suggested by the skills and attributes approach discussed earlier (Bridgstock, 2009; Hinchliffe & Jolly, 2011; Moreau & Leathwood, 2006): confidence, resilience, and good listening skills. The traditional conceptualisation of employability as a kind of individualised set of check-box attributes or skills is further indexed by Arwa on line 2 when, still reconstructing the coordinator's speech, she (begins to) report that her answers were (presumably) perfect.

From line 3 onwards Arwa reports a fairly intense reaction to being told that she looks angry, particularly as that pertains (or does not pertain, as she implies) to her suitability for the course. She seems to infer the comment to be an assessment of her character, as opposed to her demeanour, as we can see on lines 3 and 4 (between which there were some lines which I have omitted). She reports her interlocutor as saying that Arwa *look like angry* (line 3), but then by line 4, Arwa discursively equates this assessment with the suggestion that she is *crazy*, and even unstable (indicating that she could abruptly break a cup). Arwa had attempted to accomplish a professional identity in the placement interview, in which she had indicated to me (not included in excerpt) that she was *really confident*, and that she had not smiled because her interviewer was not smiling (contributing, Arwa indicated, to the evaluation of her as *angry*). Thus, in her recounting she appears to portray her attempt at professional identity performance as being rejected, and a 'crazy' identity as being imposed upon her by her storyworld interlocutor. She strongly rejects this positioning and is highly agentive in her forceful rejection of the feedback she has been given. The boundary is not really clear between when she is addressing the course coordinator in the storyworld, and when she is addressing me in the here-and-now of the interview.

The mismatch between the way Arwa intended to come across and the way her behaviour was interpreted in the narrated interactional context may be rooted in a clash of interactional norms surrounding the expression of emotion. That is, her enactment of 'enthusiastic interviewee,' or perhaps of 'sadness' (see following paragraph) may have been interpreted as anger in the local context (cf. Bamberg 1997a; Pavlenko, 2002), although it is not possible to comment further on this without access to the recounted interaction itself. Furthermore, Arwa's strong reaction to this misinterpretation in interaction with me may be linked to gender norms which sanction female anger (Gibbings, 2011; Sharkin, 1993).

On lines 5–6 she gives this alternative assessment of her character: *sad*, rather than *crazy*. At this point she discursively switches to a lower agency position. Indexing her cultural capital (*skills* and *good qualification*) she positions herself in a victim role (Bamberg's (2011b, 2011a) world-to-person agentive positioning), repeating three times that *nobody appreciate*[s] her capital. Her victim-like position is further highlighted by opposing (or complementary?) intensifiers or amplifiers *always* (line 10) and *never* (line 11), both often used to mark exaggeration in speech (Hinkel, 2003), to highlight her interaction position that her positive attributes are regularly overlooked. Arwa discursively indicates that she places a great deal of value in her own cultural capital. This lack of recognition of her capital by interviewers appears to be challenging her ability to perform a professional identity.

Later in this same interview, the start of a move away from the idea that employability is something which resides solely within her can be seen. While not demonstrating an awareness of the two-way process of employability as an identity per se, Arwa here hints at consideration of adaptation of her interactional behaviour to the local context. However, this is framed in a way which suggests Discourses of Integration or Assimilation (expectations that migrants adapt to the cultural norms of the dominant culture (Ehrkamp, 2005)) and perhaps of Gratitude, rather than as a co-constructed process. Arwa mentioned again the incident outlined in Excerpt 8.5 and went on to talk about how she believes teaching in New Zealand needs to change, noting her reluctance to *keep silent*. Then, while recounting to me ways in which she believes New Zealand teachers could improve, Arwa dynamically reorients from a position of giving advice to one of receiving it. While taking up this position, however, she retains the advice-giving role as well. As advice-giver she now appears to be double voicing her words, dialogically responding to an absent other (Bakhtin, 1981, 1990). Double voicing, as discussed earlier, points to the fundamentally dialogic nature of interaction, and the way that any 'new' statement calls to both all earlier statements and to those yet to come (Irvine, 2012).

Excerpt 8.7 3 August 2016, 29:24–29:48

```
1. Arwa:  before they they're thinking about + I mean + they need to
          [clears throat]
2.        think more + about our feeling + rather than + thinking about
3.        their I mean culture ok s- we have to respect New Zealand culture
4.        because now + I mean New Zealand my home + this will be my country
5.        + in just four years now I will get the nationality of the kiwi
6.        + so I need to learn yes I have to learn I have to respect the
          kiwi culture
```

Within this excerpt there is a shift from externally-directed advice (lines 1–2) towards internally-directed advice (line 3 onwards). Arwa has expressed to me on several occasions that she believes it is important to address any room for improvement that she perceives in New Zealand society, and this is what she has been doing leading up to this excerpt. However, here she abruptly shifts the responsibility of cultural awareness from New Zealand-born New Zealanders to herself and other migrants (or at least shares the responsibility).

This becomes evident halfway through line 3 starting with *ok*, but her changing position may be indicated earlier on lines 1 and 3 through the use of *I mean* (used again on line 4) which can be used to indicate upcoming adjustments of the speaker's position, either meta-linguistically (modifying a speaker's ideas) or meta-communicatively (modifying the speaker's intentions) (Schiffrin, 1987, p. 304). Additionally, *I mean* may also be linked to negative politeness, indicating a discursive position of a speaker not being entirely committed to what they have just said, and that they are willing to modify their statements if they have caused offense to their interlocutors (Fox Tree & Schrock, 2002, p. 741). Arwa's use of *I mean*, then, could indicate that she is re-evaluating the position she is taking even as she speaks, before deciding to shift from a high-agency position of giving advice to a lower-agency position of advice-recipient.

She introduces a claim of personal responsibility for her resettlement challenges, resonant of McKendy's (2006) observation of prisoners 'pasting in' statements of personal responsibility, as discussed in Chapter 6. Arwa does so by addressing an imagined counter-argument to what she has just been saying in an instance of Bakhtinian answerability (1981, 1990). She opens this 'response' with *ok*, an indication of agreement with – or concession of a point to – her imagined conversant. While Bakhtin's concepts can be applied to any utterance, expression of answerability is notably evident in this excerpt from Arwa, and again on line 6 when she addresses her imagined challenger saying *yes I have to learn*. She does not shy away from the responsibility she assigns herself, using verbs of necessity (*have* and *need*) repeatedly in quick succession on lines 3 and 6 (as in Chapter 7, I am comfortable assigning meaning here to second-language speaker Arwa's lexical choices, given the discursive context of obligation that characterises this excerpt as a whole).

She went on to outline how she is taking steps to address this responsibility, through a training session with a refugee support worker. She describes envisaging a positive future where change has been enacted – change within herself – by stating that with this help, *we can successful + in the next + interview and... in the life + in the all life*, sharing this imagined success with the support worker through using the first-person plural *we*. She discursively links her commitment to play her part in the two-way process of successful settlement and success in future interviews, seeming to indicate an awareness of 'employability' as negotiated. Nonetheless, this is framed here as an internalised requirement of respect on the part of both old-timer and newcomer (Norton, 2001), rather than as an identity negotiated in discourse.

To support her change of orientation, Arwa also seems to 'paste in' some statements echoing Discourses of (migrant) Integration. On line 3, then again on line 6, she states that, first *we* then *I*, *have to respect New Zealand* (then *kiwi*) culture. Interestingly, both these statements follow directly or very soon after her dialogic responses (*ok* and *yes*) to her absent interlocutor, so she may in fact be responding to actual past instantiations of being told this. The 'pasting in' of statements of personal accountability may be a discursive strategy for navigating Bamberg's (2011b) agency dilemma. As discussed in Chapter 6, claiming or ceding agency as a narrator and finding the right balance between the two to accommodate both one's sense of self as capable and agentive, and local norms of self-presentation (as well as Discourses of Gratitude) can be a precarious discursive path to navigate. Taking the interactional position of giving *herself* advice, Arwa may avoid the potentially face-threatening and low agency position of someone ignorant of, and incapable of adapting to, local norms and expectations.

Interestingly, Arwa – a permanent resident of New Zealand at the time of this interview – says that New Zealand is her *home* (line 4) but indicates that New Zealand will only be *(her) country* upon gaining citizenship (*this will be my country + in just four years now I will get the nationality of the kiwi*; lines 4–5). This calls to mind the concept of citizenship as capital (Bauder, 2008), discussed in Chapter 7 in relation to Omar being denied an interview, ostensibly based on citizenship. In the present excerpt, Arwa speaks of citizenship as a gateway to belonging – New Zealand <u>*will*</u> *be (her) country* once she has a Kiwi nationality. Furthermore, she attributes this future status (using *so* to mark the causal relationship on line 4

(Schiffrin, 1987)) to her obligation to *learn* and *respect* local culture. This is unsurprising given the relationship between citizenship and expressing "identities of belonging" (Bauder, 2008, p. 324, as discussed in Chapter 7).

It is worth noting that, throughout our interviews, Arwa frequently offered advice to the nation of New Zealand in a way which could be seen to be in violation of the Discourses of Gratitude that surround expectations of former refugees (Moulin, 2012; Nayeri, 2017; Nguyen, 2013). However, during these episodes of advice-giving, Arwa would frequently justify them in ways which *did* align with Discourses of Gratitude. For example, she told me about a time she berated other former refugees for putting up with what she saw as less-than-ideal conditions at Mangere Refugee Resettlement Centre, asking them in the storyworld *is this good thinking + you think because the food is free + and the and the place is free to sleep + is this good* (16 May 2016; 36.19–36.25). She went on to say that *not everything is ok positive positive positive you have to say if there is + negative things*, and that *if you speak you will contribute this society + if I just keep silent… this means I will not do anything for New Zealand* (16 May 2016; 39.36–40.08). Arwa's negative feedback could be seen to transgress, as Bauder (2008, p. 325) notes, nation states of the Global North's expectation that migrants "express their loyalty[,]… embrace the cultural identity of their country of settlement and demonstrate their willingness to adapt to an imagined national habitus and associated national 'values'." However, she frames her ostensive complaints as contributions; as her duty to give back to New Zealand. In doing so, she seems to be in fact aligning with Discourses of Gratitude, albeit in an idiosyncratic way.

Similarly, the 'pasting in' that Arwa engages in in Excerpt 8.7 has the discursive effect of allowing her to negotiate a realignment with Discourses of Gratitude in the interactional context with me, in the same way that McKendy's (2006, p. 481) prisoners were able to realign with institutionally-enforced Discourses of Individual Responsibility in their own narratives. Furthermore, Arwa discursively demonstrates her willingness to adapt to the norms of the imagined community of New Zealand (B. Anderson, 1991), displaying recognition of the negotiated nature of belonging, which has implications for the ongoing development – and co-construction – of a locally-valuable employable identity.

Interview 3 (November 2016)

Recognition of incongruous interactional norms played a role in a temporary research assistant position at a local university that Arwa was offered in November 2016. Some months earlier she had emailed an Associate Professor somewhat out of the blue, introducing herself and asking if he knew of any employment opportunities. His (reported) response to her indicated that he was fairly taken aback by – and unhappy with – being contacted directly in this manner, by someone he did not know. A refugee resettlement worker then acted as an intermediary (with Arwa's permission) and emailed him explaining that Arwa was a recently-arrived former refugee, and that her direct approach was aligned with the interactional norms of her previous contexts. Arwa told me that the professor's disposition softened following this intervention, and he told Arwa and the resettlement worker that he would keep an eye out for any opportunities that fit her qualifications and experience. Eventually, he arranged a summer research assistant position for her. The resettlement worker's role in mediating this interaction and its eventual result in (temporary) employment highlights the importance of social capital in job seeking.

When I spoke to Arwa in November, she seemed happier and more relaxed than the previous times I had met her. I addressed this explicitly, after we had briefly discussed once again the capital-challenging incidents outlined in Excerpts 8.5 and 8.6 above. It seemed to me that Arwa was less invested in the incidents than in previous tellings. I believe that this can be seen below, along with the effects that employment appears to be having on her *imagined* employable identity:

Excerpt 8.8 4 November 2016; 7:42–8:01

```
1. Emily: now you seem much more kind of (2)
2. Arwa:  happy
3. Emily: yeah
4. Arwa:  because now I + I + let's say now I get what I want now
5. Emily: mm
6. Arwa:  and yeah yes I get what I want and I will consider it the first step
7. Emily: mm
8. Arwa:  this is the first step and then + the next time
9.        maybe I will get another full time job maybe:: +
10.       better than this one again we'll see
```

My long pause at the end of my utterance on line 1 was caused by my re-evaluating my intended word choice. I wanted to tell Arwa that she seemed more *calm*, as in, that she seemed content and relaxed. However, given that she had previously told me that people had described her as *angry* and *emotionally unstable*, and that this had really hurt her, I was conscious that *calm* might inadvertently index an unintended binary of *calm* vs. *unreasonable* or *agitated*. When I begin to suggest that Arwa's outlook has changed in some way (line 1), Arwa infers my general sentiment and provides her own evaluation, that she is *happy* (line 2). She attributes this (opening with *because*, line 4) to being in a position where she has achieved her goal (or, as is clarified in the following moments, achieved a first step towards her goal). This assessment seems to emerge within the interaction, as she precedes it with *let's say*, which Lee (2003) suggests marks new and relevant information, and De Rycker (1990, p. 402) indicates marks the following material as "a hypothetical example, a rough guess or anything about which the speaker is not entirely sure" (cited in De Clerck, 2004, p. 227). I would argue that in this context it illustrates not uncertainty on Arwa's part, but an indexical feature indicating that this is interactionally intended to be understood as having just sprung to mind. This reading is supported by her positive affirmation on line 6, beginning with *yeah yes*, as if she is agreeing with what she has just heard herself say. She then goes on to state that she views this accomplishment as the *first step* (lines 6 and 8, perhaps invoking her employment plan (Figure 8.1, above)). In doing so Arwa is orienting to an employable identity which outranks the job she has just secured, but one which is, through *first step* framing, nonetheless validated by it.

She then indexes her imagined future (Norton, 2001) where her subsequent employment will perhaps be *full time* and *better* (lines 9 and 10), though this imagined identity is hedged through repeated use of *maybe* (line 9) and *we'll see* (line 10). Arwa's negotiation of her current and future employable identities seems supported by the recognition and validation of her capital as valuable in the labour market (cf. her remark that *I feel really painful + because... nobody appreciate these skills* in Excerpt 8.6, above). This, along with Arwa's uptake and discursive development of my incomplete comment on her disposition, demonstrates the co-constructed and interactionally negotiated nature of employable identities. Validation of Arwa's employability (in the form of a job) perhaps lends legitimacy to Arwa's imagined future identity.

Interview 7 (April 2017)

Alas, Arwa's optimism was not to last. We met again in April of 2017, two months after her research assistant position had finished. This role had not led on to additional employment as she had hoped. Eleven months and one temporary paid position after I met her, her views about her institutional cultural capital and her own employability had changed dramatically. It was from this meeting that the vignette at the start of this chapter is taken (Excerpt 8.1, above), wherein Arwa displays her emerging views of what employability might mean to *employers*, hinting at a developing understanding of the co-constructed nature of employability.

A little later in the same interview as Excerpt 8.1, Arwa speaks more explicitly about her emerging sentiments about her institutional cultural capital. She tells me about an argument she had with her parents, reporting that she told them *now just you follow me to + it's not force me yeah it's a kind of force me + study PhD* (based on the surrounding context I believe it is safe to say that Arwa here means *lead* and not *follow*). There is an interesting reversal of agentive positions in this statement, for both Arwa-as-protagonist and Arwa-as-narrator. As *protagonist*, she switches from a high-agency, person-to-world position (*not* being forced to study) to a low-agency, world-to-person position (being forced). Meanwhile, as *narrator*, she switches from a lower agency position of accepting what is, to a higher-agency position of standing up for herself – indicating that yes, she does feel that she was forced into study (and is not ok with that). She went on to tell me that her family was very highly educated (*six doctor*[s] *and two professor*[s]), and to outline her advice to her cousin, who she indicated was considering studying towards a PhD:

Excerpt 8.9 7 April 2017; 8:17–8:40

```
1. Arwa:  if my cousin now I want to ask him why you study + PhD now +
2.        I advise you don't study + it's really (2) like stupid project +
3.        one of the stupid project in the life is the PhD so I advise him
4.        I said no because now it's become like fashion + everyone have PhD
5. Emily: mm
6. Arwa:  so I said believe me you will regret + you get this PhD (1)
7.        you will regret because you will not get a job very easily +
8.        especially if you go to Western countries + it's very hard
```

After earlier having positioned herself as having been *forced* to study by her parents – a world-to-person narrative position (Bamberg, 2011a) – here Arwa starts to discursively reclaim agency, positioning herself as an authority on the value, or lack thereof, of post-graduate study. She hypothetically advises her cousin not to study and portrays the institutional cultural capital of a PhD as worthless due to its ubiquity. This high agency self-positioning is emphasised in lines 6–8 when she says *believe me*, which Janet Holmes (1984, p. 353) suggests discursively acts as a 'speaker-oriented booster,' intended to enhance the credibility of the speaker. This is followed by addressing her cousin in the storyworld, telling him that he will regret doing a PhD because it will not lead to employment.

It is interesting to note the real-world context of these sentiments, and the effect it may – or may not – be having upon the unfolding of Arwa's narrative. Discussing the (lack of) worth of PhDs in conversation with me, a PhD candidate at the time, Arwa makes no attempt to discursively mitigate her position with regards to my own current endeavours and their potential future worth (I was not offended, which I mention to make clear that Arwa was not ignoring or oblivious to any expressions of offense on my part). It may be that Arwa has momentarily forgotten my role at the time as a doctoral researcher, although this seems unlikely, as it underpinned and was very salient to our interactions at this point in our relationship. Perhaps she is taking the interactional position that she does not care about the potentially face-threatening (to me) effects of diminishing the worth of doctoral study, or perhaps she is, while addressing her storyworld cousin, also implicitly and indirectly giving me life advice as her interlocutor in the here-and-now.

In either case, Arwa is taking up a powerful position within our interaction, either as an authority on the matter, or by disregarding the conceivably face-threatening character of her statements (see, for example, Bhopal, 2010; and Doná, 2007 for discussions of dynamic power relations within research interviews). This powerful position-taking within our interaction strengthens the discursive argument she develops within this excerpt regarding the worthlessness of PhDs to employability. It is worth noting that she went to on discuss a PhD-qualified friend who had had trouble finding work, removed their PhD from their CV and then found a job quickly. So not only has Arwa come to a point where she sadly no longer sees the value in her institutional capital that she once did, she in fact sees it as a burden to her ability to effectively negotiate an employable identity in the labour market.

Some five months later, in September 2017, Arwa briefly moved to a city 500 kilometres from where she had been living. After a successful phone interview for a teaching job at a tertiary education institute, she had been asked to attend a follow up interview in person. Having been advised by others that job prospects in Computer Science were much better in this other city, Arwa decided to buy a car, sell some of her belongings, move out of her flat, and, with her remaining possessions packed into her car, move to there. I was slightly taken aback by this seemingly abrupt decision to move, with no permanent accommodation nor employment definitively arranged, but Arwa seemed hopeful and excited. She was not positive that she would get the job that she was interviewing for but was positive about her better prospects in the labour market nonetheless.

Interview 9 (December 2017)

The next time that we met three months after she had moved, Arwa had moved back to the city she had originally lived in. Although by all accounts her interview had gone well, the job had gone to someone with more teaching experience. She had not been able to find affordable and acceptable accommodation in the city she had moved to, nor employment, and had decided to return to her original city, where she had better networks and support. Although the circumstances of her return had the potential to be face-threatening for Arwa in the context of our conversation, I was pleased to find her in good spirits, and optimistic about her future prospects.

After failing to secure a job, Arwa had begun to consider returning to study, and changing her career direction. She met with career advisors at a local refugee support agency, who suggested that she pursue Business Studies, or further studies in Computer Science. Arwa was resistant to the idea of further education in Computer Science, believing a PhD to be sufficient, and that if she wanted to update her skills she could do so on her own, with library books. Business Studies, however, appealed to her, and she went to see an advisor at a university to discuss this. Arwa told me that the advisor initially encouraged her to find a job in the area she was already educated in, citing an overseas-born-and-educated friend of her own who was able to find work easily. At the beginning of this excerpt (lines 1–4) Arwa is reconstructing the advisor's dialogue; i.e., speaking in the advisor's voice:

Excerpt 8.10 12 December 2017, 2:15–2:43

```
1. Arwa:   she's Chinese from Hon- from Hong Kong she applied for a job
2.         here in [city name] and she got it + and she's overseas +
3.         and she's don't have + any permanent residence so why
4.         why you don't get the job
5. Emily:  mm
6. Arwa:   and then after some like + debating her? + she told me that um
7.         + she has like ten years' experience of teaching + after her PhD +
8.         said then that's the reason + I think this is my problem
9.         the lack of experience + and nobody give me the chance to to
10.        to start only + just to start nobody give me the chance
```

In Arwa's narrative here the advisor is positioned as conflating the experiences of Arwa and the advisor's own friend as one and the same, on account of them both being foreign nationals (lines 1–4). Furthermore, the experiences of someone who (in the storyworld of this narrative) applied for a job *from* overseas and then moved to New Zealand upon getting the job, are being compared with the experiences of Arwa's, a forced migrant who arrived in New Zealand under very different circumstances. Interestingly, Arwa herself does not appear to make the distinction salient (and thus makes no attempt to orient towards a refugee identity).

As narrator, Arwa assigns her protagonist self a rather powerful position by presenting herself as having *debate*d with her storyworld interlocutor about the difference between her and the advisor's friend until they arrive at a distinction that seems to fit Arwa's existing understanding of her own unemployment: her own lack of teaching experience. She frames this initially as a certainty: *that's the reason* their experiences have differed (line 8), and then slightly softens her position on the same line, mitigating what *her problem* is with *I think*. She takes up a lower agency, victim-like role as she laments her lack of opportunity to prove her embodied cultural capital that accompanies her institutional cultural capital, saying that *nobody give [her] the chance* to prove herself, and to gain the necessary experience (lines 9 and 10). Using minimisers *only* and *just* to depict what she needs (*to start only + just to start*) has the discursive effect of positioning this lack of opportunity as unreasonable (that to be given the opportunity is not so much to ask), and strengthening her victimlike, world-to-person self-positioning.

In Excerpt 8.6 above, Arwa opined that *nobody appreciate these skills* that she has (August 2016). Here, while still positioning herself as underappreciated, she now states that *just to start nobody give me the chance* (December 2017). There is a subtle adjustment in the framing of her embodied cultural capital – from it being unrecognised, to being denied the opportunity to *demonstrate* that capital. Furthermore, while the narrated interaction could be taken to challenge Arwa's value in the labour market, this interaction is discursively framed like a coming together of ideas, whereas previously recounted challenges to Arwa's capital and employability have been framed rather more like disputes (Excerpts 8.6, 8.6, above). It could be argued that these dynamic discursive reframings reflect a growing recognition of necessity of negotiation and co-construction in the enactment of locally valuable capital, and, in kind, a locally valuable employable identity.

This recognition is also evident a little later in the same narrated discussion with the careers advisor. Below in Excerpt 8.11, Arwa recounts a point in their interaction in which her embodied cultural capital is positioned by her storyworld interlocutor as locally invaluable. However, unlike her previous narratives of challenges to her capital, Arwa-as-narrator frames this storyworld interaction as a learning experience. Just prior to the following excerpt, the career advisor suggested to Arwa-as-protagonist that New Zealand-earnt institutional capital may be useful if Arwa intends to change her career. Arwa-as-protagonist then asked whether she should enrol in a master's or bachelor's degree in Business Administration. The excerpt opens with the advisor's response.

Excerpt 8.11 12 December 2017, 3.17–3.47

1. Arwa: she told me this one + um it's ok good for you but not to be a manager
2. + I need to have like two years' experience + of working in company
3. Emily: mm
4. Arwa: I said yes I had experience in [*origin country*] because I worked with my father
5. he learn me + about the administration
6. + [*quickly*] but that's in [*country*] not in New Zealand
7. Emily: mm
8. Arwa: she said that will be a little bit hard + for you now + to accept +
9. maybe they reject you (1) because of your background +
10. it's computer sciences + you don't know anything about business +
11. it's like zero (1) and then ok I told her what you what you what's your advice
12. she said you can start with diploma

On line 8, based on the following phrase *maybe they reject you*, it is my reading that that in using *accept*, Arwa means *to be accepted* (into either of the study programmes she had earlier suggested), rather than that she, Arwa, needs to *accept* something.

In this excerpt, Arwa orients to a novice identity, in contrast to the expert role that she discursively assigns the storyworld advisor. This might seem like expected positioning when recounting an interaction with an advisor, but as we have seen previously (Excerpts 8.5, 8.6 above), Arwa does not necessarily adhere to those expectations, particularly when she tells stories in which her world view is being challenged, or her face threatened.

This self-positioning can be seen when she explicitly asks her storyworld interlocutor for advice on line 11. Arwa recounts here that her own suggestion of studying towards a master's degree is gently discouraged by the advisor, on account of Arwa's lack of the necessary embodied cultural capital (two years' experience working in a company). Arwa-as-character contests this, saying she does have administration experience, learnt from her father (here perhaps indexing our previously established understanding of her father as a man of high status). However, she then immediately indicates recognition that this capital was earnt in her country of origin, and not New Zealand, introduced with *but* to mark an ideational adjustment to the previous utterance (Norrick, 2001, p. 857, citing Bell, 1998; and Katriel & Dascal, 1984).

The speed with which Arwa delivered this mitigation leads me to believe that it is intended to be taken as originating from Arwa herself – in the narrative world directed at her interlocutor, in the here-and-now directed at me, or both. That is, it has the effect of dialogically pre-empting an unspoken challenge to the validity of that embodied capital (Bakhtin, 1981). Implicit in this statement is that this overseas-earnt capital is not necessarily valuable in Arwa's current context. The fact she leaves this unsaid has the effect of indicating that Arwa believes both that her storyworld interlocutor, and me as here-and-now interlocutor, share this understanding of the contextually-bound nature of capital – the impact of Bourdieu's *fields* on capital (Bourdieu, 1991; Hesmondhalgh, 2006). My minimal feedback (line 7) has the effect of confirming this shared understanding. Whether or not this dialogic addressing of her capital's value took place in the actual narrated event as well, or only within our interaction, the observation of the contextual and dynamic nature of capital seems to indicate Arwa's developing recognition of the importance of the negotiation, and co-construction of employable identities (as well as aligning with the aforementioned literature on migration and the loss of useful capital upon crossing borders (Colic-Peisker & Walker, 2003; Gans, 2009; Ricento, 2015)).

Returning to a reconstruction of the career advisor's dialogue, Arwa discursively frames her interlocutor's advice as careful and hedged, as she guides Arwa-as-protagonist away from the idea of studying towards a master's degree. This hedging is indexed by a discursive minimiser (*little bit hard*, line 8) and uncertainty marker (*maybe*, line 9). The fact that Arwa reconstructs this dialogue as hedged is meaningful. While we cannot know how any interaction she has had actually played out (Tannen, 1986), the hedging incorporated in the pseudoquoted speech (Dubois, 1989) shows that it was recognised as such by Arwa at the time, and was not perceived as a challenge or threat to her sense of self.

Although Arwa goes on to recount a fairly bald and potentially face-threatening statement from the advisor on line 11 – *you don't know anything about business + it's like zero* – there is no discursive indication that Arwa received it as such. She positions herself as receptive to the feedback (*ok*, line 11) and, as mentioned above, asks for alternative advice. The advisor's recounted advice to her, *you can start with diploma* (line 12), while suggesting a lower-level qualification than either option Arwa had initially suggested, is worded in such a way to imply potential future development (in the New Zealand qualifications system, a diploma is (typically) a 12-month course beneath bachelor's degree level. It is possible that the advisor was referring to a Graduate Diploma, or Postgraduate Diploma (both also typically 12-month courses), which can be undertaken by those who have completed bachelor's degrees). In the storyworld that Arwa is narrating, this suggested diploma can be considered simply a *start*, which indexes an imagined future identity where Arwa has gone on to bigger and brighter things (Darvin & Norton, 2015; Norton, 2001). Arwa portrays the narrated interaction of the storyworld as having given her a positive view of the future, presented in a way that respected her existing embodied institutional capital even if its value was not transferable to her current context nor actualisable for the enactment of a locally-recognised employable identity.

Arwa's bright imagined future continued to discursively emerge within our conversation. Although her plans are less concrete here than in previous interactions, she is optimistic about the positive returns on her further investment in education:

Excerpt 8.12 12 December 2017; 13:37–13:58

```
1. Emily: what sort of job do you think you'd like to head into
2.        (1) with the business (2)
3. Arwa:  mm (2) I'm not sure exactly exactly but I mean what I want
4.        to open up other opportunities so when they see my CV +
5.        and then they see something from New Zealand
6. Emily: yep
7. Arwa:  which is new career + with computer sciences
8. Emily: mm
9. Arwa:  so it will be good + for me
```

Arwa expresses uncertainty towards my inquiry about future employment, making use of the utterance initial filled pause *mm* (line 3), followed by a two-second pause. After these voiced and unvoiced delays, Arwa indicates that she does not have a decisive response to my question, and then reorients her response with *but I mean* (line 3). The alternative that she provides is a desire to *open up other opportunities* (line 4), and here she may be indexing Discourses surrounding university study and employability. She orients to the idea of New Zealand-earnt institutional capital as more valuable in New Zealand (lines 4–5), although she assigns recognition of that value to (presumably) employers looking at her CV (*they*, lines 4 and 5), rather than herself.

Thus, we see Arwa's continued recognition that her employable identity is a co-construction, and that the value she sees in herself must be recognised as such by employers to be useful. Furthermore, once again the *positive* evaluation of New Zealand-earnt institutional capital is left unsaid, pointing to a presumed shared understanding between us of the benefit of this suggested new capital for her CV and thus job prospects. In fact, Arwa discursively draws a direct connection between the institutional cultural capital she is intending to earn, and a *new career* (line 7) in her imagined future, giving her evaluation on line 9 – opening with *so* to draw an inferential or causal connection (Bolden, 2006; Schiffrin, 1987) – that her decision to study will have positive outcomes in the future.

Conclusion

The successful enactment of an employable identity is a complicated and multi-faceted undertaking. While Discourses of Employability continue to promote the learning and practicing of transferable skills and attributes as a pathway to employment and personal employability (Hinchliffe & Jolly, 2011; L. Holmes, 2013; Moreau & Leathwood, 2006), approaching employability from an identity perspective recognises its emergent and discursively negotiated nature. For newcomers to a given context, unfamiliarity with local interactional norms and available discursive positions, and lack of access to (or ability to actualise) valuable capital means that the quest for locally-recognised employability may be a convoluted and frustrating one.

Throughout our conversations over 20 months, Arwa demonstrated a great trajectory in the way that she enacted, and recounted attempts to enact, her employable identity. Early on, her entire conceptualisation of herself as employable seemed to be invested in her institutional cultural capital. She later expressed awareness of, and desire to align with, local interaction norms and Discourses, as well as advising New Zealanders to do the same for newcomers, alluding to the two-way process of resettlement – and employable identity development. A temporary boost to her sense of self as employable (in the form of employment) did not prevent her eventual conclusion that her institutional capital was worthless in the New Zealand labour market, as she observed the importance of learning, enacting, and, crucially, interactively negotiating locally-valuable ways of performing an employable identity and utilising her capital *with* (potential) employers and colleagues. Over this data collection period, Arwa gradually developed her employable identity and encountered challenges to it, and opportunities to successfully co-construct it, in both her storyworlds and in interaction with me.

Through an exploration of Arwa's identity work in narrative over 20 months, the longitudinal nature of employable identities becomes clear. While no two newcomers' experiences will be the same, the struggles Arwa has encountered with her sense of self as agentive and employable, the actualisation of her social and cultural capital, and her attempts to negotiate locally-valuable identities are by no means unique. The 'rules of the game' above and beyond any 'skills and attributes' that can be taught in a university curriculum, are certainly not immediately apparent to newcomers, nor is the co-construction necessary for enacting employable identities appropriate for the New Zealand context. In Arwa's case, her journey towards employment is not complete. Once she has finished her new studies (if she takes that path) she will re-enter the employment market and put her developing employable identity to the test as she applies for, interviews for, and secures employment.

The enactment of a locally-valuable employable identity in the search for employment can be a challenging and arduous one. The enactment of a locally-valuable employable identity *in* employment is a new challenge in itself. Interaction with employers, colleagues, and clients all require the negotiation of perhaps unfamiliar norms and expectations that may be peculiar to that particular workplace's Community of Practice (J. Holmes & Meyerhoff, 1999; Lave & Wenger, 1991). The negotiation and co-construction of a workplace-specific employable identity is the focus of the following chapter, in which I explore the workplace interactions of Nina, a carer at an aged care facility, and two residents whom she visits each morning, Charlie and Ava.

CHAPTER 9

Negotiating an employable identity in the workplace

Introduction

The path to suitable, permanent employment can be a long and arduous one for former refugees, as evidenced in the narratives of Kelly, Isaac, Omar, and Arwa. We have seen the ways in which these participants encounter and navigate the social structures of unhelpful Discourses, subtle and overt discrimination, and difficulty translating and actualising cultural and social capital. All of these affect not only access to (and success in) appropriate opportunities but also former refugees' sense of selves as agentive and employable. After having secured employment, these challenges do not necessarily disappear. The performance and negotiation of an employable identity in the workplace is likely to come up against these same challenges, albeit in different and perhaps less restrictive ways.

In this chapter I explore the authentic workplace interactions of Nina with two residents, Ava and Charlie, in her role as a carer at Pinewood eldercare facility. The collection of this data, which was described in detail in Chapter 3, involved Nina wearing an unobtrusive recording device on her person when she was in Ava's and Charlie's rooms of residence, recording her interactions with them as she brought them coffee or dressed them in the morning. Nina, unlike this study's other four participants, has not undertaken tertiary education or professional training with a view to use that institutional capital to access commensurate employment. As discussed earlier (Chapter 4), while working as a cleaner she took a Salvation Army rest home carer course and soon thereafter (by virtue of social capital gained through the course) was offered a trial period as a carer at Pinewood which consequently became a full time, permanent position. Thus, I do not aim to contrast the job-seeking experiences of Nina with those of Arwa, Omar, Isaac, or Kelly. Her experiences as a former refugee employee, however, offer rich insight into the ongoing journey towards belonging that does not end with an offer of employment.

To briefly illustrate Nina's identity work in the workplace, I begin with a short excerpt in which her apparent attempt at creating solidarity through a narrative is instead used to discursively position her as vulnerable and ill-informed, albeit seemingly benevolently. As she works, Nina navigates various other-positioning and dynamic power relations, all the while maintaining a professional, employable identity. This excerpt follows on from Charlie describing his treatment for back pain, which Nina followed with a story about her own issues with back pain. Charlie had inquired about her treatment, and Nina indicated that financial constraints had prevented her from following up on this:

Excerpt 9.1 17 October 2017; 5.03–5.24

```
1. Charlie:   [reproachful] but you should've been able to get a subsidy
              at least
2.            (1) you should've been able to
3. Nina:      yes I no follow the + things and
4. Charlie:   [incredulous] you got f- + you how many children have you got?
5.            four children?
6. Nina:      [quietly] yeah [laughs]
7. Charlie:   yeah yeah but what I'm saying is that you need to get help
8. Nina:      yes + [short laugh] + we do
```

Based on Nina's consistent use of *no* as a general marker of utterance negation, and the prosody of the sentence, I believe that on line 3 this word should be read as *no* (for *I (did) not*) rather than *know* (for *yes I know*).

Charlie seems to be taking a position of 'looking out' for Nina by drawing her attention to financial assistance she may have been able to receive for therapy. However, his somewhat admonishing tone has the discursive effect of positioning Nina as irresponsible in her failure to access such assistance (lines 1–2). Nina's response indicates that she is aware of such avenues towards assistance but that she chose not to follow them (line 3). However, Charlie retakes the floor and on lines 4–5 discursively links her (interactively assigned) irresponsibility to her role as mother of four children, seemingly indexing Discourses of (good) Motherhood (that is, a dominant Discourse of a 'selfless' mother who "places her caring role before everything else in her life," often constructed in competition or opposition to a 'working mother' (Raddon, 2002, p. 394)). Furthermore, his focus on the *number* of children Nina has underscores his position that the family needs assistance (explicitly stated on line 7). Nina's short responses to these comments cedes the point without further engaging with it (lines 6 and 8), and her laugher here may be serving to mitigate the potentially face-threatening position of having her parenting skills and financial status questioned in the workplace (Billig, 2005; Warner-Garcia, 2014). At this point Nina ended the recording.

The role of the recorder, and me as a (delayed) overhearer (Bell, 1984), should be noted as well. Charlie's other-positioning of Nina may impact upon the way that she wishes to perform her identity with me. Nina's frequent use of narratives that mirror the resident's narratives (discussed in greater detail later in this chapter) suggests that it contributes to the relational work she engages in as part of her professional, workplace identity (cf. Hay's (2008) research on appropriate humour responses, of which contributing further humour and echoing responses are two).

Charlie is taking up an ostensibly benevolent discursive position here, by seemingly attempting to negotiate the pursuit of financial aid for Nina and her family. However, his endeavour can also be seen to draw upon refugee-related Discourses indexing vulnerability and naivety, perhaps infringing upon aspects of Nina's employable identity enactment associated with competence and occupational knowledgeability. Nina's short responses and mitigating laughter display a discursive orientation away from the othering through disengagement, without challenging her employable identity work evident in the courteous and professional navigation of this positioning.

In the excerpts that follow we see Nina's agentive use of her own capital in the form of narratives that mirror the residents' narratives, with the discursive effect of creating solidarity and fostering warm and friendly relationships in her role as carer, while at the same time negotiating her professional and employable identity. She skilfully navigates Discourses of Refugeehood and other-positioning from her interlocutors, and implicitly and explicitly makes claims to her belonging in the Pinewood community, as well as the imagined community of New Zealand (B. Anderson, 1991). These discursive claims are not always successful, and it appears that Nina prioritises orientation to her employable identity over emphasising her identity claims of belonging.

Eldercare interactions

Interactions in eldercare facility contexts have been explored from different perspectives. These include psychology and social psychology (e.g. Caporael, 1981; Coupland et al., 1988; Kemper, 1994; O'Conner & St. Pierre, 2004), medicine (e.g. Balsis & Carpenter, 2006; Cunningham & Williams, 2007; Grimme, Buchanan, & Afflerbach, 2015; Herman & Williams, 2009), and sociolinguistics and discourse (e.g. Backhaus, 2009; Corwin, 2017; Grainger, 1993; Makoni & Grainger, 2002; Sass, 2000). The focus of these studies tends to be exploration of what has been called 'elderspeak,' an infantilising and condescending way of speaking to the elderly. Elderspeak has variously been claimed to include such elements as slow speaking speed, careful articulation, terms of endearment, frequent praise, and regular interruptions (of residents by carers), repetition, and high frequency of modal verbs and tag questions, among others (Backhaus, 2009; Grainger, 1993; Makoni & Grainger, 2002; Marsden & Holmes, 2014).

Marsden and Holmes (2014) took a different approach to exploring eldercare interactions. Drawing on an Interactional Sociolinguistic framework and the extensive back catalogue of research of the Language in the Workplace project (e.g. J. Holmes et al., 2011; J. Holmes & Stubbe, 2003; see also Chapter 3), they took an interactive view to analysing carer-resident interactions. Analysis from this perspective accounts for both transactional and relational aspects of discourse, as well as the immediate and wider social context in which a given interaction takes place. Thus, the carer-resident interactions can be seen as co-constructed negotiations of social meaning (Marsden & Holmes, 2014, p. 20). The study reveals "rich and complex" interpersonal discourse between residents and carers (2014, p. 17), characterised by warm, friendly relationships. This is evidenced in reciprocal use of terms of endearment (2014, p. 22), carers' familiarity with residents' family lives and preferences, and the two-sided nature of their interactions (2014, p. 27). Thus, Marsden and Holmes (2014, p. 25) conclude that while past research indicates that power is the most salient aspect of carer-resident interactions, their findings suggest that solidarity may in fact be more important.

Nina in the workplace

It is this same interactive approach to resident-carer interactions that I take here with Nina's data. And, like Marsden and Holmes (2014), my analysis finds Nina's workplace interactions to be based in warm, friendly relationships characterised more by solidarity than power. However, power does factor into the data, and as will be shown below, is often evident in fleeting and dynamic self- and other-positioning (Bamberg, 2011a; Bucholtz & Hall, 2005; De Fina, 2003). Below I explore the co-construction of meaning and identity positions in Nina's interactions with Ava and Charlie.

Nina, in ethnographic data collection alongside these workplace interactions, indicated that she has good interpersonal relationships with both Charlie and Ava. This is additionally supported by the evident depth and breadth of their knowledge of each other's families and home lives in the workplace data itself, only parts of which I have the scope to include here. Nina can be seen to navigate intersectional identity positions of carer, former refugee, non-native English speaker, outsider/newcomer, and mother, undoubtedly among others. Nina employs and displays considerable cultural capital in the navigation of different aspects of her identity, agentively taking up, accepting, and resisting identity positions, moment-by-moment in interaction. She manages her relationships with the residents while fulfilling the requirements of her job, engaging in both transactional and relational talk as she performs a professional, employable, and contextually-appropriate identity.

Mirrored narratives

Issues of power and control, as Marsden and Holmes (2014) note, have been the focus of several studies of eldercare interactions, drawing upon Discourses of Aging as related to dependency or deficiency (Discourses that construct the elderly as passive, dependent, and vulnerable (Ng & McCreanor, 1999; Weicht, 2013)). In the present data the potential for drawing upon these Discourses appears to intersect with Discourses of Refugeehood which themselves index vulnerability and deficiency (cf. Greenbank, 2014; Marlowe, 2010; O'Higgins, 2012; Pupavac, 2008). Within the structure signified by these Discourses, all parties in the present chapter's interactions are able to agentively take up higher or lower status positions relative to the other, depending upon the Discourses they choose to draw upon, and the identity positions they are attempting to perform.

Nina's skilful relational work is demonstrated in the way she normalises and validates Ava's and Charlie's complaints by providing a narrative of her own which mirrors their concern. Nina's lived experience functions as cultural capital, allowing her to build solidarity between herself and the residents, and frame the interactions as conversations between equals (and not, for example, as patient-attendant relationships). In this excerpt, Nina and Charlie have been talking about that day's weather. Nina then ask Charlie about the weather report for the following day, to which he replies that he could not remember:

Excerpt 9.2 27 September 2017; 1.07–1.41

```
1.  Charlie:  I'm getting very old you see (1) I can't remember anything you see
2.  Nina:     oh no
3.  Charlie:  and ah
4.  Nina:     the another day + I was with three ladies in + m- + in some +
5.            in my another job? and someone asked me ah +
6.            what is the name of these ladies (1) and I for- a second
7.            I forget //everything\
8.  Charlie:  /[laughs]\\
9.  Nina:     and I say ah::: you can ask [laughing] because [laughs] +
10.           to pretend that but was for + ten minutes I forget and I say
11.           oh my god something wrong with me
```

Charlie links this memory lapse to his age (line 1), to which Nina expresses sympathy (line 2) and then goes on to offer a comparable situation (lines 4–7, 9–11). Nina-as-narrator assigns a low-agency position to Nina-as-protagonist, which, following Charlie's reference to his own bad memory, may serve to create solidarity with him, and normalise memory loss as not just something which older people experience. The normalisation is further evidenced by both Nina's and Charlie's laughter (lines 8–9) which co-constructs this as a light and humorous story, despite Nina's reconstructed internal dialogue that *oh my god something is wrong with me* (line 11).

In the following excerpt, Nina uses a similar technique to dynamically reorient from a position of alignment with Ava's (storyworld) daughter to one of alignment with Ava herself. In doing so she appears to successfully create solidarity with Ava and give her the discursive space to elaborate upon her complaint and take up an empowered discursive position:

Excerpt 9.3 6 November 2017; 5.44–6.32

1.	Ava:	I had my hair cut on Friday + I think she cut it too short (1)
2.		it's all sort of sticking up (1) I said to Janine I think it's too short (1)
3.		she said to me (1) no I don't think so Mum but I'm:: + got my doubts
4.	Nina:	the good thing about hair it's growing again [*laughs*]
5.	Ava:	that's what she said
6.	Nina:	yeah (1) but I don't like when I I this is why I don't like go to the: +
7.		do my hair because I say a little bit and when they go +
8.		[1]//more\[1] than what I asked for? [2]//(1)\[2] that's sad
9.	Ava:	[1]/more\\[1] [2]/yeah well she\\[2] I I I came out + the next morning I quite
10.		cause it was all sticking up like a golliwog + [*laughs*] but it will grow again
11.		//+ so\ next time I have it cut I'm gonna say to her p- +
12.		please don't cut the top too short
13.	Nina:	/[*sniffs*] yeah\\ (3) yes good

Ava's narrative about her unsatisfactory hair cut (lines 1–3) includes a tentative evaluation (*she cut it too short*) backed up with evidence (*it's all sort of sticking up*). In her storyworld she expresses her dissatisfaction to her daughter Janine, who disagrees. Ava-as-narrator sticks to her original evaluation, evidenced in the doubtful tone of *I'm::* and the explicit expression thereof: *got my doubts* (line 3). Nina does not initially align herself with Ava, providing instead the long-term outcome; that Ava's hair will grow out in any case (line 4). This may be an attempt at humour and could be taken as either sympathy towards or dismissal of Ava's complaint. While it is unclear which one Ava infers, she aligns Nina's discursive position with that of her storyworld daughter on line 5 and does not elaborate further.

Following Ava's lack of uptake of any humour, after minimal feedback and a one-second pause, Nina then reorients her self-positioning to align herself with Ava, providing her own small story (Bamberg, 2004c) about hairdressers cutting off more hair than requested (lines 6–8), which mirrors Ava's. Small stories, in contrast to the 'big' narratives of, for example, flight, are the ones told in ordinary interactions and everyday life (Bamberg, 2004b, p. 223), which may only comprise an utterance or two. Small stories allow glimpses of narrators' navigation of various versions of self in a given context, and the "fleeting moments of narrative orientation to the world [which might otherwise] easily be missed out on" (Bamberg & Georgakopoulou, 2008, p. 5). Here, Nina's fleeting evaluation of this occurrence – *that's sad* (line 8) – has the discursive effect of underscoring her solidarity with Ava's position. This realignment validates Ava's complaint, as she then returns to her grievance and makes a joke about her own appearance (lines 9–10). She comes to a seemingly satisfactory resolution, setting up an agentive position for her future self wherein she assertively instructs her storyworld future hairdresser to follow her wishes (as evidenced in her emphatic tone).

Projected future events in narrative are a kind of small story which may act as a rehearsal for future action (Georgakopoulou, 2006b). That is, narrated past events "[inform] and [shape] the future in ways that foreground the intertextual links of stories making them part of an interactional trajectory" (Georgakopoulou, 2006b, p. 126). Thus, Ava's projected action allows her to recover from her past low-agency, victim-like position (as the recipient of an undesirable haircut), and narratively rehearse for a higher-agency, assertive position of making her requirements clear. This future satisfactory resolution is co-constructed with Nina whose interactive reorientation seems to provide discursive space for it to happen. This data displays Nina's awareness and skilful negotiation of a contextually-appropriate employable identity which includes the co-construction of empowered positions for eldercare residents.

Empowering interactions

Further evidence of Nina's management of her workplace interactions can be seen in parallel interactions with Charlie and Ava, recorded on the same day, both following a residents' meeting in which a member of the Green Party (a left-wing political party with a predominant focus on environmental values, in parliamentary opposition at the time of the recording) had come to discuss policy before the upcoming national election. Discussing the very same event with both of them, Nina appears to approach each interaction with subtle differences. When speaking to Ava, Nina gives almost entirely minimal, positive feedback (after an initial query to open the topic). She contributes to the co-construction of an empowered, politically-engaged identity for Ava:

Excerpt 9.4 13 September 2017; 0.06–1.00

```
1.  Nina:  how was the meeting today + good?
2.  Ava:   well more people there than + what I thought would be there
3.  Nina:  oh
4.  Ava:   I think it was quite successful
5.  Nina:  oh it's //nice\
6.  Ava:   /so\\ he answered a lot of questions + ah w- //[unclear]\
7.  Nina:  /what you::\\ + questions about
8.  Ava:   oh I asked him about mental health + which is quite dear to
           my heart
```

```
9.  Nina:  oh it's //good\
10. Ava:   /ah\ my daughter being a psychiatrist + but I think he got +
11.        psychologist and psychiatrist mixed up
12. Nina:  oh
13. Ava:   and he didn't answer me particularly what I wanted to know +
14.        but that's life
15. Nina:  oh yeah
16. Ava:   and yeah there were a lot of + about very ah (2)
17.        good climate warming and question like that came
18.        which are also very important
19. Nina:  mm yeah
20. Ava:   yeah water tax things like that
21. Nina:  it's good mm
22. Ava:   yeah
23. Nina:  hopefully (1) there's something good coming from them
24. Ava:   I hope so=
25. Nina:  =from these new elections
```

Throughout her interaction with Ava, Nina provides verbal feedback that is engaged enough to acknowledge and encourage what Ava is saying without taking a position herself, one way or the other. In doing so, she allows space for Ava to take up a politically-engaged and knowledgeable position. In Ava's narrative storyworld, she presents the visiting politician with an issue *very dear to [her] heart* (line 8) and positions herself as more well-informed than him vis-à-vis the difference between psychiatry and psychology (lines 10–11). She continues this politically-engaged self-positioning by taking an evaluative stance on climate change-related questions – that they are *good* (line 17) and *very important* (line 18).

Nina's positive, minimal feedback throughout (lines 5, 9, 12, 15, 19, 21) supports Ava's self-positioning, and thus they co-construct Ava's political position. The only comment that Nina herself offers on the elections, that she hopes *there's something good coming from them* (line 23), is general enough that it seems unlikely that anyone could find fault with her sentiment. Certainly, an interlocutor could infer this statement as alignment with any preceding comments. Thus, Nina's minimal and somewhat ambiguous feedback allows Ava to take the lead in this interaction, lending Ava an empowered and uncontested position from which to discuss politics. Engaging in discursive solidarity with and empowerment for Ava, Nina seems to adhere to workplace norms in which residents having the discursive space to express themselves and their acumen takes precedence over a sincerely equal exchange of ideas. Thus, this excerpt provides evidence of Nina's orientation towards her employable identity as a carer, wherein expressing strong political positions one way or another may be inappropriate.

While Ava's recounting of the meeting comprised a brief summary of points salient to her, along with some evaluative commentary, Charlie's recounting included a great deal more general political background and went on for a considerably longer period of time. In this interaction, it is Charlie and not Nina who brings up the topic of the meeting. It is not clear whether Nina talked to Charlie or Ava first about the meeting, so perhaps Charlie is introducing new information to Nina. However, she remarks later in the interaction that the visiting politician *looked very young*, so evidently, she was aware of his presence before Charlie told her (as a staff member it is highly likely she would have been told about the politician's visit in a staff meeting anyway). Charlie's discursive position of informing Nina about the meeting sets the scene for an interaction in which he positions himself as a political expert, and Nina as a novice.

Excerpt 9.5 13 September 2017; 0.06–0.46

1.	Charlie:	I've been + ah: I went to a + meeting (1) ah: in the rec room
2.		(1) which was: with ah + a guy from the Green? party
3.	Nina:	oh what he offer [*laughs*]
4.	Charlie:	he well he offered all sorts a + [*carefully*] he wants
5.		he wants people to vote for the Green party + um: +
6.		because they're very (1) worried (2) ah: + the environment +
7.	Nina:	//oh\
8.	Charlie:	/an::d\\ about the state of the rivers in New Zealand and
9.		the water in New Zealand (1) and basically they're they're very keen
10.		(1) to see (1) Labour + win[1]
11.	Nina:	[*tut*] oh it's good

Despite Nina's probable awareness of the politician's visit, she nonetheless discursively indicates that this is new information, opening with utterance-initial *oh* (line 3), a 'change-of-state' discourse marker which can indicate an adjustment in the speaker's knowledge (Bolden, 2006; Schiffrin, 1987). She invites Charlie to continue his story by asking what the politician had to *offer* (line 3), framing the storyworld politician as bargaining for votes. This indexes a familiarity with Discourses of Politics (as a morally ambiguous game) and appears to be intended as humour based on her following laughter. It may also be an attempt to both create solidarity with Charlie and make a claim to belonging, drawing on what Tranekjær (2017; drawing on Holmes & Marra, 2002) calls 'common sense laughables;' that is, emphasising shared knowledge or drawing on local repertoires to highlight or create solidarity. This solidarity and identity claim is not taken up by Charlie, though he does initially mirror her usage of *offer*, before restarting, in a carefully pronounced style and at a measured pace, stating that the visitor *wants people to vote for the Green party* (lines 4–5).

1. The Green Party would be very unlikely to win an election alone, but under New Zealand's Mixed-member proportional (MMP) electoral system, the Party could (and did) form a coalition with major political party Labour.

While telling someone that what a visiting Green party candidate wants is for people to vote for the Green party could be taken to be an obvious and condescending explanation (as well as rejecting Nina's orientation to political insight), Nina gives no discursive indication that she takes it as such. Charlie's detailed and carefully articulated narrative (which continued in this fashion for some time after this excerpt), along with Nina's receptive feedback throughout, has the discursive effect of co-constructing an expert-novice dichotomy between Charlie and Nina within the interaction. Furthermore, Charlie's marked slow and careful speech, likely intended to ensure Nina's comprehension, has the discursive effect of emphasising her status as a non-native speaker of English, thus serving to position her as something of an outsider, in addition to a novice.

A little later in their conversation, Nina makes use of her embodied cultural capital as a long-time member of the Pinewood community to contribute to the political discussion, which Charlie briefly acknowledges before returning to his self-positioning as teacher, and other-positioning of Nina as student. Charlie has just questioned the logic of the Green party candidate coming to Pinewood, as he doubted that anyone living there would be likely to vote for that party:

Excerpt 9.6 13 September 20147; 2.34–3.37

```
1.  Charlie: they'd all be Labour or National go- //all traditional\
2.  Nina:    /mm last year\\ las- last time when was the votings was everyo-
3.           most of here they voting for Nationals
4.  Charlie: yeah
5.  Nina:    for John Key[2] (1) I remember
6.  Charlie: yeah yeah yeah
7.  Nina:    because by the time you remember Fran Douglas? + she was alive
8.  Charlie: who?
9.  Nina:    Fran Douglas (1) number 17 she was alive and she was say that
10.          she want to vote for (1) John Key + she always say everyone
             will be
11.          w- vote for John Key
12. Charlie: they probably were + um + and th- and I and I did too + um (1)
13.          now that he's not there + ah:: and now that I do- I don't know
14.          it's very hard (1) to decide what to do + because there's a
             new + young
15.          + you see Labour party Labour + very young woman
16.          Jacinda Ardern she's very good
17. Nina:    oh yes //I see\
18. Charlie: /she's very\\ good um + and she + brought the Labour party
19.          up to equal with National
20. Nina:    that's good
```

2. John Key was leader of the centre-right, incumbent National party and Prime Minister of New Zealand until December 2016, stepping down nine months before the 2017 election.

Backing up Charlie's suggestion that Pinewood residents would be unlikely to vote for the Green party, Nina provides some evidence for his claim, firstly attributing this to her memory of most residents voting for the National party (lines 2, 3, 5), and then increasing the claim's discursive validity by attributing it to a since-deceased resident who Nina had known (Bangerter et al., 2011; Georgakopoulou, 1995; Matoesian, 2000). In doing so she makes clear her engagement with the conversation and displays her cultural capital (in the form of useful knowledge about the Pinewood community). She makes a discursive claim to an identity of belonging, perhaps challenging Charlie's other-positioning of her as a student to his teacher by asserting her relevant knowledge (cf. van de Mieroop & Schnurr, 2017a, p. 446). Charlie acknowledges the (probable) veracity of her claim, signalling his own voting history as evidence (line 12). He then returns to his self-positioning as expert on matters political, telling Nina about the Labour party's new leader (lines 13–16, 18–19).

The previous month, low-polling (opposition) Labour leader Andrew Little had resigned with little warning, and his deputy, Jacinda Ardern had become party leader seven weeks out from a national election. The timing and unexpected nature of the change in leadership, along with Ardern's youth and sudden, widespread popularity ('Jacindamania,' (Shuttleworth, 2017)), meant that Ardern-related news occupied an enormous amount of media time and space for the remainder of the lead up to the election. Even if Nina were not an avid news-watcher, which she told me she is, it is unlikely that she would be unaware of who Jacinda Ardern was, or her significance to contemporary New Zealand politics. Nonetheless, Nina responds once more with *oh* and mirrors Charlie's indicative *you see* (line 15) with *yes I see* (line 17), validating his self-positioning as expert and positioning herself as a novice for whom what he is saying is new information (Bolden, 2006; Schiffrin, 1987). She continues to contribute to their construction of his teacher role by providing positive, minimal feedback here and throughout the remainder of their discussion of politics. After attempting to orient towards an identity of belonging to both Pinewood and New Zealand, Nina appears to acquiesce to Charlie's othering as a (New Zealand) political novice.

Throughout these parallel interactions with Ava and Charlie, Nina clearly orients to the carer-resident relationship over one of conversational equals. Despite little of the information that either of the residents offer being new to Nina, she engages in a discursive performance of information-recipient to her interlocutors as information-providers. Thus, she orients to and fulfils the requirements of a professional, employable identity in a manner contextually-appropriate for the eldercare setting.

Belonging and othering

As mentioned earlier, Nina navigates myriad identity positions in the workplace. Particularly salient in the data are the ways in which she negotiates subtle and explicit othering (cf. Hatoss, 2012; Jaworski & Coupland, 2005) in her interactions with both Ava and Charlie. Seemingly drawing on Discourses and ideologies of Refugeehood, (non)native-speaker proficiency, and outsider/newcomers, Ava and Charlie discursively position Nina as an Other, to greater and lesser degrees. Nina variously resists and brushes off this other positioning while maintaining her employable, workplace identity. She draws upon some of these same Discourses and ideologies herself when making claims for her own belonging in discursively sophisticated ways, co-constructing a binary of New Zealander vs. Other, as shown below.

In the excerpt below, Ava questions Nina's ability either to vote at Pinewood itself (hospitals and rest homes are visited by teams that issue votes to patients and residents in the 12 days leading up to national elections (Electoral Commission New Zealand, 2017)) or perhaps to vote in New Zealand. Nina responds to the potential challenge to her status with a claim for her own belonging.

Excerpt 9.7 13 September 2017; 1.01–1.23

1.	Nina:	what day is the elections?
2.	Ava:	we vote here but y- next + Fri- ah Saturday the 23rd
3.	Nina:	oh=
4.	Ava:	=are you you w- you'd probably I don't know whether
5.		you'd be able to vote here probably not
6.	Nina:	yeah + ah no here in the rest home no
7.	Ava:	no
8.	Nina:	but I vote last year in Drummond school
9.		last year last elections //[*laughs*]\
10.	Ava:	/[*laughs*]\\ that seems a long time ago

While it is unclear whether Ava is asking Nina if she is able to vote at Pinewood, or if she is eligible to vote in New Zealand (lines 4–5), it appears from Nina's response that she initially infers the latter, and then quickly thereafter the former (line 6), 'correcting' Ava with *yeah* then indicating a realisation with *ah*, and following this with *no* to confirm agreement that she would not be able to vote at Pinewood. However, she then goes on to make clear her eligibility to vote in New Zealand, noting that she voted in the last national election (which was three years earlier). This is introduced with *but* which serves to mark a cancellation or contrast with the possibility of ineligibility to vote at the eldercare facility (Norrick, 2001). Nina positions herself within the imagined community of New Zealanders (B. Anderson, 1991), making an identity claim through her small story of past voting (Bamberg, 2004c; Bamberg & Georgakopoulou, 2008). Her fleeting orientation towards her eligibility to vote seems to indicate its importance to her sense of belonging. Further, this is achieved skilfully within an easy-flowing conversation, maintaining the friendly atmosphere as might be expected of a carer in this context.

Nina appears to use her status as a voter to make a discursive claim of belonging with Charlie as well, which was rather less successful. Charlie's comment about being impressed, below, refers to the same politician who had been visiting Pinewood that day:

Excerpt 9.8 13 September 2017; 4.49–5.17

```
1.  Charlie:  I was very impressed yeah very //impressed\
2.  Nina:     /it's funny\\ in my all my life in my country I never vote +
3.            and when I coming here I vote + I vote the last elections (1)
4.            and + maybe I will vote these ones too
5.  Charlie:  maybe you won't BOTE anything
6.  Nina:     [laughs] VOTE
7.  Charlie:  maybe you won't BOTE anything
8.  Nina:     [laughs] ok you wanna cup //of coffee\
9.  Charlie:  /maybe you'll\\ v::ote everything
10. Nina:     [laughs] you wanna cup of coffee
11. Charlie:  yes please
12. Nina:     ok
```

Nina makes a tentative claim to belonging in her small story (Bamberg, 2004c), which although small, contains plenty of information and identity work: the unusualness of what she is to say (*it's funny*), an orientation towards Colombia as *[her] country* juxtaposed with her remark that she never voted there, a reference to her status as a newcomer, a claim to belonging through having voted in New Zealand, and perhaps an indication of her intention to continue her engagement with her new society by voting again in the future (lines 2–4). She seems to be straddling her Colombian and New Zealand identities, referring to Colombia with possessive *my*, but displaying her greater engagement with New Zealand via civic participation.

However, the content of what Nina is saying is overlooked by Charlie in favour of a metalinguistic comment. Nina, not unusually for someone whose mother tongue is Spanish (Whitley, 1986), pronounces *vote* beginning with something closer to bilabial plosive /b/ than labiodental fricative /v/, which accounts for Charlie's rather emphatic imitation of her pronunciation. Nina's reaction does not initially indicate any offense or threat to her face, as her laughter sounds genuine, and she complies with the implied requirement of 'corrected' pronunciation. Charlie repeats his imitation word-for-word (line 7) and Nina, laughing again, opts to move on to the transactional task of serving coffee (line 8), orienting away from her earlier identity claim and towards her institutional identity. Despite Nina's earlier uptake of the 'correction,' Charlie nevertheless interrupts her offer of coffee to provide his own explicit recast, drawing out the /v/ in a way which emphasises the exact point of 'error.' Nina laughs again and repeats her orientation towards her professional identity, and away from the metalinguistic exchange. Once this offer is finally taken up by Charlie, Nina abruptly ended the recording.

Although Nina complies with Charlie's 'correction,' it is worth noting that the two had been talking for over five minutes at this point, and it was directly after this challenge to her linguistic capital that Nina chose to move on to the transactional task of offering coffee, and then end the recording. In this firm switch away from relational matters and towards transactional, and the abrupt ending of the conversation, Nina arguably orients towards her professional, carer identity at the same time as orienting away from the linguistically-deficient position that Charlie is attempting to assign her. She appears to be resisting the (probably unintentional) othering Discourses indexed by Charlie by dynamically realigning with transactional elements of her employable identity.

Nina similarly makes an explicit and unprompted claim to belonging within the imagined (and institutionalised) community of New Zealanders (B. Anderson, 1991) in an interaction with Ava, in which their individual orientations toward citizenship as valuable cultural capital can be seen (Bauder, 2008). Those who arrive in New Zealand as UNHCR refugees are granted permanent residence upon arrival, and thus their status in New Zealand is 'secure' without citizenship (Immigration New Zealand, 2018a). It is likely that Nina knows this; however, I could not speak to whether Ava does. Citizenship is thus in some ways largely symbolic in its differences from Permanent Residence, in terms of the rights and access to services it affords (Controller and Auditor General, 2018). Nonetheless, its value as a signifier of belonging seems evident in both Nina's and Ava's enthusiasm. While the excerpts to follow are, at a purely interactive level, concerned with nationality and citizenship, they are linked to Nina's employable identity at a Discursive level. That is, Nina's ongoing negotiation of a legitimate employable identity is contingent upon her *belonging*, which itself may be legitimated by being state-sanctioned:

Excerpt 9.9 6 November 2017; 4.04–4.17

```
1. Nina:  AH you know what I::: received the letter for:: the immigration
2. Ava:   [very enthusiastic] GOOD //good\ that's excellent news
3. Nina:  /yes I will\\ (1) I will have my citizenship
4. Ava:   oh that's wonderful
```

The established – and good – relationship between these two is evidenced in Nina's sudden and loud exclamation (line 1), which discursively implies that Nina has suddenly remembered something which she believes will be of interest to Ava. The implication is that their relationship is good enough that Nina can safely assume Ava's investment in her imminent status as a citizen. Ava's enthusiastic response backs this up, particularly emphasised by the fact that Nina had not, at this point, said what news the letter included, but Ava was able to correctly infer its content regardless. Nina's enthusiasm in telling Ava, and Ava's even more enthusiastic response reveal their positive positions on citizenship.

Nina went on to say that she would need to wait until the day of the ceremony to become a citizen. Ava remarked that sometimes those receiving citizenship wear the national dress of their country of origin at the ceremony, and then asked Nina if she intended to do so:

Excerpt 9.10 6 November 2017; 4.26–4.38

```
1. Ava:  you- not gonna wear national dress are you? or
2. Nina: no no + some people wear a- some people wear costumes
3.       from their own country but I not see the point
4. Ava:  ah no no
5. Nina: if I gonna receive //the\
6. Ava:  [singsong] /you're\ gonna be a New Zealander now [laughs]
```

Ava phrases her question about national dress in the negative, which may act to index an ideological argument that Nina should not wear Colombian national dress when receiving New Zealand citizenship. At any rate, this negative phrasing suggests a confidence in their relationship (that this will not cause offense), as well as a certain level of surety that the answer to this question will be no (line 1). She is correct in her assumption, as Nina explains that while some people do wear the national dress of their countries of origin, she *[does not] see the point* as she will be receiving something from New Zealand, not from Colombia (as she goes on to further explain outside of this excerpt). Ava aligns herself with Nina's discursive position, reminding her, in a singsong tone not without a hint of infantilization, that she *will* be a New Zealander upon gaining citizenship (line 6).

Interestingly, Ava's slightly infantilising tone (line 6) and negative tag question (line 1) have, as noted above, been identified as characteristic of elderspeak in the literature (e.g. Caporael, 1981; Herman & Williams, 2009; Makoni & Grainger, 2002). Negative tag questions are "considered dependency-inducing, since they pre-empt a desired response," and assigning infant-like status "[implies] a lack of autonomy and [emphasises] powerlessness" (Marsden & Holmes, 2014, p. 19). These features of elderspeak, however, are generally attributable to those speaking *to* the elderly, so Ava's use of them is indicative of the complex power dynamics of any relationship, and perhaps also speaks to the low power status associated with Discourses of Refugeehood. That is, the intersectional nature of Nina's and Ava's identities means that interaction between them, and the discursive positions available to them at a given point, are not determined by a singular and fixed power relationship. Both have the possibility to assign themselves and their interlocutor higher or lower power discursive positions – and in turn to accept or reject that positioning – by drawing upon or avoiding Discourse(s) and ideologies associated with their various and intersecting identity 'categories' (Crenshaw, 1989; Davis, 2008; McCall, 2005; Yuval-Davis, 2006).

Continuing on the topic of what she might wear to the citizenship ceremony, Nina then appears to begin to draw upon Discourses of Gratitude. Contrasting with the established – and rejected – idea of wearing Colombian national clothing, Nina begins to state something that she is *supposed* to wear, before reframing this obligation more generically as one of pride, and opportunity:

Excerpt 9.11 6 November 2017; 4.50–5.00

1. Nina: I'm supposed to + [*sniffs*] wear (1) be + proud [*inhales*]
2. it's a + good //opportunity\
3. Ava: /oh::\\ yeah that's really wonderful news

Nina seems to index civic or national obligation on line 1, mentioning what she is *supposed* to wear. Although Nina does not state what it is she feels she is expected to wear, the utterance's positioning between her rejection of wearing national dress, earlier, and her reference to pride later on line 1 has the discursive effect of suggesting an obligation to wear something which aligns with the new New Zealander identity which is to be bestowed upon her with citizenship. The suggested expectation of pride, along with Nina's claim that to receive citizenship is *a + good opportunity* could be seen to index both Discourses of Integration or Assimilation and refugee-related Discourses of Gratitude. Ava supports her discursive position and reinforces the co-constructed stance on the value of citizenship, reiterating her assertion that this is *really wonderful news.*

The complexity of the power dynamics involved in Nina's interactions with residents is apparent in the following excerpts where she and Charlie position one another in undesirable and low-power roles. Charlie was to move to a different eldercare facility in another city to be closer to his daughter. He and Nina had been discussing his moving arrangements and the journey to the new city:

Excerpt 9.12 13 December 2017; 4.49–5.01

1. Nina: someone will be fly with you?
2. Charlie: no
3. Nina: oh you by yourself
4. Charlie: yeah well it's mm //sort of + doesn't matter\
5. Nina: /but it's a lot of people assisting there\\ and it's //only\
6. Charlie: [*indignantly*] /it doesn't\\ matter no
7. Nina: couple hours

Nina's implicit assumption that Charlie needs someone to accompany him on his flight (line 1), along with the assurance, once corrected, that there will be *a lot of people assisting* at, presumably, the airport (line 5), seems to be something of an affront to Charlie. Nina, perhaps drawing on Discourses of Aging and vulnerability, positions Charlie in a vulnerable, low agency position by suggesting his dependence upon others to take a flight. Charlie resists this positioning through his indignant tone and dismissal of her concerns (line 6). He went on to reclaim a higher agency position by describing some technical details of the aeroplane he believed he would be travelling on, and reminding Nina that *I've flown a lot before*, orienting away from Discourses of Aging.

Nina went on to tell Charlie that the only time that she had flown on an aeroplane was when she came to New Zealand. Indexing her own inexperience could be inferred as an attempt to mitigate Charlie's apparent (mild) offense at the suggestion that he requires assistance to fly. However here it appears to index Nina's former refugee status for Charlie, who suggests he wants to, in the future, hear what seems like Nina's narrative of flight:

Excerpt 9.13 13 December 2017; 5.51–6.25

1.	Charlie:	yeah you got to one day you've got to start telling me about
2.		um + have to do it by Skype
3.	Nina:	oh yeah
4.	Charlie:	do you //know\ what Skype is
5.	Nina:	/I\\ + [*indignantly*] yeah //but I\\ but I no have + Skype
6.	Charlie:	/yeah\\ (1) you no you haven't got a computer have you
7.	Nina:	um I have Skype before and not anymore I don't know
8.		but I can make one
9.	Charlie:	you can make a computer
10.	Nina:	no I can make a Skype thing
11.	Charlie:	[*laughs*]
12.	Nina:	and we can keep in contact
13.	Charlie:	yeah yeah + well what I'm- because what I'm saying is that
14.		you need to I would lov- I'd like to know (1) all the background +
15.		//you know we talked\ we've talked about it
16.	Nina:	/oh yeah\\ (1) yeah

Seemingly prompted by Nina's reference to her one and only flight to New Zealand, Charlie begins to state his desire to hear a particular story from Nina, noting that this telling will need to take place over Skype (likely due to his impending departure from Pinewood). Nina's response (line 3) gives no indication of any miscomprehension, but nonetheless Charlie queries whether Nina knows *what Skype is* (line 4). Given the ubiquity of Skype as a communication tool worldwide, Nina's seemingly indignant response on line 5 is unsurprising (the fact that she *can* be indignant in this interaction and not simply acquiesce speaks to the comfort of her relationship with Charlie). By questioning her familiarity with such a widely-used and fifteen-year-old technology, Charlie perhaps draws on Discourses of Refugeehood, positioning Nina as technologically incompetent and in need of assistance. Nina's indignant tone when she responds that she is familiar with Skype suggests a rejection of this other-positioning. Charlie goes on to unintentionally or wilfully (for comedic effect) misinterpret Nina's claim that she will create a new Skype account (lines 7–8) to mean that she intends to make a new computer (line 9). His laughter on line 11 suggests that his 'paraphrase' of her claim was meant in jest, but Nina's clarifying response does not acknowledge or ratify the attempt at humour (line 10), thus rejecting Charlie's implicit other-positioning of her as technologically backward. However, she orients towards their existent friendly relationship with her confirmation that they will be able to stay in contact with one another (line 12). Charlie in line 14 clarifies that the story he wants from Nina is her *background* which, in the interactional context of following her revelation that her UNHCR-organised flight from Ecuador to New Zealand for resettlement was the only time in her life that she's flown, suggests he is interested in the story of her refugee experience.

This indexicality of Nina's (former) refugee status is accentuated by Charlie's discursive hedging and downgrading of his request (lines 13–15). This begins with a false start and then metacommentary on what is to come (*what I'm saying is*, line 13). Then in quick succession he reduces the illocutionary force (Austin, 1975) of his request in three steps, from stating that Nina *needs* (to tell him), to that he would *lov(e)* to know, to finally that he would *like* to know her story (line 14). He appears to engage in further hedging by indexing their existent relationship and previous discussion of the topic (line 15), introduced with *you know* to appeal to their shared understanding (Erman, 2001, p. 1348). All of this hedging has the effect of suggesting caution on Charlie's part when broaching the topic of Nina's *background*. This lends support to the idea that he is indexing Discourse of Refugeehood within which former refugees are presumed to have, importantly, traumatic or at the very least sensitive narratives of flight and arrival in their societies of resettlement. Nina's response is accommodating to Charlie's request, without indicating any particular enthusiasm to comply with the implied request (cf. Kelly's, Omar's, and Arwa's hesitance and redirection in the telling of their stories of flight, Chapters 5 and 8). At this point Charlie changed the conversation's focus to the eldercare facility that he would soon be moving to, and thus any further examination of Nina's self-positioning regarding this request is not possible.

Charlie and Nina's evidently undesirable positioning of one another in these two excerpts seems to indicate that they are indexing the vulnerability or dependence associated with Discourses of Refugeehood and Aging, respectively. This illustrates the complex intersectional nature of identity, as well as Nina's skilful and dynamic management of her employable identity alongside other identities discursively made salient by both herself and others.

Discussion

The negotiation of an employable identity in the workplace, as Nina's data has shown, involves complex and dynamic negotiation. Her skilful relational work and pragmatic dexterity allows her to forge genuine interpersonal relationships in the workplace (within the constraints of her role as carer and the employable identity work it entails), while attending to the transactional requirements of her role. Any issues arising from her status as a second language speaker seem to be easily overcome by her sophisticated and contextually-appropriate interpersonal skills. As a former refugee, non-native speaker of English and relative newcomer to New Zealand, Nina encounters other-positioning in her interaction with residents, which she appears to either resist or deflect, all the while maintaining an orientation to her professional, employable identity. Sometimes in response to this other-positioning, and sometimes unprompted, Nina can be seen to make discursive claims to her belonging, as she negotiates various and changing identity roles in the workplace.

Despite minor issues with grammatical proficiency in English, Nina displays considerable pragmatic skills – highly valuable cultural capital in carer roles (see Marsden & Holmes, 2014). Through the telling of her own narratives which reflect the residents' stories, Nina fosters friendly relationships that project an interactional equality between them, despite the contextually-appropriate discursive positions available for Nina to take up being restricted by her role as carer. These mirrored narratives may be intended to normalise and validate the residents' concerns, countering any potentially indexed Discourses of Aging that might suggest that their issues are solely worries for the elderly. It is worth noting Harwood's (2008, p. 3) observation that "anti-ageist [Discourses] can also themselves be seen as ageist at times, for instance when they reinforce ideas that older adults need protection from ageism, are unable to think critically about their own lifespan position, and need to be shielded from certain 'realities'" (cf. Coupland & Coupland, 1999). Accordingly, Nina's discursive attempts to normalise aging may in fact *contribute* to ageism – but the data seems to suggest that her competent and seemingly easy relational work is effective in cultivating warm and cordial relationships in the workplace. Thus, her mirroring and normalisation of residents' stories seems to contribute to a contextually-appropriate employable identity.

She also engages in small talk with residents that allows them to take up empowered discursive positions, such as in her discussion of the Green Party candidate's visit with Ava (Excerpt 9.4). When discussing the same event with Charlie (Excerpt 9.6), she makes a discursive claim to belonging through the use of her cultural capital, which is briefly acknowledged by Charlie, but his overall positioning of her as a politically-uninformed novice has the interactional effect of situating her as an outsider to the imagined community of New Zealand. Nina seems to take this in her stride and accepts Charlie's apprentice-positioning. She makes claims to belonging without insisting upon their uptake, creating an amiable atmosphere in which residents are engaged and have the space to take up knowledgeable and agentive roles in discourse, while still having an active conversational partner.

Nina's sense of her own belonging and her status as a (relative) newcomer to New Zealand become salient in instances of explicit othering, such as Charlie's focus on her pronunciation after Nina's discursive attempt to position herself within the civic community of New Zealand (Excerpt 9.8). Charlie and Nina by all accounts have a good, friendly relationship, and it is probable that Charlie's metalinguistic comments come from a benevolent place, that is, he likely believes that he is helping Nina by 'correcting' her pronunciation. While Nina's linguistic message is entirely clear, Charlie appears to be orienting to standard language ideologies in which linguistic capital is believed to "[reside] in the standardised forms of speech used by dominant social groups" (Menard-Warwick, 2005, p. 256; also Milroy, 2001). In 'helping' Nina with her pronunciation, he dismisses her identity claim of belonging. His attempt to guide Nina towards standard pronunciation could in fact be an instance of benevolent discrimination (cf. Araeen, 2000; Barreto & Ellemers, 2005; Holmes, 2014), whereby his attempts to 'help' her actually contribute to and reinforce standard language ideologies and Discourses of Refugeehood that suggest deficiency, vulnerability, or incompetency.

Ava and Nina co-construct a claim to Nina's (future) insider status (Excerpts 9.9, 9.10, 9.11), simultaneously co-constructing an ideological binary of New Zealander vs. Other. It is a binary in which they both place Nina on the 'New Zealander' side, in part based upon the cultural capital of citizenship (Bauder, 2008). We see here no drawing upon of ideologies of transnationalism or straddling of boundaries between multiple national identities (cf. Duff, 2015; Ehrkamp & Leitner, 2006; Vertovec, 2001). Transnationalism is a concept which suggests that migrants maintain linguistic, familial, economic, cultural, ideological and political ties and identities that straddle geopolitical borders after migration (Duff, 2015; Ehrkamp & Leitner, 2006), though as Duff (2015, p. 57) notes, the reality "can be much more complex and distributed than this kind of binary (origin-settlement) suggests." Nina seems to orient to her New Zealander identity in a way which draws upon Discourses of (migrant) Integration or Assimilation.

In an increasingly globalised world that allows migrants to sustain robust transnational ties, Ehrkamp (2005, p. 1673) observes, Discourses of Assimilation, which create pressure for migrants to accommodate their behaviour to the norms and values of the receiving society, "may 'other' transnational practices." In describing her own experiences of forced migration to the United States, Nayeri (2017, n.p.) notes that "as refugees, we owed them our previous identity. We had to lay it at their door like an offering, and gleefully deny it to earn our place in this new country. There would be no… third culture here." It seems that transnational straddling of cultural boundaries may be at odds with an ideological binary of citizen vs. Other, along with Discourses of Gratitude.

Nina and Ava's co-construction of citizenship as highly valuable, along with Ava's suggestion that Nina is *gonna be a New Zealander* upon receiving citizenship, is reminiscent of Arwa's claim (Excerpt 8.7; previous chapter) that New Zealand will be *(her) country* upon gaining citizenship, and her framing of citizenship as a gateway to belonging (it is worth noting that the website of the Office of the Controller and Auditor-General (2018) itself notes that one of the benefits of citizenship over permanent residence is "a greater sense of national identity"). This kind of framing suggests that belonging to New Zealand is something which is proved by an institutionalised, official document, and not a relational and ongoing negotiation that Nina (and Arwa) is already involved in (cf. Bucholtz & Hall's (2005) discussion of discursive *authorisation*). While this excerpt in fact provides evidence of Nina's belonging within the Pinewood community, in Nina and Ava's easy rapport and Ava's enthusiastic investment in Nina's affairs, this explicit claim to institutionalised belonging also displays Nina's multifaceted, intersectional negotiation of position within the workplace.

This intersectional negotiation is highlighted in Excerpts 9.12 and 9.13, in which Charlie and Nina appear to position one another in ways that are undesirable for the recipient of the positioning. New Zealand's Ministry of Health requires eldercare facilities to "promote the independence and quality of life of residents" (Ministry of Health, 2012 cited in Marsden & Holmes, 2014, p. 20). The role of carers in eldercare facilities thus involves accommodating residents' relational needs, alongside performing transactional tasks (Backhaus, 2009; Grainger, 1993; Marsden & Holmes, 2014). However, in an eldercare context, complex power relations pervade any and all interactions between staff and residents (Herman & Williams, 2009; Makoni & Grainger, 2002). Discourses of Aging frame the elderly as dependent and vulnerable, and may contribute to a discursive power imbalance, impacting upon both staff's positioning of residents, and the residents' reaction to that positioning. On the other hand, carers are employees of the residents, and attend to them in their homes. This dynamic may result in a power imbalance in the opposite direction, in which carers (employees) are interactionally subordinate to residents (employees).

In Nina's case, relationships of power in the workplace are further complexified by social structures related to her former refugee status, due to Discourses of Refugeehood (and Gratitude) that may suggest vulnerability and deficiency. Power, as Tannen (1987, cited in Al Zidjaly, 2009, p. 179) notes, does not arise from a single source but is co-constructed by all participants, moment-by-moment, as well as being impacted upon by the intersectional facets of the identity salient in a given moment (Crenshaw, 1989; Davis, 2008). As discussed in Chapter 3, navigating power differentials becomes particularly acute in interactions with a historically or socially marginalised community (Bhopal, 2010; K. Block et al., 2012). As members of two such (imagined) communities, the elderly and former refugees, Charlie (and Ava) and Nina find themselves in both higher and lower status interactive positions relative to the other.

In Excerpts 9.12 and 9.13, it seems that both Charlie and Nina are drawing on ideas of vulnerability or dependence, informed by different Discourses: those of Aging, and those of Refugeehood. As such they must navigate undesirable other-positioning by their interlocutors in order to orient to the identity they are attempting to accomplish at the time. Nina and Charlie's established relationship seems robust enough for them to openly reject such positioning (through tone and redirection). Nina's skilful intersectional management of her employable and (former) refugee identities in the workplace is evident, as she manoeuvres the rejection of other-positioning while maintaining the discursive power balances required of her workplace role.

For former refugees in the labour market and workplace, it seems that the path to belonging is beset on all sides by the inequities of social power and the benevolent discrimination of the well-meaning. Nina's skilful negotiation of her employable identity in her carer role involves the dynamic navigation of discourse and Discourses that challenge her identity as a member of the imagined community of New Zealand. This highlights the dialectic nature of the journey towards belonging: oldtimers and newcomers (Norton, 2001) are mutually involved in the co-construction of successful and acceptable resettlement outcomes. The enactment of employable identities, likewise, is a two-way process in which employees' performances must be negotiated with, ratified, and accepted by colleagues, clients, and employers. Nina's extensive pragmatic skills, knowledge of and adherence to workplace norms and expectations, employment of her own capital, and agentive navigation of Discourses and self- and other-positioning in her workplace interactions appear to be successful, resulting in the (co)construction of a ratified professional and employable identity well-suited to her workplace environment.

Nina's workplace interactions, and the narratives of Omar, Kelly, Arwa, and Isaac, have provided remarkable insight into the discursive challenges former refugees may encounter in their attempts to negotiate locally-appropriate employable identities in New Zealand, both in the search for work and in the workplace. Their identity work in the stories and time they have shared provide invaluable understanding of journeys towards belonging, and I explore the wider social implications of this insight upon resettlement and employment outcomes in the following chapter.

CHAPTER 10

Discussion

Introduction

Over the previous five chapters' micro-level analysis of moment-to-moment identity navigation, this study has made clear that former refugees encounter numerous structural obstacles along their journeys to negotiating locally-valuable and recognised employable identities. In fact, every jobseeker faces structural obstacles in attempts to gain acceptable employment commensurate with their skills, qualifications and experience. The gender and culture orders (J. Holmes, 2006a, 2018), various forms of social discrimination, the navigation of Discourses, access to education and interviews, and so forth – all of these impact upon our ability to actualise our capital and enact appropriate employable identities. We need to know how to discursively 'package' our embodied capital in such a way that it is recognised as such by others, and in ways that adhere to the rules governing the particular field in which we are attempting to negotiate an employable identity (Bourdieu, 1991; Brown et al., 2016; van de Mieroop & Schnurr, 2017a). Exploring this from an Interactional Sociolinguistics approach focuses on (little-d) discourse as "the basic research site" (Gumperz, 2005, p. 215), although as discussed in Chapter 2, this kind of approach also depends upon the researcher's "understanding of the socio-cultural context of the interaction under investigation" (Vine, Holmes, Marra, Pfeifer, & Jackson, 2008, p. 345). That is, IS pays close attention to the wider social context within which the interactive data is located. Indeed, it is the social context of former refugees' employability struggles which has motivated this study. Thus, I return here to discuss the wider (macro) implications of former refugees' employable identity navigation, in light of the challenges illuminated through my (micro) Interactional Sociolinguistic analysis.

Being born into the middle classes (or above) of a society's culturally-dominant group provides a head start of sorts in education, status, employment opportunities and success (Bourdieu, 1986). Those born outside of this culturally-dominant group are forced to 'catch up' from birth, and this is similarly the case for newcomers to a society, unfamiliar with or unpractised in the rules of the new (Bourdieusian) field. This is accentuated in the case of forced migrants whose conditions for migration allow little choice and preparation, and whose social and cultural capital can become worthless in a new context. Social Discourses of Refugeehood and (refugee)

Gratitude may hinder efforts to enact and have recognised erstwhile valuable capital and locally-useful employable identities. Within this social structure, former refugees have agency to resist or exploit disempowering Discourses, but identity is a co-construction and negotiation, and any self-positioning they attempt to take up must be ratified by their interlocutors – interviewers, colleagues, and employers – in order to be successful. For forced migrants, ideologies of employability and those of refugeehood may conflict with one another, with subsequent implications for their sense of self as employable, and their resilience in the labour market.

Migration of capital

As discussed in Chapter 2, the embodied cultural capital of dispositions and knowledge that is aligned with socially dominant practices facilitates academic success and allows for transformation into institutional cultural capital in the form of awarded qualifications. As Bourdieu (1986, p. 48) notes, "the economic and social yield of the educational qualification depends on the social capital… which can be used to back it up." The kind of social capital that an individual can tap into is also dependent, in part, upon the embodied cultural capital that facilitated its creation. That is, appropriate, useful cultural capital is necessary to create and maintain useful social capital, and that cultural capital in turn relies upon social capital to provide economic and social benefits.

This cycle or loop suggests that neither institutional cultural capital, nor embodied cultural capital, nor social capital are sufficient alone to discursively co-construct a legitimate employable identity (Brown et al., 2016; Hinchliffe & Jolly, 2011). Each seems to require the support of the other(s) in order to actualise value in the enactment of employable identities. The migration context, as has been discussed throughout this book, further complexifies the intersection of these types of capital and the negotiation of locally-valuable employable identities. Capital of any kind which is valuable in one place – e.g. someone's country of origin – may lose some or all of its value in another – e.g. a country of resettlement – presenting difficulties for getting a foot into this capital loop.

For forced migrants, the depreciating effects of migration upon capital can be further amplified, comparative to voluntary migrants. Refugees have little, if any, choice in their destination, often receiving little forewarning of their departure, and likely have more pressing and immediate concerns to attend to than future employment, such as their personal welfare and that of their families. This means that consideration of the countries in which one's institutional capital would be valued and recognised, investigation of local labour markets, becoming acquainted with local norms and practices, and preparation for the (re)creation of useful social networks are far less possible and practical for those fleeing persecution than for those choosing to migrate for voluntary pull factors (Kunz, 1973). The 'depreciation' of a certain type of capital can be rooted in the bearer's ability to display and negotiate that capital discursively.

Newcomers to a given context can find ways to transform at least some of their existent capital to *locally-useful* capital through the adoption of *locally-recognised* ways of enacting and negotiating it. Furthermore, the ability to do so appears to be important in allowing former refugees to imagine their future identities and communities and to maintain their senses of self as capable and competent. This was shown in my participants' allusions to their futures. Isaac drew on his high status social capital to warrant his imagined future as a politician (Excerpt 7.8); validation from employers of Arwa's institutional cultural capital allowed her to imagine future success (Excerpt 8.8); challenges to Kelly's institutional cultural capital restricted her ability to imagine beyond the steps immediately in front of her (Excerpt 7.3); and Omar's inability to have his embodied cultural capital recognised and validated led to him focusing on the imagined futures of his children rather than himself (Excerpt 7.9).

Migrants and refugees can continually renegotiate their identities "… as they understand that, in order to increase the value of their overall cultural capital and acquire social goods such as status, power or employment, individuals must act within the approved patterns of a particular Discourse" (Kerekes et al., 2013, p. 272). When the prevailing Discourses are disempowering, however, this can put former refugees in the position of having to choose between aligning or disaligning with such undesirable Discourse, with ensuing effects on the success of transformation of capital in the local context.

Discourses of Refugeehood

Discourses surrounding (former) refugees do not emerge as 'truth' from an objectively appreciable world made up of factual observations. Rather, they are borne of "particular epistemic and ideological assumptions" (Schwöbel-Patel & Ozkaramanli, 2017, p. 2). One of the ways that these ideological assumptions become visible is in the media, in the ways that discourse frames how refugees are spoken and written about, what is assumed, what is included, what is omitted. Media coverage both reflects and helps shape public opinion, and thus its effects on Discourses are clear.

Studies exploring media discourse surrounding refugees and asylum seekers in the United Kingdom and elsewhere have found that these groups are frequently framed in ways that are homogenising, dehumanising, and criminalising (e.g. Baker et al., 2008; Baker & McEnery, 2005; Gabrielatos & Baker, 2008;

Khosravinik, 2008, 2009; Leach & Mansouri, 2003; Leudar et al., 2008; Martínez Lirola, 2014). New Zealand's media appears to be more benevolent and less inflammatory than, for example, the United Kingdom's, perhaps owing to the absence of tabloid-type newspapers. However, in a study I conducted in 2014 on the framing of refugees and asylum seekers in New Zealand newspapers (Greenbank, 2014), I found that media discourses suggested vulnerability, victimhood, low agency, and, less frequently but still present, burden and criminality (see also Spoonley & Butcher, 2009; Sulaiman-Hill et al., 2011). Common to almost every newspaper article in my corpus was a sense of the 'otherness' of refugees and asylum seekers (whether through trauma, spectacle, or threat), and a persistence of the 'refugee' label which was liberally applied to former refugees, including those newsworthy for reasons independent of their former refugeehood, long after their settlement in New Zealand.

The image of the helpless, vulnerable victim refugee is frequently employed by the UNHCR, perhaps unsurprisingly as it is the organisation's function to help those in need. Images on the UNHCR's website, as Schwöbel-Patel and Ozkaramanli (2017, pp. 3–4) note, "[depict] women and children, in the open, often wearing traveling clothes, huddled in groups; the images of children are ones in which they stand alone, looking directly at the camera," and the only foregrounded men are (largely white) UNHCR officials. This aesthetic contrast hints at "predetermined ideas about race, vulnerability, and weakness" (Schwöbel-Patel & Ozkaramanli, 2017, p. 4). This has been called the *fundraising image* of the refugee, intended to engender compassion and support from viewers of the image in the Global North (Schwöbel-Patel, 2016), and prove that these (UNHCR) refugees are genuine, and deserving of outside help. The unintended consequence of such suggestive framing is the creation of an ideological binary between genuine/deserving UNHCR refugees, and 'bogus'/undeserving asylum seekers and displaced persons. The downsides of using such simplified imagery, however, are purportedly outweighed by the role they play in raising awareness of refugee plight (Schwöbel-Patel, 2016, p. 250), as well as sympathy toward claims for asylum.

The discursive navigation of such Discourses of Refugeehood has been demonstrated throughout this study's data, and nowhere clearer than in the participants' narratives of flight. In telling these stories, (or even being asked to do so, which can easily result in a refusal to tell), this study's storytellers are necessarily and explicitly positioned as (former) refugees – both by me as question-asker, and by themselves as they take up the telling. That 'becoming' a refugee involves a well-founded fear of persecution and an unwillingness to avail oneself of the protection of the country of one's nationality (UNHCR, 2011) means that a narrative of flight could be expected to include frightening or upsetting elements that portray the teller as a victim, a low-agency recipient of terrible circumstances out of their control.

Indeed, Chan (2006, p. 251), in exploring the migration experiences of Vietnamese refugees, found that "immense suffering, deprivation, loss, and violent uprooting" were commonalities of many of these stories (cited in Nguyen, 2013, p. 23). The telling of these stories of suffering may be a valuable way for those who have suffered the trauma, loss, and indignities of involuntary migration to personally make sense of the disruption to their lives. Storytelling can be a way to "remember, bear witness, or seek to restore continuity and identity, [and] can be a symbolic resource enlisted to alleviate suffering and change [one's] situation" (Eastmond, 2007, p. 251). As discussed in Chapter 5, suffering can gain meaning through being shared, and can become meaningless if it is untold and "socially invisible" (Eastmond, 1996, cited in 2007, p. 252). Thus, visibility of suffering is important and necessary, but reductionist imagery and framing of former refugees as victims is not.

Furthermore, the Discourses which highlight victimhood that former refugees must discursively navigate fail to account for several elements of refugeehood that contradict such representation. The first of these is that the refugee label can drown out all other facets of an individual's identity. Refugees and former refugees "are people with an identity, a past, a history, a cultural heritage" (Lacroix, 2004, p. 147). That is, they are "ordinary people in extraordinary circumstances" (Harrell-Bond, 1999, p. 158). The experiences that led to becoming refugees, while likely critical moments or periods in their lives, are not the only important aspect of their identities. For any of us to have our entire life's accumulated history and experiences distilled perpetually into a single, disempowering label, would be painful, no matter the safety, freedom, or new life it has allowed. Dina Nayeri, speaking on her forthcoming book about her own experiences as a former refugee, has noted that "a single moment of displacement can shape everything that comes after," and that in countries of resettlement, the refugee label "can become a permanent siphon of identity and power" (Canongate, 2018).

The apparent perpetuity of the refugee label relates to the second element of refugeehood that contradicts Discourses of Refugeehood: that refugeehood is an experience, or a process, not a static identity (Korac, 2009, p. 7). Lacroix (2004) argues that a refugee is "a new kind of person, one who has been constructed by transnational forces" (p. 147; following Moussa, 1993). That is, a person's well-founded fear of persecution, their flight, and the cooperation of nations and supranational organisations together 'create' a refugee. The refugee label is a "tangible representation of policies and programmes… [which] institutionalise and differentiate categories of eligibility and entitlements" (Zetter, 2007, p. 180). It is a functional label which becomes a kind of convenient shorthand for a group of people (Zetter, 2007, p. 180) but which really describes a process – claiming (and being granted) asylum and awaiting resettlement – but often seems to be hard to lose once the process has been completed – once the former refugee has permanently resettled in their new country.

Thirdly, Discourses of Refugeehood overlook the fact that refugeehood is not *only* devastating or disempowering but can be emancipating and empowering. Those who experience refugeehood do not simply encounter abhorrent circumstances and then end up in a country of resettlement. Their own actions and decisions lead to their safety and new lives. Nyers (2006) notes that refugees are thus "courageous citizens who, because of their words, actions, or thoughts, [have been] forced out of their political identities (citizens) and communities (state). The… fear [sometimes felt by refugees] is thus a product of a prior bravery or courage" (p. 50; cited in Moulin, 2012). Thus, the refugee experience can be transformative,

> [opening] up new social spaces and opportunities… because displacement or a loss of place, in specific circumstances and concepts, can be experienced as freedom from the pre-established sociocultural norms of the native society and country that often constrain individual behaviour and actions. (Korac, 2009, p. 7)

The experience of refugeehood is not only about loss, but is also about reclaiming governance of one's destiny and re-establishing a life in new circumstances (Korac, 2009, p. 7). It can thus be both disempowering *and* empowering. Korac (2009, p. 8) recommends viewing refugee victimhood as being necessarily intertwined with agency, noting that doing so helps to lessen the 'gap' between the oldtimers and the newcomers, positioning refugees as "people like us, who have agency, sound judgement and reasons for action embedded in their past, politics, experiences of flight, and life way away from home." To consider refugeehood without recognising refugee agency is to dehumanise those who are forced to migrate (Korac, 2009, p. 7; Malkki, 1996).

The elements of the (former) refugee experience which contradict Discourses of Refugeehood are based in the irreducibility of human experience (Rampton et al., 2014) and the functionality of the term *refugee*. The complexity of refugee experiences and the need to able to create and implement policy, and engender social tolerance and empathy, requires a discursive shorthand (Zetter, 2007). That these Discourses have, in all likelihood, emerged out of individual and social empathy and benevolence makes challenging them a delicate business, especially when 'leaning in' to them can prompt greater, much-needed support with both tangible (e.g. increasing refugee quotas) and intangible (e.g. tolerance) outcomes.

For this study's former refugees themselves, orienting to refugee identities allowed access to assistance or opportunities that may have otherwise been unavailable to them. For Kelly, however, her willingness to orient to her refugee identity by attending a function intended to make connections between former refugees and employers (Excerpt 6.2) was negatively impacted upon by her observation of disempowering discourse at the event. For Isaac in Excerpt 6.5, orienting to his refugee identity appeared to present no challenge to his sense of self (at least in our interactional context) as he offered his story to his lecturer in a (successful) bid for advice and assistance with his work. Arwa, as discussed in Chapter 8, did not orient to her refugee identity directly when contacting a local professor about job opportunities. However, she reported relaying his unfavourable response to refugee resettlement workers, who contacted the professor pointing to Arwa's former refugee status. This additional information appears to have softened the professor's disposition towards her, and eventually resulted in her temporary employment. At the same time, Arwa has made it clear to me in conversation that she is not interested in orienting to her refugee identity in her job search. In these participants' reported experiences, the tension between the utility and hindrance of such Discourses is clear.

The Spectacle of Refugeehood

The Discourses surrounding (former) refugees create something of a *Spectacle of Refugeehood*. By *spectacle* I refer to something which is on to display, something to be viewed or consumed (in the media sense); a performance or event worthy of attention. A spectacle creates a dichotomy between a passive, viewable and viewed object, and an active viewer of the object; between the seeing spectator and the spectacularised 'seen' (Schwöbel-Patel, 2016, p. 249). Here, the spectators are those who have not experienced refugeehood, viewing it from the outside. The spectacle is refugeehood, enveloping millions of diverse, disparate refugees and former refugees, and homogenising them through both dominant media imagery and social Discourses as low agency, pitiable objects of suffering.

The concept of the spectacle "concerns the social construction of people and events in order to make a striking impression" (Schwöbel-Patel, 2016, p. 249). Positioned as passive 'seen' for the viewing of the dominant ingroup, former refugees cannot but be othered by such a spectacle. As Sontag (2003) notes, "... the other, even when not an enemy, is regarded only as someone to be seen, not someone (like us) who also sees" (cited in Schwöbel-Patel, 2016, p. 247). This is perhaps hinted at in the ways that Charlie seems to undervalue Nina's embodied cultural capital by either explaining issues in excessive detail, or not acknowledging her claims of relevant knowledge (Excerpts 9.1, 9.5, 9.6, 9.8, 9.13). While this may of course be Charlie's usual modus operandi, it is possible that he is influenced by the Spectacle of Refugeehood which others former refugees as receptacles of outside gaze and information, not producers of them. Viewing the Spectacle of Refugeehood in this way highlights the low agency, victim-like positions associated with forced migrants.

Discussing the social construction of 'the victim' in international law courts, Schwöbel-Patel (2016, p. 251) discusses how a spectacle is not only a viewable phenomenon but is representative of a social relationship of domination. This domination, she argues, is not only the effect but the *purpose* of spectacle:

> The current predominant capitalist model, which creates and maintains inequalities, is seen as natural, criminalising those who are already disenfranchised and hiding from view the relationship between privileged and disenfranchised… Our spectacularised archive of images is, then, representative of a particular ideology. The images are representations of common ideas, which have been given significance; their purpose is to trigger predictable thoughts and feelings.
> (Schwöbel-Patel, 2016, p. 267)

Spectacle thus maintains the status quo in terms of the social distribution of power by reinforcing and reproducing the Us-Them binary between host country 'natives' – an in-group of those who belong (in New Zealand), and forced migrants – an out-group of those who do not (yet) belong, and who are Other. This is not a binary relationship of equals. Power, Hall (1997, p. 259) remarks, should be understood here "… not only in terms of economic exploitation and physical coercion, but also in broader cultural or symbolic terms, including the power to represent someone or something in a certain way… [and] includes the exercise of symbolic power through representational practices." Further, Derrida (1972, p. 41) argues that this kind of binary opposition does not suggest a happy coexistence but rather a 'violent hierarchy' in which one side of the binary has power over the other (cited in Hall, 1997, p. 258).

The 'stickiness' of the refugee label means that this division is maintained indefinitely and hinders social inclusion and belonging. Furthermore, given the Discourses that contribute to this ideological hierarchy between the active viewer and the passive viewed, and the low-agency positions they index, former refugees are placed in subordinate roles in the Spectacle of Refugeehood. It is clear that an inescapable refugee label hinders forced migrants from moving from the peripheries of society toward the centre – toward a sense of belonging in their new homes. The undesirability of this label and its associations was demonstrated in the narratives of flight of this study's participants (Chapters 5 and 8), who oriented away from Discourses that index vulnerability and low agentivity. Arwa in particular avoided telling almost any detail of the impetus for her former refugee status (Excerpts 8.2, 8.3, 8.4) and instead reoriented to her academic identity when I probed for further detail.

Discourses of Refugeehood that paint refugees as 'ultimate' victims (Korac, 2009, p. 7) risk encouraging the expectation that just being safe in New Zealand should 'be enough' for refugees, that to expect, or desire, more than simply being alive may call the authenticity of their refugeehood into question, as discussed above. Kelly seems to reject such an idea in her discussion of former refugees being expected to work like slaves and be grateful for the opportunity (Excerpt 6.2). This expectation that former refugees who left full lives to live out their days in the shadow of a disempowering Discourse keeps open a wound. It does not allow former refugees to heal and move on to normal lives in which they are 'allowed' to strive for better, to pick up the following of their dreams that were disrupted by well-founded fears of persecution. For Omar, who wavered between determination and despair with regards to his employment prospects, it seemed to become necessary to transfer his hopes for the future onto his children in lieu of himself (Excerpt 7.9). Perhaps for some, shaking off the weight of refugeehood is only possible for the second generation.

Discourses of Gratitude

Discourses of the traumatised, ideal, victim-refugee are closely connected to Discourses of (refugee) Gratitude. As Schwöbel-Patel and Ozkaramanli (2017, p. 8) note, "the ideal or deserving refugee is… the 'grateful' refugee." A feeling of gratitude is likely a common part of the refugee resettlement experience, but it is one feeling among many in what can be a long, drawn out, complicated process involving many conflicting and contradictory feelings. The almost axiomatic assumption that refugees should and will be perpetually grateful for their relative safety in their countries of resettlement, and an unspoken requirement of a perpetual performance thereof, can be disempowering and can hinder social inclusion (Colic-Peisker, 2009; Marlowe, 2010; Spouse, 1999).

While it is important to celebrate and encourage the receiving of refugees, it is also important to remember that doing so, for New Zealand and for all other signatories of the 1951 United Nations Convention and/or the 1967 Protocol Relating to the Status of Refugees, is an obligation, not a gift. The New Zealand government's Immigration website refers to the country's "international humanitarian obligations and responsibilities to provide protection to refugees" (Ministry of Business, Innovation and Employment, 2007). This obligation, as Nayeri (2017, n.p.) points out, can also be considered to be a fundamental human obligation: "It is the obligation of every person born in a safer room to open the door when someone in danger knocks," and could more helpfully be thought of as an act of compassion rather than as a gift (CBC Radio, 2017).

Discourses of 'Asylum as a gift,' however, are fairly prevalent on the part of refugee-receiving nations. This granting of status is often represented as "a gratuitous and benevolent act" (Moulin, 2012, p. 61). Those on the receiving end of these benevolent acts may then be expected not only to be grateful but also to reciprocate the gift of asylum in some way. The problematic element underlying this normative belief is that the benefactor-beneficiary relationship is not one of equals. Gratitude is a reflection of a hierarchical social structure which places "the one who receives into a subordinate position, from which they are expected to obey the rules, natural or civil, as a form of reciprocity" (Moulin, 2012, p. 62). 'Obeying the rules' might mean, in the case of newcomers to a society (and particularly so 'visible' minorities (cf. Colic-Peisker, 2005, 2009; Hatoss, 2012; Ricento, 2015)), accepting one's lot and not complaining about or criticising any unsatisfactory elements of their new societies. Evidence of such thinking can be seen in a recent bill proposed by New Zealand First (a nationalist political party that is part of a centre-left coalition government at the time of writing) that would require migrants and refugees to sign a 'New Zealand values' contract that outlines 'rules' for respecting 'core New Zealand values' (Morning Report, 2018).

Being expected to weather such unsatisfactory elements as poverty, underemployment, loss of status, racism, classism, and other forms of intolerance without criticism or comment is dehumanising, disempowering, and humiliating. Both Kelly and Arwa were shown to flout this expectation by criticising perceived treatment of former refugees (Kelly, Excerpt 6.2), and language teachers, Mangere Refugee Resettlement Centre, and New Zealand society generally (Arwa, Excerpt 8.7 and in-text excerpts, Chapter 8). While Kelly actively distanced herself from expectations of silent gratitude, Arwa's comments, framed as contributions or giving back to New Zealand in the form of constructive feedback, could be seen to simultaneously violate and align with Discourses of Gratitude. Moulin (2012, p. 63) argues that the framing of refugee status as a gift relegates refugees to a position of "subordination and dependency," where the generosity is not expected to be repaid but rather "reciprocated with long-term subordination to the benefactor" (van Wees, 1998, p. 41). Thus, Arwa's constructive feedback to New Zealand sits in opposition to Discourses of Gratitude, as her attempts to contribute are not subordinate but critical, a higher agency position to take.

Expectations of gratitude may mutate into indebtedness, and, for the former refugee, "enshackled in an endless debt-payment relationship to the state… recompense through gratefulness is always incommensurate to the gift" (Nguyen, 2013, p. 25). This gift is in fact an imposed identity – the grateful refugee (Schwartz, 1967, pp. 1–2, cited in Moulin, 2012, p. 63). But what does this imposed identity mean for multi-faceted individuals leading "… multi-dimensional lives – laughing, crying, celebrating, grieving and hoping, just like the rest of us" (Scheyvens et al., 2003,

p. 168)? While refugee status affords essential rights and much-needed assistance, this ostensibly temporary identity, as discussed in Chapter 2, may end up obscuring other facets of a person's identity or sense of self (Marlowe, 2010, p. 1). A tacit social expectation for former refugees to experience gratitude endlessly, or at least perform it, is to permanently consign them to a position of low power and dependency.

This "tedium of constant gratitude" (Spouse, 1999, p. 396) may result in resentment, and feelings of social exclusion (Colic-Peisker, 2009; Marlowe, 2010; Moulin, 2012). Additionally, and importantly for official measures of resettlement success, a constant orientation to Discourses of Gratitude may affect an individual's ability to be resilient in the labour market, if they are to view themselves as competent candidates for employment and be able to enact employable identities in their chosen professions. Generally-held assumptions of what it means to be employable, as discussed in Chapter 1 and throughout this study, involve such traits as competence and adaptability (Hinchliffe & Jolly, 2011; Moreau & Leathwood, 2006). Discourses of Gratitude threaten to undermine the enactment of these traits, by expecting perpetual subordination and dependency from former refugees.

Despite the expectations of subjective dependency and gratitude (and thus low agency) involved with Discourses of Gratitude, former refugees are nonetheless expected to become economically self-sufficient, which of course requires agentivity and self-determination. Nguyen (2013, p. 23) argues that

> … the figure of the grateful refugee is closely related to that of the highly assimilated and successful "good refugee"… [who is] often also constructed as a model minority, who is perceived as hardworking and resourceful and, through both innate and cultural qualities, is able to achieve educational, economic, and social success with no or very little assistance from the state.

The dilemma of a grateful (former) refugee, both deferential and entrepreneurial "has been referred to as 'Schrödinger's immigrant,' who is 'simultaneously stealing your job and too lazy to work,' epitomising the ungrateful refugee" (Schwöbel-Patel & Ozkaramanli, 2017, p. 9) This 'immigrant' who occupies, or is socially expected to occupy, both high and low agency positions, brings us back to Bamberg's (2011b, 2011a) agency dilemma.

Agency dilemma

Bamberg's (2011b, 2011a) *agency dilemma*, as discussed in Chapter 6, suggests that speaking subjects are faced with the discursive predicament of using narrative devices that position them as having high agency, in control, and capable of acting upon the world, or as low-agency, victim-like, and acted upon by the world.

Furthermore, in telling stories, narrators are faced with this choice of positioning for themselves both as narrator of the story, and as protagonist within their own storyworlds. Variously higher and lower agency self-positioning contributes towards orientation to various identity positions within discourse, as well as allowing post hoc reframing of past events or identity positions which might challenge or support the identity work being undertaken in the interaction at hand.

Furthermore, telling stories in an interview allows storytellers to collaboratively negotiate their identities with interviewers, and allows the possibility of "[becoming] empowered to construct 'new' or 'revised' identities for themselves during the interview, which they may be able to draw on in the future" (van de Mieroop & Schnurr, 2017a, p. 451). This has been shown in this study's data. In Excerpt 5.1 Kelly recounts a low-agency situation of being publicly berated, then takes up a high agency position as narrator in dismissing and reacting to her storyworld adversary in a way she seemingly was unable to – or at least did not – in the narrated event. Similarly, in Excerpt 6.4, Omar dynamically reorients from a position of despair, to vowing to continue fighting to have his capital recognised and validated, in seconds. In light of the societal Discourses that former refugees are situated within, and the Spectacle of Refugeehood which looms over their attempts to enact employable identities in the New Zealand context, this agency dilemma becomes particularly acute.

The simplification of representation involved with such Discourses stigmatises those who have experienced suffering and homogenises their experiences. Schwöbel-Patel (2016, p. 250) remarks that this can be problematic in two ways, "for those who do not fall within the accepted image (because they may struggle for recognition of their victim-status) but also for those who do fall within the accepted image (because this image is dependent on an understanding of victims as lacking agency)." This issue may then be linked to refugee legitimacy. That is, appearing to fulfil the expected role of a victim may allow an individual to more closely match external expectations of what a refugee 'is,' whether those expectations come from an organisation like the UNHCR or a general member of the public.

However, if an 'ideal,' low-agency, victim-like refugee is the epitome of a legitimate refugee, then a refugee who exercises agency and shows no visible signs of victimhood perhaps invokes the notion of an illegitimate refugee. This puts refugees and former refugees in a situation where they may have to choose between orienting towards their experiences of refugeehood (and thus, dependency, which is a critical element of 'ideal' victimhood (Schwöbel-Patel, 2015; drawing on Christie, 1986)), or exercising agency, acting upon the world, and directing their own lives, and thus risking inadvertent orientation to refugee illegitimacy and related criminality (Moulin, 2012; Schwöbel-Patel & Ozkaramanli, 2017). Moulin (2012) argues that this is a choice between protection from a state – along with an expectation of gratitude and dependency – and political autonomy (no state protection) and the freedom from expectations of gratitude (ironically the latter also matching the 'good refugee' ideology discussed above (Nguyen, 2013, p. 23)).

Members of social 'outgroups' "are frequently exposed to… binary form[s] of representation" (Hall, 1997, p. 229). That is, those considered 'others' are often represented as "sharply opposed, polarised, binary extremes" such as good/bad, civilised/primitive, grateful/ungrateful – and frequently, contradictorily, required to be both at once (Hall, 1997, p. 229). These binaries are simplifying and reductionist, inhibiting nuance and distinction. Furthermore, as Derrida (1972; cited in Hall, 1997, p. 235) argues, binary oppositions are rarely neutral; there is always evaluative distinction between the two poles of any binary opposition. Thus, former refugees are 'between a rock and a hard place' in their discursive navigation of Discourses of Refugeehood and Gratitude, choosing between gratitude and dependency on the one hand (perhaps threatening employability), and ingratitude and autonomy on the other.

The dynamic navigation of higher and lower agency positions in discourse was shown in Omar's reorientation from a position of acceptance or resignation to one of vowing to continue fighting for his future (Excerpt 6.4), as well as Kelly's swift discursive repairs after seemingly unintentionally assigning herself a high agency (blameworthy) position when discussing a public reprimand (Excerpt 6.7). Arwa, too, appears to 'catch' herself mid-utterance when providing advice to New Zealand (Excerpt 8.7), reorienting to the role of advice recipient. For Nina, who is negotiating these binaries in the workplace, the navigation occurs within the enactment of a contextually-appropriate employable identity at Pinewood. Thus, rejection or avoidance of low-agency other-positioning, for example, may be achieved through reorientation towards transactional tasks (Excerpt 9.8). The stakes, it seems, are higher for former refugees in the discursive navigation of Bamberg's (2011b, 2011a) agency dilemma.

It should be noted that refugees and former refugees are both spectators of, and subsumed within the spectacle of, refugeehood. Before their own experiences with refugeehood they would have observed the Spectacle of Refugeehood from the 'outside;' from the spectator role. Having now gone through the process of refugeehood, this study's participants do not, at any point in the collected interactional data, problematise the Spectacle of Refugeehood nor Discourses of Refugeehood and Gratitude. Rather, in various ways, they distance themselves from these Discourses personally and individually. They do not reject the validity of the Discourses regarding refugeehood in general, but they largely discursively disalign with them (e.g. throughout narratives of flight, and Kelly in Excerpts 5.1 and 6.2, and Arwa in Excerpt 8.7). This, then, is an instantiation of Bourdieu's (1991) symbolic violence, in which the ideologies imposed by the powerful can lead to the oppressed reproducing the conditions of their own oppression, reinforcing and legitimating existing structures of inequality (Bourdieu, 1991). 'Victims' of a stereotype, Hall (1997, p. 263) notes, can "unconsciously confirm it by the very terms in which they try to oppose and resist it."

Faced with these structural barriers and the ideological hierarchy within which they are (inadvertently) positioned in discourse, former refugees are not without the power to take up multiple and dynamic identity positions. Power, Foucault (1977) suggests, is everywhere. Power is not only "a negative, coercive, or repressive social phenomenon that forces us to act against our wishes… [but] can also be a necessary, productive, and positive force in that it provides space for creative openings" (Faist, 2018, p. 420). Thus, in attempting to enact employable identities – or take up any given desirable identity position – former refugees can resist or exploit the disempowering Discourses and orient to variously agentive subject positions (even, as discussed above, without problematising them). As narrators and as protagonists they can "act upon themselves to construct identities that are 'dissident' in relation to the dominant group's norms… they may challenge them by drawing on other [Discourses] or even produce counter narratives" (van de Mieroop & Schnurr, 2017a, p. 451; drawing on Bamberg, 2004a; and Clifton & van de Mieroop, 2016).

That is, if counter-Discourses and 'dissident' identities are enacted frequently enough, they can contribute towards the creation of new norms and social change (Bamberg et al., 2007; van de Mieroop & Schnurr, 2017a). Isaac, for example, believes that the turning point in his life in New Zealand came when he was able to transcend his low-status role as a cleaner at a university by a fortuitous opportunity to display his embodied cultural capital to an audience of his desired peers (Excerpt 7.1), thereby challenging dominant Discourses of what a former-refugee cleaner might be capable of. This unexpected opportunity, Isaac explains, opened avenues for him to go on to enact employable identities in a range of other contexts.

For former refugees attempting to enact employable identities, navigating a dilemma of agency is particularly critical. Aligning with Discourses of Refugeehood is problematic because being an object of pity is not positively associated with employability. And disaligning with Discourses of Refugeehood and Gratitude is problematic as it risks appearing 'ungrateful' for New Zealand's benevolence, which may hinder locally-valued employability. This reductionist and non-neutral binary by which social outgroups are often represented (Hall, 1997), as discussed above, puts former refugees into something of a bind. Where is the life of "happy mediocrity" for these groups, as Nayeri (2017, n.p.) asks? Is it "a privilege reserved for those who never stray from home?"

As this book has explored, attempts to orient to high agency discursive positions in the service of attempting to enact locally-valuable employable identities are not always successful. Identity positions are negotiated and co-constructed conjointly with other interlocutors, colleagues, interviewers and employers. And as noted by Holmes and Marra (2017, p. 128), "discourse is a core means through which individuals gradually adopt behaviours which they perceive as normative, and which conform to the systems of belief subscribed to by members of the desired ingroup." Lack of locally-valuable cultural capital, particularly related to socio-cultural norms, may undermine newcomers' attempts to align themselves with the ingroup's practices and expectations, along with the complexity added by the discursive navigation of Discourses.

Conclusion

The implications of capital's low fungibility, disempowering Discourses, and the limited effects of personal, discursive agency (as demonstrated in this study's five chapters of interactional analysis), are that former refugees' attempts to enact and co-construct employable identities are constrained in intersecting ways, with obvious ramifications for their ability to access and secure acceptable, appropriate employment. If participation in society is hindered, and movement from society's peripheries is denied, "participants may be kept on the boundaries and may even be excluded from the community, thus become complete outsiders or non-participants" (Clifton & van de Mieroop, 2016, p. 226). Such continued marginalisation in the face of ongoing attempts to agentively resist and navigate these barriers impacts upon former refugees' self-esteem, imagined futures, and resilience in the labour market, as this study has shown. Furthermore, the labour market effects can already be seen in former refugees' high levels of unemployment and underemployment in New Zealand and across refugee-receiving nations. The exploration of employable identity negotiation that this study has undertaken contributes to a wider discussion on addressing employment-related resettlement challenges. In the following chapter I return to this study's research questions in light of this discussion and consider the contributions my research has made.

CHAPTER 11

Conclusion

Introduction

The discursive negotiation of employable identities is a complex and situated process, and this is particularly the case for those of refugee background. This book has explored the navigation of social and discursive challenges to enacting employable identities in the narratives of former refugees in naturalistic interviews and in authentic workplace communication. In this final chapter, I return to my research questions, discuss the contributions this study has made, and consider future research directions.

Research questions

In my research I have endeavoured to address, in a systematic and complex manner, the overarching research question I presented in Chapter 1: *How do refugee-background jobseekers and employees enact employable identities in discourse?* I have broken this research question into four, more specific research questions which I have addressed over the course of five chapters of data and analysis.

Research question 1a

How do this study's participants make use of narrative to position themselves in the New Zealand context?

As the analysis has demonstrated, narratives are excellent research sites within which to explore complex and dynamic identity negotiation. In the stories that we tell, we locate ourselves in two worlds: the storyworld of the unfolding narrative, and the interactional context in the social world in which the story is being told. In telling a story we frame the 'events' we are recounting such that they build towards a particular identity position that we are attempting to accomplish, both for the storyworld protagonist, and for the 'real world' narrator. As an example of self-positioning in narrative, the participants' narratives of flight (Chapters 5 and 8) were told to me, prompted, in the context of an informal, conversational interview, in a context where both their former refugee status and their employment status/employability were highly salient. The stories they told me variously contained danger, violence, and fear, as we might expect from journeys towards refugeehood. But these disquieting elements were not foregrounded nor dwelled upon; instead they created a backdrop against which the storytellers could interactively negotiate more desirable – and potentially, useful, in terms of employability – identity positions. They told me stories in which they were the masters of their own destinies, forging paths towards new lives in the face of adversity. Nonetheless, in taking up these resilient, competent, and adaptable identities, this study's participants also navigate Discourses of Refugeehood and Gratitude which permeate our interactions and threaten to undermine or contradict the identity positions they are attempting to negotiate.

The participants are necessarily former refugees, but frequently through their stories they make it clear that while refugeehood is salient to their lives, a refugee was not something that they are (any longer); or they discursively make a distinction between themselves and an imagined community (B. Anderson, 1991) of other refugees. This imagined community that they index explicitly or by implicit contrast appears to reinforce Discourses of Refugeehood. That is, in distancing themselves from Discourses of refugee vulnerability, incompetence, and victimhood, this study's participants made little discursive challenge to the Discourses themselves. So in telling their stories of flight, the participants frame themselves not as *refugees* (which they of course ceased to 'be' upon arrival in New Zealand) but as people who have experienced refugeehood in the course of lives filled with other equally, or more, salient experiences which have impacted upon who they are, or who they are attempting to negotiate in interaction.

Through the telling of their stories, they reveal simultaneously the extraordinariness and the ordinariness of former refugees: their lives were, and are, just as full and complex as anyone else's, and are not reducible to their refugee identity. At the same time, they have experienced extraordinary circumstances (Harrell-Bond, 1999), and these circumstances necessarily impact upon their negotiation of identity roles in discourse (particularly in the context of a refugee-related research interview). They use storytelling to position themselves as capable, resilient, and agentive – all important both to self and to the enactment of employable identities. They acquiesce to telling (particular versions of) their narratives of flight but avoid positioning themselves as victims. Any trauma or victimhood they experience is perhaps personal, but in telling their stories to someone they do not know well (at the time they told them to me), they take up stronger positions. This is not only seen in their narratives of flight (Chapters 5 and 8), but also throughout their interviews. In their storytelling, they negotiate belonging – making sense of and attempting to navigate their way out of the liminality of refugeehood.

Research question 1b

What do this study's participants understand to be important to employability, and how is this relevant to the ways that they attempt to negotiate employable identities in discourse?

I have demonstrated that the participants place great importance on their institutional cultural capital as well as the embodied cultural capital of experience in their attempts to negotiate employable identities. This can be seen both in their choices of topic and in the ways that they index their capital in discourse. Their *investment* in their own institutional and embodied cultural capital can be seen in their discursive positioning of themselves, in both their storyworlds and in the context of the interaction with me, when their capital is challenged – such as Arwa's fiery storyworld response to a language teacher's perceived lack of respect for her status (Excerpt 8.5), and Kelly's recounted strategy of only focusing on the steps in front of her to maintain her investment in her undergraduate qualification display (Excerpt 7.3).

The social capital that these participants have at their disposal also plays a role in their conceptualisations of employability. This can be seen in Isaac's recounting of advising friends to develop wider social networks, and Kelly positioning herself as unfairly disadvantaged because she is not able to access the employment that her classmates with CEO fathers can, as well as an account of having no social network to support her when she had to weather multiple job rejection letters.

The ways that opportunities to display embodied cultural capital impact upon participants' success in negotiating employable identities is emergent in the data. This was seen in Isaac's story about having an unusual opportunity to display his embodied cultural capital – his skills as an orator and activist – in a public speech addressing his desired imagined community (B. Anderson, 1991). The inverse can be seen in Omar's narrated frustration surrounding attempts to implement a more efficient maintenance schedule at his workplace (Excerpts 6.3 and 6.4). Doing so would have been a display and validation of his embodied cultural capital built upon decades of experience in the field. Similarly, his recounted inability to convince a recruiter to secure him an interview despite his suitability for the role was rooted in a lack of 'the right type' of capital (Excerpt 7.4), in this case the cultural capital of citizenship (which of course may be a pretext and an instance of 'new racism' (Augoustinos et al., 2005; M. Barker, 1981; van Dijk, 2000)).

The challenges and setbacks that the participants encountered in their attempts to enact, draw upon, and negotiate the value of their various forms of capital in the pursuit of employable identities appear to impact upon their senses of self, self-esteem, imagined futures, and resilience in the labour market. While Isaac's success has left him positive and hopeful about his future, Arwa, Kelly, and Omar have had much less optimistic outlooks throughout this study's duration (however, I note that Isaac had long periods of underemployment and general employability challenges before being involved in this study which I do not wish to discount). Arwa's classification of her hard-earned doctorate as worthless (Excerpt 8.1 and 8.9), Kelly's decision to give up after a year of fruitless job searching with no social support (Excerpt 7.7), and Omar's transferral of hopes for the future from himself onto his children (Excerpt 7.9) show the effects that loss of status and ongoing marginalisation can have on former refugee jobseekers in their attempts to enact employable identities.

Research question 2

How does a participant's navigation of an employable identity develop over time?

As exploration of the previous research questions has demonstrated, negotiating employable identities in new contexts can be fraught with challenges, in the face of a lack of familiarity with interactional norms and available discursive positions, as well as obstacles to the recognition of erstwhile valuable social and cultural capital. Consequently, the path to enacting a locally-recognised employable identity can be a long and convoluted one. This was certainly the case for Arwa who, over twenty months, appeared to experience the full gamut of human emotion with regards to her own employability.

In some ways, Arwa's trajectory resembles the Kübler-Ross (1969) model of grief, in which those who are grieving or processing a terminal illness are purported to progress through the emotional states of denial, anger, bargaining, depression, and acceptance (my use of this model as an analogy should not be taken to suggest that I subscribe to Kübler-Ross's description of the stages of grief, which has been criticised for its cultural specificity and lack of evidence (Corr, Doka, & Kastenbaum, 1999), but rather to explore the range of interpretations of experience Arwa reported and the identity positions she took up therein). I refer here to the identity positions which Arwa took up in narrative and interaction with me over the data collection period, and not to any cognitive state that I cannot speak for. When we first met her initial sense of herself as employable was strongly tied to the ostensive value of her institutional capital, and she recounted the insult and disrespect she felt when that capital, and her attempts to present herself as employable and educable, were challenged (Excerpts 8.5, 8.6) – mapping on to the 'grief stages' of denial and anger. In later interviews Arwa expressed desire to align with local interaction norms and Discourses, at the same time as encouraging New Zealanders to respect newcomers' norms and needs, hinting at recognition of the negotiated nature of belonging (Excerpt 8.7) – the bargaining stage. A year after we met, she maligned her institutional cultural capital as worthless (Excerpts 8.1, 8.9) – depression, and began to orient to the idea of interactively negotiating locally-valuable ways of performing an employable identity (Excerpts 8.10, 8.11) – perhaps an acceptance stage.

Although I believe that loss of status, the invalidation of a lifetime's amassed capital, as well as of course the refugee experience generally, are likely to induce a grieving process in individuals, I stress again that I am not applying Kübler-Ross's (1969) model as an analytic tool, but rather as a helpful descriptor of the roller-coaster of challenges Arwa encountered and her reported reactions and identity work surrounding them. To say that Arwa is in a stage of acceptance at the end of my study is of course not to say that Arwa's journey has a happy ending, or that it has ended at all. However, over the data collection period, my analysis has shown that Arwa's negotiation of an employable identity has evolved. She has developed appreciation of to the idea of an interactionally negotiated phenomenon, as she has encountered both challenges to it, and opportunities to successfully co-construct it in interaction with me and in her narrated storyworlds.

This longitudinal exploration of Arwa's identity work has shown that developing a locally-valuable employable identity and moving inward from society's peripheries to its centre and a sense of belonging or inclusion, can be a long and arduous journey (cf. Lave & Wenger, 1991; Norton, 2001). Furthermore, this journey is commonly not a linear one but cyclical. Any 'progress' towards successful negotiation of an employable identity in one arena may be set back by unexpected obstacles in the form of lengthy, unsuccessful job searches, encountering unfamiliar communities of practice, and undesirable positioning by others.

Research question 3

How does a participant negotiate an employable identity in a specific workplace context?

Analysis of data collected in Nina's workplace further highlighted the co-construction of belonging (Greenbank & Marra, 2020; Holmes, 2018), and the extent to which successfully negotiating an employable identity in the workplace requires dynamic navigation of norms and Discourses. Evident in the data are the ways that Nina's former refugee status, her status as a non-native speaker of English and relative newcomer lead to her being othered by Pinewood residents Ava and Charlie, albeit seemingly benevolently intentioned. Nina's skilful relational work and pragmatic dexterity allowed her to variously resist or deflect such othering, all the while forging developing interpersonal relationships and maintaining an orientation to her professional, employable identity.

She frequently told stories which mirrored the narratives that the residents told her, projecting interactional equality and cultivating warm relationships with them. She also engaged in small talk with the residents in a manner that allowed them to take up empowered discursive positions, such as when she discussed a local politician's visit (Excerpts 9.4, 9.5, 9.6). Throughout these interactions Nina made claims to belonging, both unprompted, and in response to othered positioning from the residents. However, she did not insist upon the uptake of her claims to belonging, thus maintaining an amiable atmosphere for residents to take up knowledgeable and agentive positions, contributing to an employable identity appropriate for her role (Marsden & Holmes, 2014). That is, the discursive positions available for Nina to take up may have been constrained by her role as carer (Holmes & Schnurr, 2017).

Nina skilfully and graciously navigated Discourses of Refugeehood that the residents sometimes oriented towards, taking up alternate positions or changing the subject, all the while maintaining a professional identity. Further, Nina and the residents together navigated potentially overlapping Discourses that suggested vulnerability – Discourses of Refugeehood and of Aging; evidence of the complexity of power relations in a given context and the ways in which power can be drawn from many sources (cf. Lammers, 2007).

In analysis of Nina's workplace data, it became clear that former refugees continue to encounter benevolently-enacted yet disempowering Discourses of Refugeehood once employed, not just in the search for suitable employment. Nina's skilful negotiation of an employable identity contextually appropriate for her role as a carer involves various challenges to her identity as a member of the imagined community of New Zealanders. However, her extensive pragmatic skills and agentive navigation of Discourse and self- and other-positioning allows her to co-construct, conjointly with the residents she cares for, a validated employable identity.

Contributions

In the previous chapter I outlined the theoretical contributions that this study has made: an exploration of some of the structural barriers (however benevolently enacted) that former refugees encounter in their attempts to enact employable identities, the ideological implications of these, and the limited potential of former refugees' agentive behaviour and discursive manoeuvring in light of the negotiated nature of belonging in general, and locally-valuable employable identities in particular. In addition to these, I now outline the methodological, analytical, and sociological contributions that this study makes.

Methodological contributions

As discussed throughout this book and particularly in Chapter 8, the journey towards the successful enactment of a locally-valuable employable identity can be a long, unsteady and challenging one. For this reason, the longitudinal approach that I took to collecting interview data, particularly in Arwa's case, provided invaluable insight into the obstacles Arwa encountered, as well as displaying development in her understanding of and engagement with what it means to be employable in the local context.

The first time I met Arwa she was sure of her own value in the labour market based on her institutional cultural capital. A year later, having secured a temporary research position she was enthusiastic about her imagined future, her confidence boosted by long-awaited validation of her qualifications. Four months after that, when the job did not lead on to further, better employment, Arwa dismissed her PhD as having been a waste of time, lamenting her inability to prove herself. Still later Arwa's narratives involve stories of discursive negotiation and plans to work towards some New Zealand-earnt institutional capital.

Conversational interviews with Arwa over this twenty-month period provided fuller, richer data than any one-off interview could provide, allowing analysis of her development of an employable identity over time (cf. Kraus, 2000; Morita, 2004; Ortega & Iberri-Shea, 2005). Furthermore, the relationship that we built meant that Arwa became willing to share things with me that she had earlier held back, trusting me to judge how to use the data, and occasionally explicitly telling me to exclude certain topics (cf. McKay & Snyder, 2009). Thus, Arwa's data shows the greater depth of insight that can be achieved through a longitudinal approach to narrative identity.

A further methodological contribution this study provides is insight into the challenges involved with attempting to access workplaces for data collection, especially in the context of former refugee employees. Arwa and Kelly were largely unemployed for the duration of this study, taking on only short-term volunteer and entry-level positions. Both Isaac and Omar changed roles during the duration of the study. The temporary and changeable nature of their employment – sadly fairly typical of former refugee experiences (ChangeMakers Refugee Forum, 2012; Feeney, 2000) – meant that accessing workplace data with the four initial participants proved impossible.

Former refugees, as discussed throughout this study, are overrepresented in unemployment and underemployment (ChangeMakers Refugee Forum, 2012; Searle, Prouse, L'Ami, Gray, & Gruner, 2012), and thus these challenges may be common to research in former refugee contexts. I also speculate that employers of former refugees, especially those who are new to the workplace and/or in low-status positions, may be wary of engaging with researchers who are unknown to them, perhaps concerned that their work practices may be under particular scrutiny in the context of research with the marginalised (cf. Tilbury & Colic-Peisker, 2006). Thus, in highlighting methodological challenges to accessing workplace data with former refugee participants, this study provides a methodological backdrop for further research in this area.

Analytical contributions

In exploring the participants' experiences though the analytical lens of an employable identity emergent from and co-constructed within interaction, I have brought further attention to the negotiated nature of employability and of belonging more generally (following Holmes & Marra, 2005; Reissner-Roubicek, 2017; van de Mieroop & Schnurr, 2017 and others). Further, exploring the enactment of employable identities in the analysis of narratives has provided rich, emic, longitudinal analysis, allowing for deep exploration of the identity struggles that former refugees encounter in their trajectories towards full involvement in their new contexts.

Furthermore, in applying Bamberg's (2011a, 2011b) agency dilemma to analysis of former refugees' narratives, this study has emphasised the dynamic ways that these newcomers must negotiate world-to-self and self-to-world positioning in order to navigate wider social Discourses surrounding refugeehood. Additionally, I have highlighted the ways that these Discourses permeate discourse in both research interviews and naturalistic workplace data – as complementary data sets, not auxiliary to one another. Doing so has shed light on the prevalence of these Discourses and the ways in which they can limit discursive positions available to former refugees.

Wider societal contributions

This research has contributed to a wider discussion of the challenges involved with successful, ongoing (former) refugee resettlement. Exploration of the Discourses surrounding former refugees and refugeehood generally is illuminating, in that the ways that former refugees are talked about – and to – matters. The Christchurch mosque shootings of March 2019 made this appallingly clear. The xenophobic, isolationist, and white supremacist rhetoric which has been gaining traction around the world this century, from online fora to the speech of some of the world's most prominent leaders and politicians, has resulted in horrific, real-world violence and death. The outpouring of national grief that emerged in New Zealand as a result of the Christchurch massacre, moving to witness, has of course not resolved the underlying ideologies that led to it happening in the first place. As Prime Minister Jacinda Ardern said in a speech given at a memorial service two weeks after the attack, confronting what had happened "… comes [with] a responsibility. A responsibility to be the place that we wish to be. A place that is diverse, that is welcoming, that is kind and compassionate" (The Guardian, 2019). While demonstrably present in New Zealand society, the kinds of Discourses that other newcomers in malevolent, threatening ways happily did not in fact emerge out of this study's data. Nonetheless, the benevolently-rooted Spectacle of Refugeehood, for all its utility in drawing much-needed attention to the plight of forced migrants and engendering empathy and tolerance (Schwöbel-Patel, 2016), also deserves problematisation in light of its disempowering and hindering real-world effects on former refugees in their attempts to negotiate belonging in their new homes.

Further, this study has drawn attention to the wasted potential of first generation forced migrants for their host nations. Countries such as New Zealand claim skill shortages in various areas (Immigration New Zealand, 2018c), and yet there are qualified doctors and engineers and computer scientists and so forth here in New Zealand, fully qualified and available to work, unemployed and underemployed (Jansen & Grant, 2015; Statistics New Zealand, 2004). This, for New Zealand, is a wasted generation of newcomers, including their skills and talents and contributions. I hope that my discussions of challenges involved with the translation of social and cultural capital in new social contexts contributes to a wider discussion of the long-term challenges of refugee resettlement.

However, equally important, to the economic argument of wasted potential, in my eyes, is the contribution this study makes to examining the personal effects of employable identity struggles for former refugees. This study's participants have taken courageous action to escape untenable conditions and improve their – and their families' – welfare, brought their considerable institutional and cultural capital to New Zealand, and embarked on long journeys to rebuild their lives. The ongoing obstacles and challenges they encounter, from clear instantiations of rejection or discrimination, to micro level marginalisation in the navigation of disempowering Discourses, cannot but impact upon their senses of self, resilience in the labour market and society generally, and their dignity. While only a limited data set, this study's examination of five former refugees' identity struggles has offered demonstrable evidence of the personal effects of continual marginalisation. This has the potential to serve as a starting point for continuing research.

Future research

I see future research stemming from this study taking three directions. The first of these would be an expansion of the authentic workplace interaction phase of this research, as well as further longitudinal explorations of employable identities over time. Thus, a longitudinal study of the detail involved in Arwa's interview case study, for example, following a participant (or participants) from unemployment to employment and collecting authentic workplace data, could provide extra insight into of the development of employable identities in the workplace, and the situational context impacting upon these. Furthermore, collecting data with employers themselves could provide further insight into the co-construction of employable identities, and the ways in which employers' and former refugee employees' interpretations and understandings of interactions align or differ.

Secondly, it would be valuable to explore the effects that gender has upon resettlement experiences and upon the development of employable identities. The intersection of gender and refugeehood as it pertains to employability has been explored in various studies (e.g. Bloch, 2007b; Hunt, 2008; Koyama, 2014; McSpadden & Moussa, 1993; M. Tomlinson, 2010). However, examining this facet of resettlement could benefit from being approached through the lens of employable identity navigation. I noted that of my four participants in the interview phase of this study, the two men ended up in full time work (although only one of these was satisfied with his position), and the two women remained unemployed throughout most of the study's duration. The number of participants in this study is too small to make any kind of inference from this observation, but nonetheless this intersectional aspect of resettlement, employment opportunities and outcomes, and the negotiation of employable identities deserves further attention.

Lastly, I believe that to take practical steps towards improving resettlement outcome for former refugees generally, and employability issues specifically, a broad range of research perspectives is necessary. For this reason, following in the footsteps of New Zealand's Migration Research Network (Migration Research Network, 2018), I would like to see the coming together of specifically refugee-related research in a given context, here Aotearoa/New Zealand, from diverse disciplines such as (human) geography, international relations, gender studies, psychology, and beyond, in addition to (socio)linguistics. A collaborative project of this kind would be valuable in exploring what kind of richer, fuller picture of former refugee resettlement outcomes could come out of it.

Concluding remarks

In 2018, around 44,400 people were forcibly displaced from their homes each day, contributing to a global total of 65.5 million displaced persons, 25.4 million of whom are UN mandated refugees (UNHCR, 2018). With these numbers unlikely to abate over the coming century as the effects of climate change and other impetus exacerbate inequality and political instability, research contributing to resettlement outcomes that are effective and satisfactory to both newcomers and host societies is more important than ever. Successful resettlement, in whatever way that is interpreted by a given individual, can entail a long and formidable journey from the peripheries of society towards a true sense of belonging and acceptance. This journey may be beset with challenges to former refugees' sense of their own (social) worth, and to their dignity.

Undertaking this research with Arwa, Isaac, Kelly, Nina, and Omar has challenged my own ideas of refugeehood and illustrated the many, variable, frequent, and out-of-site challenges that former refugees can encounter, not only in the development of locally-valuable employable identities, but in their lives in New Zealand generally. I hope that my work contributes towards a wider discussion of improving resettlement outcomes, particularly the ways in which former refugees can be allowed to get on with living normal lives, after navigating their way out of extraordinary circumstances.

References

Ahearn, L. M. (2001). Language and agency. *Annual Review of Anthropology*, 30, 109–137. https://doi.org/10.1146/annurev.anthro.30.1.109

Ahearn, L. M. (2010). Agency and language. In J. Jürgen, J.-O. Östman, & J. Verschueren (Eds.), *Society and language use* (pp. 28–48). Amsterdam: John Benjamins. https://doi.org/10.1075/hoph.7.03ahe

Aijrner, K. (1984). 'Sort of' and 'kind of' in English conversation. *Studia Linguistica*, 38(2), 118–128. https://doi.org/10.1111/j.1467-9582.1984.tb00738.x

Al Zidjaly, N. (2009). Agency as an interactive achievement. *Language in Society*, 38(2), 177–200. https://doi.org/10.1017/S0047404509090320

Allen, K. (2015). Self-appreciation and the value of employability: integrating un(der) employed immigrants in post-Fordist Canada. In *The post-Fordist sexual contract: working and living in contingency* (pp. 49–69). New York: Palgrave Macmillan.

Allen, R. (2009). Benefit or burden? Social capital, gender, and the economic adaptation of refugees. *The International Migration Review*, 43(2), 332–365. https://doi.org/10.1111/j.1747-7379.2009.00767.x

Anderson, B. (1991). *Imagined communities: Reflections on the origin and spread of nationalism (Revised)*. London: Verso.

Anderson, G. (2000). The role of the pragmatic marker *like* in utterance interpretation. In G. Anderson & T. Fretheim (Eds.), *Pragmatic markers and propositional attitude* (pp. 17–38). Amsterdam: John Benjamins. https://doi.org/10.1075/pbns.79.02and

Angouri, J., Marra, M., & Holmes, J. (2017). Introduction: Negotiating boundaries at work. In *Negotiating boundaries at work: talking and transitions* (pp. 1–8). Edinburgh: Edinburgh University Press.

Araeen, R. (2000). The art of benevolent racism. *Third Text*, 51, 57–64. https://doi.org/10.1080/09528820008576853

Archer, L., Hollingworth, S., Maylor, U., Sheibani, A., & Kowarzik, U. (2005). *Challenging barriers to employment for refugees and asylum seekers in London*. Guildford: The SEQUAL Development Partnership.

Attanucci, J. S. (1993). Timely characterization of mother-daughter and family-school relations: Narrative understandings of adolescence. *Journal of Narrative and Life History*, 3(1), 99–116. https://doi.org/10.1075/jnlh.3.1.04tim

Augoustinos, M., Tuffin, K., & Every, D. (2005). New racism, meritocracy and individualism: constraining affirmative action in education. *Discourse & Society*, 16(3), 315–340. https://doi.org/10.1177/0957926505051168

Austin, J. L. (1975). *How to do things with words*. Oxford: Oxford University Press. https://doi.org/10.1093/acprof:oso/9780198245537.001.0001

Backhaus, P. (2009). Politeness in institutional elderly care in Japan: a cross-cultural comparison. *Journal of Politeness Research: Language, Behaviour, Culture*, 5(1), 53–71. https://doi.org/10.1515/JPLR.2009.004

Baker, P., Gabrielatos, C., Khosravinik, M., Krzyzanowski, M., McEnery, T., & Wodak, R. (2008). A useful methodological synergy? Combining critical discourse analysis and corpus linguistics to examine discourses of refugees and asylum seekers in the UK press. *Discourse & Society*, 19(3), 273–306. https://doi.org/10.1177/0957926508088962

Baker, P., & McEnery, T. (2005). A corpus-based approach to discourses of refugees and asylum seekers in UN and newspaper texts. *Journal of Language and Politics*, 4(2), 197–226. https://doi.org/10.1075/jlp.4.2.04bak

Bakhtin, M. (1981). *The dialogic imagination: Four essays*. Austin: University of Texas Press.

Bakhtin, M. (1984). *Problems of Dostoevsky's poetics*. Minneapolis: University of Minnesota Press. https://doi.org/10.5749/j.ctt22727z1

Bakhtin, M. (1990). *Art and answerability: Early philosophical essays*. Austin: University of Texas.

Balsis, S., & Carpenter, B. D. (2006). Evaluations of elderspeak in a caregiving context. *Clinical Gerontologist*, 29(1), 79–96. https://doi.org/10.1300/J018v29n01_07

Bamberg, M. (1997a). Emotion talk(s). The role of perspective in the construction of emotions. In S. Niemeier & R. Dirven (Eds.), *The language of emotions* (pp. 209–225). Amsterdam: John Benjamins. https://doi.org/10.1075/z.85.15bam

Bamberg, M. (1997b). Positioning between structure and performance. *Journal of Narrative and Life History*, 7(1–4), 335–342. https://doi.org/10.1075/jnlh.7.42pos

Bamberg, M. (2003). Positioning with Davie Hogan: Stories, tellings, and identities. In C. Daiute & C. Lightfoot (Eds.), *Narrative analysis: Studying the development of individuals in society* (pp. 135–157). London: Sage.

Bamberg, M. (2004a). Considering counter narratives. In M. Bamberg & M. Andrews (Eds.), *Considering counter-narratives: Narrating, resisting, making sense* (pp. 351–371). Amsterdam: John Benjamins. https://doi.org/10.1075/sin.4.43bam

Bamberg, M. (2004b). Narrative discourse and identities. In J. C. Meister, T. Kindt, W. Schernus, & M. Stein (Eds.), *Narratology beyond literary criticism* (pp. 213–237). Berlin: Walter de Gruyter.

Bamberg, M. (2004c). Talk, small stories, and adolescent identities. *Human Development*, 47(6), 366–369. https://doi.org/10.1159/000081039

Bamberg, M. (2005). Master narratives. In D. Herman, M. Jahn, & M. L. Ryan (Eds.), *The Routledge encyclopedia of narrative theory* (pp. 287–288). New York: Routledge.

Bamberg, M. (2006). Biographic-narrative research, quo vadis? A critical review of 'big stories' from the perspective of 'small stories.' *Narrative, Memory, and Knowledge: Representations, Aesthetics, and Contexts*, 63–79.

Bamberg, M. (2009). Identity and narration. In P. Hühn, W. Schmid, J. Schönert, & J. Pier (Eds.), *Handbook of narratology* (pp. 132–143). New York: Walter de Gruyter.

Bamberg, M. (2011a). Narrative practice and identity navigation. In J. A. Holstein & J. F. Gubrium (Eds.), *Varieties of narrative analysis* (pp. 99–124). Thousand Oaks: Sage.

Bamberg, M. (2011b). Who am I? Narration and its contribution to self and identity. *Theory & Psychology*, 21(1), 3–24. https://doi.org/10.1177/0959354309355852

Bamberg, M. (2017, July). *Narrative practices: Contextualizing a sense of who we are (identities)*. Conference Workshop presented at the New Zealand Discourse Conference, Auckland University of Technology.

Bamberg, M., De Fina, A., & Schiffrin, D. (2007). Introduction to the Volume. In M. Bamberg, A. De Fina, & D. Schiffrin (Eds.), *Selves and identities in narrative and discourse* (pp. 1–8). Amsterdam: John Benjamins. https://doi.org/10.1075/sin.9.02bam

Bamberg, M., Fina, A. D., & Schiffrin, D. (2011). Discourse and identity construction. In S. J. Schwartz, K. Luyckz, & V. L. Vignoles (Eds.), *Handbook of identity theory and research* (pp. 177–199). New York: Springer. https://doi.org/10.1007/978-1-4419-7988-9_8

Bamberg, M., & Georgakopoulou, A. (2008). Small stories as a new perspective in narrative and identity analysis. *Text & Talk-An Interdisciplinary Journal of Language, Discourse Communication Studies*, 28(3), 377–396.

Bangerter, A., Mayor, E., & Doehler, S. P. (2011). Reported speech in conversational storytelling during nursing shift handover meetings. *Discourse Processes*, 48(3), 183–214. https://doi.org/10.1080/0163853X.2010.519765

Baran, D. M. (2018). Narratives of migration on Facebook: Belonging and identity among former fellow refugees. *Language in Society*, 47(2), 245–268. https://doi.org/10.1017/S0047404518000027

Barker, C. (2008). *Cultural studies*. London: Sage.

Barker, M. (1981). *The new racism: Conservatives and the ideology of the tribes*. London: Junction Books.

Barreto, M., & Ellemers, N. (2005). The burden of benevolent sexism: How it contributes to the maintenance of gender inequalities. *European Journal of Social Psychology*, 35, 633–642. https://doi.org/10.1002/ejsp.270

Bauder, H. (2008). Citizenship as capital: The distinction of migrant labor. *Alternatives*, 33(3), 315–333. https://doi.org/10.1177/030437540803300303

Baumgarten, N., & House, J. (2010). *I think* and *I don't know* in English as lingua franca and native English discourse. *Journal of Pragmatics*, 42, 1184–1200. https://doi.org/10.1016/j.pragma.2009.09.018

Baxter, J. (2008). Is it all tough talking at the top?: A feminist post-structuralist analysis of the construction of gendered speaker identities of British business leaders within interview narratives. *Gender & Language*, 2(2), 197–222. https://doi.org/10.1558/genl.v2i2.197

BBC News Service. (2015, December 22). Lebanon: One in four a refugee. Retrieved August 25, 2016, from https://www.bbc.com/news/av/world-middle-east-35163273/lebanon-one-in-four-a-refugee

BBC News Service. (2016, March 4). Migrant crisis: Migration to Europe explained in seven charts. Retrieved August 2, 2016, from http://www.bbc.com/news/world-europe-34131911

Beck, E., Williams, I., Hope, L., & Park, W. (2001). An intersectional model: Exploring gender with ethnic and cultural diversity. *Journal of Ethnic & Cultural Diversity in Social Work*, 10(4), 63–80. https://doi.org/10.1300/J051v10n04_04

Bell, D. (1998). Cancellative discourse markers: A core/periphery approach. *Pragmatics*, 8, 515–541. https://doi.org/10.1075/prag.8.4.03bel

Benwell, B., & Stokoe, E. (2006). *Discourse and identity*. Edinburgh: Edinburgh University Press.

Berg, L., & Millbank, J. (2009). Constructing the personal narratives of lesbian, gay and bisexual asylum claimants. *Journal of Refugee Studies*, 22(2), 195–223. https://doi.org/10.1093/jrs/fep010

Berger, P. L., & Luckmann, T. (1967). *The social construction of reality*. London: Allen Lane.

Berger, R. J., & Quinney, R. (2005). The narrative turn in social inquiry. In *Storytelling sociology* (pp. 1–11). Boulder: Lynne Rienner Publishers.

Bhopal, K. (2010). Gender, identity and experience: Researching marginalised groups. *Women's Studies International Forum*, 33(3), 188–195. https://doi.org/10.1016/j.wsif.2009.12.005

Billig, M. (2005). *Laughter and ridicule*. London: Sage Publications.

Binghalib, Y. (2011). Family dynamics between Arab Muslim parents, Western parents and their bi-ethnic children (Master's Dissertation). California State University, Sacramento.

Blackledge, A., & Pavlenko, A. (2001). Negotiation of identities in multilingual contexts. *International Journal of Bilingualism*, 5(3), 243–257. https://doi.org/10.1177/13670069010050030101

Blakemore, D. (1988). "So" as a constraint on relevance. In R. M. Kempson (Ed.), *Mental representations: The interface between language and reality* (pp. 183–195). New York: Cambridge University Press.

Bloch, A. (2000). Refugee settlement in Britain: The impact of policy on participation. *Journal of Ethnic and Migration Studies*, 26(1), 75–88. https://doi.org/10.1080/136918300115651

Bloch, A. (2007a). Methodological challenges for national and multi-sited comparative survey research. *Journal of Refugee Studies*, 20(2), 230–247. https://doi.org/10.1093/jrs/fem002

Bloch, A. (2007b). Refugees in the UK labour market: The conflict between economic integration and policy-led labour market restriction. *Journal of Social Policy*, 37(1), 21–36.

Block, D. (2006). Identity in applied linguistics. In T. Omoniyi & G. White (Eds.), *The sociolinguistics of identity* (pp. 34–49). London: Continuum.

Block, D. (2010). Problems portraying migrants in applied linguistics research. *Language Teaching*, 43(4), 480–493. https://doi.org/10.1017/S0261444809990280

Block, D. (2013). Issues in language and identity research in applied linguistics. *ELIA; Sevilla*, (13), 11–46.

Block, K., Warr, D., Gibbs, L., & Riggs, E. (2012). Addressing ethical and methodological challenges in research with refugee-background young people: Reflections from the field. *Journal of Refugee Studies*, 69–87.

Blommaert, J., & Bulcaen, C. (2000). Critical discourse analysis. *Annual Review of Anthropology*, 29, 447–466. https://doi.org/10.1146/annurev.anthro.29.1.447

Boden, R., & Nedeva, M. (2010). Employing discourse: universities and graduate 'employability.' *Journal of Education Policy*, 25(1), 37–54. https://doi.org/10.1080/02680930903349489

Bolden, G. B. (2006). Little words that matter: Discourse markers "So" and "Oh" and the doing of other-attentiveness in social interaction. *Journal of Communication*, 56(4), 661–688. https://doi.org/10.1111/j.1460-2466.2006.00314.x

Bolden, G. B. (2009). Implementing incipient actions: The discourse marker 'so' in English conversation. *Journal of Pragmatics*, 41(5), 974–998. https://doi.org/10.1016/j.pragma.2008.10.004

Bourdieu, P. (1977a). Cultural reproduction and social reproduction. In J. Karabel & A. H. Halsey (Eds.), *Power and ideology in education* (pp. 487–511). New York: Oxford University Press.

Bourdieu, P. (1977b). *Outline of a theory of practice*. Cambridge: Cambridge University Press. https://doi.org/10.1017/CBO9780511812507

Bourdieu, P. (1977c). The economics of linguistic exchanges. *Social Science Information*, 16(6), 645–668. https://doi.org/10.1177/053901847701600601

Bourdieu, P. (1986). The forms of capital. In J. G. Richardson (Ed.), *Handbook of theory and research for the sociology of education* (pp. 241–258). New York: Greenwood.

Bourdieu, P. (1991). *Language and symbolic power*. (J. B. Thompson, Ed., G. Raymond & M. Adamson, Trans.). Cambridge: Polity Press.

Bourdieu, P., & Passeron, J.-C. (1979). *The inheritors: French students and their relations to culture*. Chicago: Chicago University Press.

Bourdieu, P., & Wacquant, L. J. D. (1992). *An invitation to reflexive sociology*. Chicago: University of Chicago Press.

Bradshaw, J. (2013). The ecology of minority languages in Melbourne. *International Journal of Multilingualism*, 10(4), 469–481. https://doi.org/10.1080/14790718.2013.832358

Bridgstock, R. (2005). Australian artists, starving and wellnourished: What can we learn from the prototypical protean career? *Australian Journal of Career Development*, 14(3), 40–48. https://doi.org/10.1177/103841620501400307

Bridgstock, R. (2009). The graduate attributes we've overlooked: enhancing graduate employability through career management skills. *Higher Education Research & Development*, 28(1), 31–44. https://doi.org/10.1080/07294360802444347

Brinkman, S., & Kvale, S. (2005). Confronting the ethics of qualitative research. *Journal of Constructivist Psychology*, 18(2), 157–181. https://doi.org/10.1080/10720530590914789

Britain, D. (1992). Linguistic change in intonation: The use of high rising terminals in New Zealand English. *Language Variation and Change*, 4(1), 77–104. https://doi.org/10.1017/S0954394500000661

Brown, P., & Hesketh, A. (2004). *Mismanagement of talent: Employability and jobs in the knowledge economy*. Oxford: Oxford University Press. https://doi.org/10.1093/acprof:oso/9780199269532.001.0001

Brown, P., Power, S., Tholen, G., & Allouch, A. (2016). Credentials, talent and cultural capital: a comparative study of educational elites in England and France. *British Journal of Sociology of Education*, 37(2), 191–211. https://doi.org/10.1080/01425692.2014.920247

Bucholtz, M. (1999). You da man: Narrating the racial Other in the linguistic production of white masculinity. *Journal of Sociolinguistics*, 3(4), 443–460. https://doi.org/10.1111/1467-9481.00090

Bucholtz, M., & Hall, K. (2005). Identity and interaction: a sociocultural linguistic approach. *Discourse Studies*, 7(4–5), 585–614. https://doi.org/10.1177/1461445605054407

Bull, T. (2013). Linguistic emancipation and the linguistic market place. *Sociolinguistic Studies; Galicia*, 7(1/2), 33–55. https://doi.org/10.1558/sols.v7i1-2.33

Burr, V. (2003). *Social constructionism* (2nd ed.). New York: Routledge.

Butcher, A., Spoonley, P., & Trlin, A. (2006). *Being accepted: The experience of discrimination and social exclusion by immigrants and refugees in New Zealand*. Auckland: New Settlers Programme, Massey University.

Cameron, D. (2009). Theoretical issues for the study of gender and spoken interaction. In P. Pichler & E. M. Eppler (Eds.), *Gender and spoken interaction* (pp. 1–17). London: Palgrave Macmillan. https://doi.org/10.1057/9780230280748_1

Canongate. (2018). The ungrateful refugee by Dina Nayeri, coming 2019. Retrieved October 7, 2018, from https://canongate.co.uk/news/the-ungrateful-refugee-by-dina-nayeri-coming-out-spring-2019/

Caporael, L. R. (1981). The paralanguage of caregiving: baby talk to the institutionalized aged. *Journal of Personality and Social Psychology*, 40(5), 876–884. https://doi.org/10.1037/0022-3514.40.5.876

Carspecken, P. F. (1996). *Critical ethnography in educational research*. New York: Routledge.

Carter, P. L. (2003). "Black" cultural capital, status positioning, and schooling conflicts for low-income African American youth. *Social Problems*, 50(1), 136–155. https://doi.org/10.1525/sp.2003.50.1.136

Carter, R., & McCarthy, M. (1997). *Exploring spoken English*. Cambridge: Cambridge University Press.

CBC Radio. (2017, May 4). Expecting gratitude from refugees can be toxic, says author. Retrieved from https://www.cbc.ca/radio/thecurrent/the-current-for-may-3-2017-1.4095703/expecting-gratitude-from-refugees-can-be-toxic-says-author-1.4095737

Cemalcilar, Z., & Gökşen, F. (2014). Inequality in social capital: Social capital, social risk and drop-out in the Turkish education system. *British Journal of Sociology of Education*, 35(1), 94–114. https://doi.org/10.1080/01425692.2012.740807

Chafe, W. (2003). Laughing while talking. In D. Tannen & J. E. Alatis (Eds.), *Linguistics, language, and the real world: Discourse and beyond (Georgetown University Round Table on Languages and Linguistics)* (pp. 36–49). Washington: Georgetown University Press.

Chan, S. (2006). *The Vietnamese American 1.5 generation: Stories of war, revolution, flight, and new beginnings*. Philadelphia: Temple University Press.

ChangeMakers Refugee Forum. (2012). *'People with refugee backgrounds can do the job.': Refugee-background experiences of employment in Wellington*. Wellington: ChangeMakers Refugee Forum.

Chavez, L. R. (1991). Outside the imagined community: Undocumented settlers and experiences of incorporation. *American Ethnologist*, 18(2), 257–278. https://doi.org/10.1525/ae.1991.18.2.02a00040

Christie, N. (1986). The ideal victim. In E. A. Fattah (Ed.), *From crime policy to victim policy* (pp. 17–30). Basingstoke: Macmillan. https://doi.org/10.1007/978-1-349-08305-3_2

Clifton, J., & van de Mieroop, D. (2016). *Master narratives, identities and the stories of former slaves*. Amsterdam: John Benjamins. https://doi.org/10.1075/sin.22

Coalter, F. (2007). Sports clubs, social capital and social regeneration: 'Ill-defined interventions with hard to follow outcomes'? *Sport in Society*, 10(4), 537–559. https://doi.org/10.1080/17430430701388723

Colburn, S. (2015). Filming concerts for youtube: Seeking recognition in the pursuit of cultural capital. *Popular Music and Society*, 38(1), 59–72. https://doi.org/10.1080/03007766.2014.974373

Colic-Peisker, V. (2005). 'At least you're the right colour': Identity and social inclusion of Bosnian refugees in Australia. *Journal of Ethnic and Migration Studies*, 31(4), 615–638. https://doi.org/10.1080/13691830500109720

Colic-Peisker, V. (2009). Visibility, settlement success and life satisfaction in three refugee communities in Australia. *Ethnicities*, 9(2), 175–199. https://doi.org/10.1177/1468796809103459

Colic-Peisker, V., & Tilbury, F. (2007). *Refugees and employment: The effect of visible difference on discrimination*. Perth: Murdoch University.

Colic-Peisker, V., & Walker, I. (2003). Human capital, acculturation and social identity: Bosnian refugees in Australia. *Journal of Community & Applied Social Psychology*, 13(5), 337–360. https://doi.org/10.1002/casp.743

Collie, P., Kindon, S., Liu, J. H., & Podsiadlowski, A. (2010). Mindful identity negotiations: The acculturation of young Assyrian women in New Zealand. *International Journal of Intercultural Relations*, 34, 208–220. https://doi.org/10.1016/j.ijintrel.2009.08.002

Collins, S. (2016, January 30). Extra intake of Syrians grateful for NZ asylum. *The Northern Advocate*.

Connell, R. W. (1987). *Gender and power*. Palo Alto: Stanford University Press.

Connolly, P., & Healy, J. (2004). Symbolic violence, locality and social class: The educational and career aspirations of 10–11-year-old boys in Belfast. *Pedagogy, Culture & Society*, 12(1), 15–33. https://doi.org/10.1080/14681360400200187

Controller and Auditor General. (2018). Citizenship and permanent residency. Retrieved July 24, 2018, from https://www.oag.govt.nz/2013/citizenship/part3.htm

Corr, C. A., Doka, K. J., & Kastenbaum, R. (1999). Dying and its interpreters: A review of selected literature and some comments on the state of the field. *Omega: The Journal of Death and Dying*, 39(4), 239–259.

Correa-Velez, I., Gifford, S. M., & Barnett, A. G. (2010). Longing to belong: Social inclusion and wellbeing among youth with refugee backgrounds in the first three years in Melbourne, Australia. *Social Science & Medicine*, 71(8), 1399–1408. https://doi.org/10.1016/j.socscimed.2010.07.018

Corwin, A. I. (2017). Overcoming elderspeak: A qualitative study of three alternatives. *The Gerontologist, Advance online publication*, 1–6.

Coupland, N. (1980). Style-shifting in a Cardiff work-setting. *Language in Society*, 9(1), 1–12. https://doi.org/10.1017/S0047404500007752

Coupland, N. (2010). "Other" representation. In J. Jaspers, J.-O. Östman, & J. Verschueren (Eds.), *Society and language use* (pp. 241–259). Amsterdam: John Benjamins. https://doi.org/10.1075/hoph.7.16cou

Coupland, N., & Coupland, J. (1999). Ageing, ageism, and anti-ageism: Moral stance in geriatric medical discourse. In H. E. Hamilton (Ed.), *Language and communication in old age: Multidisciplinary perspectives* (pp. 177–208). New York: Garland.

Coupland, N., Coupland, J., Giles, H., & Henwood, K. (1988). Accommodating the elderly: invoking and extending a theory. *Language in Society*, 17(1), 1–41. https://doi.org/10.1017/S0047404500012574

Crenshaw, K. (1989). Demarginalizing the intersection of race and sex: A black feminist critique of antidiscrimination doctrine, feminist theory, and antiracist politics. *University of Chicago Legal Forum*, 1989, 139–167.

Cronin, A., & King, A. (2014). Only connect? Older lesbian, gay and bisexual (LGB) adults and social capital. *Ageing & Society*, 34, 258–279. https://doi.org/10.1017/S0144686X12000955

Cunningham, J., & Williams, K. N. (2007). A case study of resistiveness to care and elderspeak. *Research and Theory for Nursing Practice; New York*, 21(1), 45–56. https://doi.org/10.1891/rtnpij-v21i1a006

Daly, N., Holmes, J., Newton, J., & Stubbe, M. (2004). Expletives as solidarity signals in FTAs on the factory floor. *Journal of Pragmatics*, 36, 945–964. https://doi.org/10.1016/j.pragma.2003.12.004

Darvin, R., & Norton, B. (2015). Identity and a model of investment in applied linguistics. *Annual Review of Applied Linguistics*, 35, 36–56. https://doi.org/10.1017/S0267190514000191

Davies, B. (1990). Agency as a form of discursive practice. A classroom scene observed. *British Journal of Sociology of Education*, 11(3), 341–361. https://doi.org/10.1080/0142569900110306

Davies, B., & Harré, R. (1990). Positioning: The discursive production of selves. *Journal for the Theory of Social Behavior*, 20(1), 43–63. https://doi.org/10.1111/j.1468-5914.1990.tb00174.x

Davis, K. (2008). Intersectionality as buzzword: A sociology of science perspective on what makes a feminist theory successful. *Feminist Theory*, 9(1), 67–85. https://doi.org/10.1177/1464700108086364

Dawson, S. (2019). Identities and ideologies in study abroad contexts: Negotiating nationality, gender, and sexuality (Doctoral Dissertation). Victoria University of Wellington, Wellington.

Dawson, S. (2017). An investigation into the identity/imagined community relationship: A case study of two language learners in New Zealand. *Language, Discourse & Society*, 1(9), 15–33.

De Clerck, B. (2004). On the pragmatic functions of *let's* utterances. In K. Aijmer & B. Altenberg (Eds.), *Advances in corpus linguistics* (pp. 213–233). Amsterdam: Rodopi.

De Fina, A. (2003). *Identity in narrative*. Amsterdam: John Benjamins. https://doi.org/10.1075/sin.3

De Fina, A. (2006). Group identity, narrative and self-representations. In A. De Fina, D. Schiffrin, & M. Bamberg (Eds.), *Discourse and identity* (pp. 351–375). Cambridge: Cambridge University Press. https://doi.org/10.1017/CBO9780511584459.018

De Fina, A. (2012). Discourse and identity. In *The encyclopedia of applied linguistics*. Blackwell. Retrieved from http://onlinelibrary.wiley.com/doi/abs/10.1002/9781405198431.wbeal0326. https://doi.org/10.1002/9781405198431.wbeal0326

De Fina, A., & Georgakopoulou, A. (2008). Analysing narratives as practices. *Qualitative Research*, 8(3), 379–387. https://doi.org/10.1177/1468794106093634

De Fina, A., Schiffrin, D., & Bamberg, M. (2006). Introduction. In A. De Fina, D. Schiffrin, & M. Bamberg (Eds.), *Discourse and identity* (pp. 1–23). Cambridge: Cambridge University Press. https://doi.org/10.1017/CBO9780511584459.002

De Graaf, N. D., De Graaf, P. M., & Kraaykamp, G. (2000). Parental cultural capital and educational attainment in the Netherlands: A refinement of the cultural capital perspective. *Sociology of Education*, 73(2), 92–111. https://doi.org/10.2307/2673239

De Rycker, T. (1990). Imperative subtypes in conversational British English: An empirical investigation (Doctoral Dissertation). University of Antwerp.

Del Casino, V. J. (2009). *Social geography: A critical introduction*. Chichester: John Wiley & Sons.

Derrida, J. (1972). *Positions*. Chicago: University of Chicago Press.

Doná, G. (2007). The microphysics of participation in refugee research. *Journal of Refugee Studies*, 20(2), 210–229. https://doi.org/10.1093/jrs/fem013

Dubois, B. L. (1989). Pseudoquotation in current English communication: "Hey, she didn't really say it." *Language in Society*, 18(3), 343–359. https://doi.org/10.1017/S0047404500013646

Duff, P. A. (2015). Transnationalism, multilingualism, and identity. *Annual Review of Applied Linguistics*, 35, 57–80. https://doi.org/10.1017/S026719051400018X

Duranti, A. (2004). Agency in language. In A. Duranti (Ed.), *A companion to linguistic anthropology* (pp. 451–473). Malden: Blackwell.

Eastmond, M. (1996). Luchar y sufrir – Stories of life and exile: Reflexions on the ethnographic process. *Ethnos*, 61(3–4), 231–250. https://doi.org/10.1080/00141844.1996.9981537

Eastmond, M. (2007). Stories as lived experience: Narratives in forced migration research. *Journal of Refugee Studies*, 20(2), 248–264. https://doi.org/10.1093/jrs/fem007

Edge, S., Newbold, K. B., & McKeary, M. (2014). Exploring socio-cultural factors that mediate, facilitate, & constrain the health and empowerment of refugee youth. *Social Science & Medicine*, 117, 34–41. https://doi.org/10.1016/j.socscimed.2014.07.025

Edley, N., & Litosseliti, L. (2010). Contemplating interviews and focus groups. In L. Litosseliti (Ed.), *Research methods in linguistics* (pp. 155–179). London: Continuum.

Ehrkamp, P. (2005). "We Turks are no Germans": Assimilation discourses and the dialectical construction of identities in Germany. *Environment and Planning A*, 38, 1673–1692. https://doi.org/10.1068/a38148

Ehrkamp, P., & Leitner, H. (2006). Rethinking immigration and citizenship: New spaces of migrant transnationalism. *Environment and Planning A*, 38, 1591–1597. https://doi.org/10.1068/a38349

Electoral Commission New Zealand. (2017). Candidate handbook: Ways to vote. Retrieved July 12, 2018, from https://www.elections.org.nz/candidate-handbook/part-6-ways-vote

Erman, B. (2001). Pragmatic markers revisited with a focus on you know in adult and adolescent talk. *Journal of Pragmatics*, 33, 1337–1359. https://doi.org/10.1016/S0378-2166(00)00066-7
Faist, T. (2018). The moral polity of forced migration. *Ethnic and Racial Studies*, 41(3), 412–423. https://doi.org/10.1080/01419870.2017.1324170
Feeney, A. (2000). Refugee employment. *Local Economy*, 15, 343–349. https://doi.org/10.1080/026909400750068086
Finlay, L. (2012). Five lenses for the reflexive interviewer. In J. F. Gubrium, J. A. Holstein, A. B. Marvasti, & K. D. McKinney (Eds.), *The Sage handbook of interview research* (2nd ed., pp. 317–331). Thousand Oaks: Sage Publications.
Foucault, M. (1977). *Discipline and punish: The birth of the prison*. New York: Pantheon.
Foucault, M. (1978). *The history of sexuality* (Vol. 1, 2). New York: Pantheon.
Fox Tree, J. E., & Schrock, J. C. (2002). Basic meanings of *you know* and *I mean*. *Journal of Pragmatics*, 34(6), 727–747. https://doi.org/10.1016/S0378-2166(02)00027-9
Frank, J. (1990). You call that a rhetorical question? Forms and functions of rhetorical questions in conversation. *Journal of Pragmatics*, 14, 723–738. https://doi.org/10.1016/0378-2166(90)90003-V
Franklin, K. J. (2009). Etic and emic stories. *Graduate Institute of Applied Linguistics (GIALens)*, 2, 1–11.
Freeman, J. (1989). *Hearts of sorrow: Vietnamese-American lives*. Stanford: Stanford University Press.
Fuller, C. (2014). Social capital and the role of trust in aspirations for higher education. *Educational Review*, 66(2), 131–147. https://doi.org/10.1080/00131911.2013.768956
Fuller, J. M. (2003). The influence of speaker roles on discourse marker use. *Journal of Pragmatics*, 35, 23–45. https://doi.org/10.1016/S0378-2166(02)00065-6
Gabrielatos, C., & Baker, P. (2008). Fleeing, sneaking, flooding – A corpus analysis of discursive constructions of refugees and asylum seekers in the UK press 1996–2005. *Journal of English Linguistics*, 36(1), 5–38. https://doi.org/10.1177/0075424207311247
Gans, H. J. (2009). First generation decline: Downward mobility among refugees and immigrants. *Ethnic and Racial Studies*, 32(9), 1658–1670. https://doi.org/10.1080/01419870903204625
Gee, J. P. (1990). *Social linguistics and literacies: Ideology in discourses*. London: Taylor & Francis.
Gee, J. P. (2015). Discourse, small d, big D. In *The international encyclopedia of language and social interaction* (pp. 1–5).
Georgakopoulou, A. (1995). Women, men, and conversational narrative performances: Aspects of gender in Greek storytelling. *Anthropological Linguistics*, 37(4), 460–486.
Georgakopoulou, A. (2006a). Small and large identities in narrative (inter)action. In A. De Fina, D. Schiffrin, & M. Bamberg (Eds.), *Discourse and identity* (pp. 83–102). Cambridge: Cambridge University Press. https://doi.org/10.1017/CBO9780511584459.005
Georgakopoulou, A. (2006b). Thinking big with small stories in narrative and identity analysis. *Narrative Inquiry*, 16(1), 122–130. https://doi.org/10.1075/ni.16.1.16geo
Giampapa, F. (2004). The politics of identity, representation, and the discourses of self-identification: Negotiating the periphery and the center. In A. Pavlenko & A. Blackledge (Eds.), *Negotiation of identities in multilingual contexts* (pp. 192–218). Clevedon: Multilingual Matters.
Gibbings, S. L. (2011). No angry women at the United Nations: Political dreams and the cultural politics of United Nations Security Council Resolution 1325. *International Feminist Journal of Politics*, 13(4), 522–538. https://doi.org/10.1080/14616742.2011.611660
Giddens, A. (1981). *A contemporary critique of historical materialism*. London: Macmillan. https://doi.org/10.1007/978-1-349-16638-1

Giddens, A. (1984). *The constitution of society: Outline of the theory of structuration*. Berkley: University of California Press.

Giles, H., Coupland, N., & Coupland, J. (1991). Accommodation theory: Communication, context, and consequence. In H. Giles, N. Coupland, & J. Coupland (Eds.), *Contexts of accommodation: Developments in applied sociolinguistics* (pp. 1–68). Cambridge: Cambridge University Press. https://doi.org/10.1017/CBO9780511663673.001

Giles-Mitson, A. (2016). Address terms in New Zealand English: Tracking changes to the social indexicality of gendered terms of address (Master's Dissertation). Victoria University of Wellington, Wellington.

Glover, T. D. (2004). Social capital in the lived experiences of community gardeners. *Leisure Sciences*, 26(2), 143–162. https://doi.org/10.1080/01490400490432064

Gobo, G. (2011). Ethnography. In D. Silverman (Ed.), *Qualitative research* (3rd ed., pp. 15–34). London: Sage Publications.

Goffman, E. (1967). On face work. In E. Goffman (Ed.), *Interaction ritual*. New York: Anchor Books.

Goffman, E. (1974). *Frame analysis*. New York: Harper & Row.

Goffman, E. (1981). *Forms of talk*. Philadelphia: University of Pennsylvania Press.

Goffman, E. (1989). The interaction order. *American Sociological Review*, 48, 1–17. https://doi.org/10.2307/2095141

Goodson, I. F., & Gill, S. R. (2011). The narrative turn in social research. *Counterpoints*, 386, 17–33.

Goodson, L. J., & Phillimore, J. (2008). Social capital and integration: The importance of social relationships and social space to refugee women. *International Journal of Diversity in Organisations, Communities & Nations*, 7(6), 181–193. https://doi.org/10.18848/1447-9532/CGP/v07i06/39510

Gottlieb, A. (2006). Ethnography: Theory and methods. In E. Perecman & S. R. Curran (Eds.), *A handbook for social science field research* (pp. 47–68). London: Sage.

Gracia, P. (2015). Parent–child leisure activities and cultural capital in the United Kingdom: The gendered effects of education and social class. *Social Science Research*, 52, 290–302. https://doi.org/10.1016/j.ssresearch.2015.02.005

Grainger, K. (1993). "That's a lovely bath dear": Reality construction in the discourse of elderly care. *Journal of Aging Studies*, 7(3), 247–262. https://doi.org/10.1016/0890-4065(93)90014-B

Gramsci, A. (1971). *Selections from the prison notebooks*. (Q. Hoare & G. Nowell-Smith, Eds. & Trans.). London: Lawrence and Wishart.

Greenbank, E. (2014). Othering and voice: How media framing denies refugees integration opportunities. *Communication Journal of New Zealand*, 14(1), 35–58.

Greenbank, E., & Marra, M. (2020). Addressing societal discourses: negotiating an employable identity as a former refugee. *Language and Intercultural Communication Special Issue on Translational Research: Language, Intercultural Communication and Social Action*, 20(2), 110–124.

Grimme, T. M., Buchanan, J., & Afflerbach, S. (2015). Understanding elderspeak from the perspective of certified nursing assistants. *Journal of Gerontological Nursing*, 41(11), 42–49. https://doi.org/10.3928/00989134-20151015-05

Guerin, P., Ho, E., & Bedford, R. (2004). Who are the most unemployed people in New Zealand and what can we do about it? Presented at the 11th Labour, Employment and Work Conference, Wellington.

Gumperz, J. J. (1981). Conversational inference and classroom learning. In J. Green & C. Wallat (Eds.), *Ethnography and language in educational settings* (pp. 3–23). Norwood: Ablex.

Gumperz, J. J. (1982). *Discourse strategies*. Cambridge: Cambridge University Press. https://doi.org/10.1017/CBO9780511611834

Gumperz, J. J. (2005). Interactional sociolinguistics: A personal perspective. In D. Schiffrin, D. Tannen, & H. E. Hamilton (Eds.), *The handbook of discourse analysis* (pp. 215–228). Malden: Blackwell Publishing Ltd.. https://doi.org/10.1002/9780470753460.ch12

Hall, S. (1997). The spectacle of the other. In S. Hall (Ed.), *Representations: Cultural representations and signifying practices* (pp. 223–290). London: Sage.

Hammack, P. L., Thompson, E. M., & Pilecki, A. (2009). Configurations of identity among sexual minority youth: Context, desire, and narrative. *Journal of Youth and Adolescence*, 38(7), 867–883. https://doi.org/10.1007/s10964-008-9342-3

Harrell-Bond, B. (1999). The experience of refugees as recipients of aid. In A. Ager (Ed.), *Refugees: Perspectives on the experience of forced migration*. New York: Continuum.

Hart, C. (2014). *Discourse, grammar and ideology: Functional and cognitive perspectives*. London: Bloomsbury Publishing.

Harwood, J. (2008). Age identity and communication. In W. Donsbach (Ed.), *The international encyclopedia of communication* (pp. 136–140). Malden: Wiley-Blackwell. https://doi.org/10.1002/9781405186407.wbieca034

Hatoss, A. (2012). Where are you from? Identity construction and experiences of 'othering' in the narratives of Sudanese refugee-background Australians. *Discourse & Society*, 23(1), 47–68. https://doi.org/10.1177/0957926511419925

Hatoss, A., & Sheely, T. (2009). Language maintenance and identity among Sudanese-Australian refugee-background youth. *Journal of Multilingual and Multicultural Development*, 30(2), 127–144. https://doi.org/10.1080/01434630802510113

Hay, J. (2008). The pragmatics of humor support. *International Journal of Humor Research*, 14(1), 55–82.

Haynes, K. (2006). Linking narrative and identity construction: using autobiography in accounting research. *Critical Perspectives on Accounting*, 17(4), 399–418. https://doi.org/10.1016/j.cpa.2004.08.005

Hek, R. (2005). The role of education in the settlement of young refugees in the UK: The experiences of young refugees. *Practice: Social Work in Action*, 17(3), 157–171. https://doi.org/10.1080/09503150500285115

Herman, R., & Williams, K. M. (2009). Elderspeak's influence on resistiveness to care: Focus on behavioral events. *American Journal of Alzheimer's Disease & Other Dementias*, 24(5), 417–423. https://doi.org/10.1177/1533317509341949

Hesmondhalgh, D. (2006). Bourdieu, the media and cultural production. *Media, Culture & Society*, 28(2), 211–231. https://doi.org/10.1177/0163443706061682

Hilgers, M., & Mangez, E. (2014). *Bourdieu's theory of social fields: Concepts and applications*. London: Routledge. https://doi.org/10.4324/9781315772493

Hinchliffe, G. W., & Jolly, A. (2011). Graduate identity and employability. *British Educational Research Journal*, 37(4), 563–584. https://doi.org/10.1080/01411926.2010.482200

Hinkel, E. (2003). Adverbial markers and tone in L1 and L2 students' writing. *Journal of Pragmatics*, 35, 1049–1068. https://doi.org/10.1016/S0378-2166(02)00133-9

Hodges, A. (2015). Intertextuality in discourse. In D. Tannen, H. E. Hamilton, & D. Schiffrin (Eds.), *The handbook of discourse analysis* (pp. 42–60). Oxford: Wiley-Blackwell.

Hoffman Clark, E. (2007). "I'm a product of everything I've been through": A narrative study of the cultural identity construction of Bosnian Muslim female refugee students (Doctoral Dissertation). Florida State University, Tallahassee.

Holmes, J. (1984). Modifying illocutionary force. *Journal of Pragmatics*, 8, 345–365. https://doi.org/10.1016/0378-2166(84)90028-6

Holmes, J. (2000). Politeness, power and provocation: How humour functions in the workplace. *Discourse Studies*, 2(2), 159–185. https://doi.org/10.1177/1461445600002002002

Holmes, J. (2005a). Story-telling at work: A complex discursive resource for integrating personal, professional and social identities. *Discourse Studies*, 7(6), 671–700. https://doi.org/10.1177/1461445605055422

Holmes, J. (2005b). When small talk is a big deal: Sociolinguistic challenges in the workplace. In M. H. Long (Ed.), *Second language needs analysis* (pp. 344–372). Cambridge: Cambridge University Press. https://doi.org/10.1017/CBO9780511667299.012

Holmes, J. (2006a). *Gendered talk at work*. Oxford: Blackwell. https://doi.org/10.1002/9780470754863

Holmes, J. (2006b). Workplace narratives, professional identity and relational practice. In A. De Fina, D. Schiffrin, & M. Bamberg (Eds.), *Discourse and identity* (pp. 166–187). Cambridge: Cambridge University Press. https://doi.org/10.1017/CBO9780511584459.009

Holmes, J. (2014). Joining a new community of workplace practice: Inferring attitudes from discourse. In E. Stracke (Ed.), *Intersections: Applied linguistics as a meeting place* (pp. 2–21). Newcastle upon Tyne: Cambridge Scholars Publishing.

Holmes, J. (2018). Negotiating the culture order in New Zealand workplaces. *Language in Society*, 47(1), 33–56. https://doi.org/10.1017/S0047404517000732

Holmes, J., & Major, G. (2003). Talking to patients: The complexity of communication on the ward. *Vision–A Journal of Nursing*, 11(17), 4–9.

Holmes, J., & Marra, M. (2002a). Having a laugh at work: How humour contributes to workplace culture. *Journal of Pragmatics*, 34(12), 1683–1710. https://doi.org/10.1016/S0378-2166(02)00032-2

Holmes, J., & Marra, M. (2002b). Over the edge? Subversive humor between colleagues and friends. *Humor*, 15(1), 65–68. https://doi.org/10.1515/humr.2002.006

Holmes, J., & Marra, M. (2004). Relational practice in the workplace: Women's talk or gendered discourse? *Language in Society*, 33(3), 377–398. https://doi.org/10.1017/S0047404504043039

Holmes, J., & Marra, M. (2005). Narrative and the construction of professional identity in the workplace. In J. Coates & J. Thornborrow (Eds.), *The sociolinguistics of narrative: Theory, context and culture in oral story-telling* (pp. 192–213). Amsterdam: John Benjamins. https://doi.org/10.1075/sin.6.10hol

Holmes, J., & Marra, M. (2011). Leadership discourse in a Māori workplace: Negotiating gender, ethnicity and leadership at work. *Gender & Language*, 5(2), 317–342. https://doi.org/10.1558/genl.v5i2.317

Holmes, J., & Marra, M. (2017). You're a proper tradesman mate: Identity struggles and workplace transitions in New Zealand. In D. van de Mieroop & S. Schnurr (Eds.), *Identity struggles: Evidence from workplaces around the world* (pp. 127–146). Amsterdam: John Benjamins. https://doi.org/10.1075/dapsac.69.07hol

Holmes, J., Marra, M., & Lazzaro-Salazar, M. (2017). Negotiating the tall poppy syndrome in New Zealand workplaces: Women leaders managing the challenge. *Gender & Language*, 11(1), 1–29. https://doi.org/10.1558/genl.31236

Holmes, J., Marra, M., & Vine, B. (2011). *Leadership, discourse and ethnicity*. Oxford: Oxford University Press. https://doi.org/10.1093/acprof:oso/9780199730759.001.0001

Holmes, J., & Meyerhoff, M. (1999). The community of practice: Theories and methodologies in language and gender research. *Language in Society*, 28(2), 173–183. https://doi.org/10.1017/S004740459900202X

Holmes, J., & Riddiford, N. (2009). Talk at work: Interactional challenges for immigrants. In V. K. Bhatia, W. Cheng, & B. Du-Babcock (Eds.), *Language for professional communication: Research, practice & training* (pp. 217–234). Hong Kong: Asia-Pacific LSP and Professional Communication.

Holmes, J., & Riddiford, N. (2010). Professional and personal identity at work: Achieving a synthesis through intercultural workplace talk. *Journal of Intercultural Communication*, 22.

Holmes, J., & Schnurr, S. (2017). (Im)politeness in the Workplace. In J. Culpeper, M. Haugh, & D. Z. Kadar (Eds.), *The Palgrave handbook of linguistic (im)politeness* (pp. 635–660). Basingstoke: Palgrave Macmillan. https://doi.org/10.1057/978-1-137-37508-7_24

Holmes, J., & Stubbe, M. (2003). *Power and politeness in the workplace*. London: Longman.

Holmes, J., & Woodhams, J. (2013). Building interaction: The role of talk in joining a community of practice. *Discourse & Communication*, 7(3), 275–298. https://doi.org/10.1177/1750481313494500

Holmes, L. (1999). Competence and capability: from "confidence trick" to the construction of the graduate identity. In L. Cunningham, S. Lester, & D. O'Reilly (Eds.), *Developing the capable practitioner: Professional capability through higher education* (pp. 83–98). London: Kogan Page.

Holmes, L. (2001). Reconsidering graduate employability: The "graduate identity" approach. *Quality in Higher Education*, 7(2), 111–119. https://doi.org/10.1080/13538320120060006

Holmes, L. (2013). Realist and relational perspectives on graduate identity and employability: A response to Hinchliffe and Jolly. *British Educational Research Journal*, 39(6), 1044–1059. https://doi.org/10.1002/berj.3022

Holstein, J. A., & Gubrium, J. F. (1995). *The active interview*. Thousand Oaks: Sage. https://doi.org/10.4135/9781412986120

Holt, L. (2008). Embodied social capital and geographic perspectives: Performing the habitus. *Progress in Human Geography*, 32(2), 227–246. https://doi.org/10.1177/0309132507087648

Holt, L. (2010). Young people's embodied social capital and performing disability. *Children's Geographies*, 8(1), 25–37. https://doi.org/10.1080/14733280903500158

Horrell, R. (2009, June 17). Families grateful for peaceful new lives. *Central Leader, Fairfax NZ*.

Human Rights Watch. (2018). Eritrea. Retrieved July 28, 2018, from https://www.hrw.org/africa/eritrea

Hunt, L. (2008). Women asylum seekers and refugees: Opportunities, constraints and the role of agency. *Social Policy and Society*, 7(3), 281–292. https://doi.org/10.1017/S1474746408004260

Hymes, D. (1962). The ethnography of speaking. In T. Gladwin & W. Sturtevant (Eds.), *Anthropology and human behavior* (pp. 15–53). Washington, DC: Anthropological Society of Washington.

Hymes, D. (1964). Introduction: Toward ethnographies of communication. *American Anthropologist*, 66(6), 1–34. https://doi.org/10.1525/aa.1964.66.suppl_3.02a00010

Immigration New Zealand. (2012). *Refugee settlement: New Zealand refugee resettlement strategy*. Wellington: Immigration New Zealand.

Immigration New Zealand. (2018a). Information for asylum seekers. Retrieved July 24, 2018, from https://www.immigration.govt.nz/audiences/supporting-refugees-and-asylum-seekers/asylum-seekers

Immigration New Zealand. (2018b). New Zealand refugee quota programme. Retrieved October 1, 2018, from https://www.immigration.govt.nz/about-us/what-we-do/our-strategies-and-projects/supporting-refugees-and-asylum-seekers/refugee-and-protection-unit/new-zealand-refugee-quota-programme

Immigration New Zealand. (2018c). Skill shortages: Essential skills in demand lists (ESID). Retrieved September 20, 2018, from Immigration New Zealand website: https://www.immigration.govt.nz/employ-migrants/explore-your-options/before-you-start-hiring-migrants/skill-shortages

Íñigo-Mora, I. (2004). On the use of the personal pronoun *we* in communities. *Journal of Language & Politics*, 3(1), 27–52. https://doi.org/10.1075/jlp.3.1.05ini

Irvine, M. (2012). Bakhtin: Main theories. dialogism, polyphony, heteroglossia, open interpretation. Retrieved July 3, 2017, from http://faculty.georgetown.edu/irvinem/theory/Bakhtin-MainTheory.html

Jansen, A., & Grant, L. (2015). *Migrant journeys*. Wellington: Bridget Williams Books.

Jaworski, A., & Coupland, J. (2005). Othering in gossip: "You go out you have a laugh and you can pull yeah okay but like…" *Language in Society*, 34, 667–694. https://doi.org/10.1017/S0047404505050256

Jelle, H. A., Guerin, P., & Dyer, S. (2006). Somali women's experiences in paid employment in New Zealand. *New Zealand Journal of Employment Relations*, 31(2), 61–69.

Johnson, C. (2005). Narratives of identity: Denying empathy in conservative discourses on race, class, and sexuality. *Theory and Society*, 34(1), 37–61. https://doi.org/10.1007/s11186-005-3295-2

Johnson, G. C. (2006). The discursive construction of teacher identities in a research interview. In A. De Fina, D. Schiffrin, & M. Bamberg (Eds.), *Discourse and identity* (pp. 213–232). Cambridge: Cambridge University Press. https://doi.org/10.1017/CBO9780511584459.011

Johnstone, B. (1993). Community and contest: Midwestern men and women creating their worlds in conversational storytelling. In D. Tannen (Ed.), *Gender and conversational interaction* (pp. 62–80). New York: Oxford University Press.

Jucker, A. H., & Smith, S. W. (1998). And people just you know like 'wow': Discourse markers as negotiating strategies. In A. H. Jucker & Y. Ziv (Eds.), *Discourse markers: Descriptions and theory* (pp. 171–201). Amsterdam: Benjamins. https://doi.org/10.1075/pbns.57.10juc

Julien, C. (2015). Bourdieu, social capital and online interaction. *Sociology*, 49(2), 356–373. https://doi.org/10.1177/0038038514535862

Katriel, T., & Dascal, M. (1984). What do indicating devices indicate? *Philosophy and Rhetoric*, 17, 1–15.

Kemper, S. (1994). Elderspeak: Speech accommodations to older adults. *Aging, Neuropsychology, and Cognition*, 1(1), 17–28. https://doi.org/10.1080/09289919408251447

Kerekes, J. (2007). The co-construction of a gatekeeping encounter: An inventory of verbal actions. *Journal of Pragmatics*, 39(11), 1942–1973. https://doi.org/10.1016/j.pragma.2007.07.008

Kerekes, J., Chow, J., Lemak, A., & Perhan, Z. (2013). Trust or betrayal: Immigrant engineers' employment-seeking experiences in Canada. In C. N. Candlin & J. Crichton (Eds.), *Discourses of trust* (pp. 269–285). New York: Palgrave Macmillan.

Kettle, M. (2005). Agency as discursive practice: From 'nobody' to 'somebody' as an international student in Australia. *Asia Pacific Journal of Education*, 25(1), 45–60. https://doi.org/10.1080/02188790500032525

Khosravinik, M. (2008). British newspapers and the representation of refugees, asylum seekers and immigrants between 1996 and 2006. *Centre for Language in Social Life Working Papers, Lancaster University*.

Khosravinik, M. (2009). The representation of refugees, asylum seekers and immigrants in British newspapers during the Balkan conflict (1999) and the British general election (2005). *Discourse & Society*, 20(4), 477–498. https://doi.org/10.1177/0957926509104024

Kidner, K. (2015). Beyond greenwash: Environmental discourses of appropriation and resistance (Doctoral Dissertation). Victoria University of Wellington, Wellington.

Kiesling, S. F. (2006). Hegemonic identity-making in narrative. In A. De Fina, D. Schiffrin, & M. Bamberg (Eds.), *Discourse and identity* (pp. 261–287). Cambridge: Cambridge University Press. https://doi.org/10.1017/CBO9780511584459.014

King, B. W. (2014). Inverting virginity, abstinence, and conquest: Sexual agency and subjectivity in classroom conversation. *Sexualities*, 17(3), 310–328. https://doi.org/10.1177/1363460713516337

Korac, M. (2009). *Remaking home: Reconstructing life, place and identity in Rome and Amsterdam.* New York: Berghahn Books.

Korobov, N., & Bamberg, M. (2007). "Strip poker! They don't show nothing!'": Positioning identities in adolescent male talk about a television game show. In M. Bamberg, A. De Fina, & D. Schiffrin (Eds.), *Selves and identities in narrative and discourse* (pp. 253–271). Amsterdam: Benjamins. https://doi.org/10.1075/sin.9.12kor

Koyama, J. (2013). Resettling notions of social mobility: Locating refugees as "educable" and "employable." *British Journal of Sociology of Education*, 34(5–6), 947–965. https://doi.org/10.1080/01425692.2013.816033

Koyama, J. (2014). Constructing gender: Refugee women working in the United States. *Journal of Refugee Studies*, 28(2), 258–275. https://doi.org/10.1093/jrs/feu026

Krahn, H., Derwing, T., Mulder, M., & Wilkinson, L. (2009). Educated and underemployed: Refugee integration into the Canadian labour market. *Journal of International Migration and Integration*, 1, 59–84. https://doi.org/10.1007/s12134-000-1008-2

Kraus, W. (2000). Making identity talk. On qualitative methods in a longitudinal study. *Forum Qualitative Sozialforschung / Forum: Qualitative Social Research*, 1(2), 1–14.

Kübler-Ross, E. (1969). *On death and dying*. New York: Macmillan.

Kunz, E. F. (1973). The refugee in flight: Kinetic models and forms of displacement. *The International Migration Review*, 7(2), 125–146. https://doi.org/10.2307/3002424

Kyratzis, A. (1999). Narrative identity: Preschoolers' self-construction through narrative in same-sex friendship group dramatic play. *Narrative Inquiry*, 9(2), 427–455. https://doi.org/10.1075/ni.9.2.10kyr

Labov, W. (1972). *Sociolinguistic patterns*. Oxford: Blackwell.

Labov, W. (1997). Some further steps in narrative analysis. *Journal of Narrative and Life History*, 7(1–4), 395–415. https://doi.org/10.1075/jnlh.7.49som

Labov, W. (2014). The transformation of experience in narrative. In A. Jaworski & N. Coupland (Eds.), *The discourse reader* (3rd ed., pp. 200–212). New York: Routledge.

Labov, W., & Waletsky, J. (1967). Narrative analysis: Oral accounts of personal experiences. In J. Helm (Ed.), *Essays on the verbal and visual arts: Proceedings of the 1967 annual spring meeting of the American Ethnological Society* (pp. 12–44). Seattle: University of Washington Press.

Lacroix, M. (2004). Canadian refugee policy and the social construction of the refugee claimant subjectivity: Understanding refugeeness. *Journal of Refugee Studies*, 17(2), 147–166. https://doi.org/10.1093/jrs/17.2.147

Ladegaard, H. J. (2013). Laughing at adversity: Laughter as communication in domestic helper narratives. *Journal of Language and Social Psychology*, 32(4), 390–411. https://doi.org/10.1177/0261927X13489301

Lagenhove, L. van, & Harré, R. (1999). Introducing positioning theory. In R. Harré & L. van Lagenhove (Eds.), *Positioning theory* (pp. 14–31). Oxford: Blackwell Publishing Ltd.
Lakoff, G. (1993). The contemporary theory of metaphor. In A. Ortony (Ed.), *Metaphor and thought* (2nd ed., pp. 202–251). Cambridge: Cambridge University Press. https://doi.org/10.1017/CBO9781139173865.013
Lakoff, G., & Johnsen, M. (2003). *Metaphors we live by*. London: University of Chicago Press. https://doi.org/10.7208/chicago/9780226470993.001.0001
Lamba, N. K. (2003). The employment experiences of Canadian refugees: Measuring the impact of human and social capital on quality of employment. *Canadian Review of Sociology/Revue Canadienne de Sociologie*, 40(1), 45–64. https://doi.org/10.1111/j.1755-618X.2003.tb00235.x
Lamba, N. K., & Krahn, H. (2003). Social capital and refugee resettlement: The social networks of refugees in Canada. *Journal of International Migration and Integration*, 4(3), 335–360. https://doi.org/10.1007/s12134-003-1025-z
Lambert, A. (2016). Intimacy and social capital on Facebook: Beyond the psychological perspective. *New Media & Society*, 18(11), 2559–2575. https://doi.org/10.1177/1461444815588902
Lammers, E. (2007). Researching refugees: Preoccupations with power and questions of giving. *Refugee Survey Quarterly*, 26(3), 72–81. https://doi.org/10.1093/rsq/hdi0244
Language in the Workplace. (2014). The Language in the Workplace Project. Retrieved January 15, 2016, from http://www.victoria.ac.nz/lals/centres-and-institutes/language-in-the-workplace
Lanza, E. (2012). Empowering migrant identity: Agency in narratives of a work experience in Norway. *Sociolinguistic Studies*, 6(2), 285–307.
LaPointe, K. (2010). Narrating career, positioning identity: Career identity as a narrative practice. *Journal of Vocational Behavior*, 77(1), 1–9. https://doi.org/10.1016/j.jvb.2010.04.003
Lareau, A., & Horvat, E. M. (1999). Moments of social inclusion and exclusion race, class, and cultural capital in family-school relationships. *Sociology of Education*, 72(1), 37–53. https://doi.org/10.2307/2673185
Lave, J., & Wenger, E. (1991). *Situated learning: Legitimate peripheral participation*. Cambridge: Cambridge University Press. https://doi.org/10.1017/CBO9780511815355
Lawler, S. (2009). Symbolic violence. In D. Southerton (Ed.), *Encyclopedia of consumer culture*. London: Routledge. Retrieved from http://sk.sagepub.com/reference/consumerculture/n534.xml
Leach, M., & Mansouri, F. (2003). "Strange words": Refugee perspectives on government and media stereotyping. *Overland*, 172, 19–26.
Lee, C. (2003). The use of the discourse marker *say* in conversational English. *SNU Working Papers in English Language and Linguistics*, 2, 133–156.
Leudar, I., Hayes, J., Nekvapil, J., & Turner Baker, J. (2008). Hostility themes in media, community and refugee narratives. *Discourse & Society*, 19(2), 187–221. https://doi.org/10.1177/0957926507085952
Lillrank, A. (2012). Managing the interviewer self. In J. F. Gubrium, J. A. Holstein, A. B. Marvasti, & K. D. McKinney (Eds.), *The Sage handbook of interview research* (2nd ed., pp. 281–294). Thousand Oaks: Sage Publications.
Lin, A. (2014). Critical discourse analysis in applied linguistics: A methodological review. *Annual Review of Applied Linguistics*, 34, 213–232. https://doi.org/10.1017/S0267190514000087
Lindemann, S., & Mauranen, A. (2001). "It's just real messy": The occurrence and function of *just* in a corpus of academic speech. *English for Specific Purposes*, 20(1), 459–475. https://doi.org/10.1016/S0889-4906(01)00026-6

Long, Z., King, A. S., & Buzzanell, P. M. (2018). Ventriloqual voicings of parenthood in graduate school: An intersectionality analysis of work-life negotiations. *Journal of Applied Communication Research*, 46(2), 223–242. https://doi.org/10.1080/00909882.2018.1435901

Madison, D. S. (2012). *Critical ethnography: Method, ethics, and performance* (2nd ed.). Thousand Oaks: Sage.

Major, G., & Holmes, J. (2008). How do nurses describe health care procedures?: Analysing nurse-patient interaction in a hospital ward. *Australian Journal of Advanced Nursing*, 25(4), 58.

Makoni, S., & Grainger, K. (2002). Comparative gerontolinguistics: Characterizing discourses in caring institutions in South Africa and the United Kingdom. *Journal of Social Issues*, 58(4), 805–824. https://doi.org/10.1111/1540-4560.00291

Malkki, L. H. (1996). Speechless emissaries: Refugees, humanitarianism, and dehistoricization. *Cultural Anthropology*, 11(3), 377–404. https://doi.org/10.1525/can.1996.11.3.02a00050

Mann, S. (2010). A critical review of qualitative interviews in applied linguistics. *Applied Linguistics*, 32(1), 6–24. https://doi.org/10.1093/applin/amq043

Marlowe, J. M. (2010). Beyond the discourse of trauma: Shifting the focus on Sudanese refugees. *Journal of Refugee Studies*, 23(2), 183–198. https://doi.org/10.1093/jrs/feq013

Marra, M. (2012). Disagreeing without being disagreeable: Negotiating workplace communities as an outsider. *Journal of Pragmatics*, 44(12), 1580–1590. https://doi.org/10.1016/j.pragma.2012.06.009

Marra, M., & Holmes, J. (2004). Workplace narratives and business reports: Issues of definition. *Text*, 24(1), 59–78. https://doi.org/10.1515/text.2004.004

Marra, M., & Holmes, J. (2008). Constructing ethnicity in New Zealand workplace stories. *Text & Talk*, 28(3), 397–419. https://doi.org/10.1515/TEXT.2008.019

Marra, M., & Holmes, J. (2016). Indirect reports and workplace norms. In A. Capone, F. Kiefer, & F. Lo Piparo (Eds.), *Indirect reports and pragmatics* (pp. 151–165). Cham: Springer. https://doi.org/10.1007/978-3-319-21395-8_8

Marra, M., & Lazzaro-Salazar, M. (2018). Ethnographic methods in pragmatics. In A. H. Jucker, K. P. Schneider, & W. Bublitz (Eds.), *Methods in pragmatics* (Vol. 10, pp. 343–366). Berlin: De Gruyter Mouton.

Marsden, S., & Holmes, J. (2014). Talking to the elderly in New Zealand residential care settings. *Journal of Pragmatics*, 64, 17–34. https://doi.org/10.1016/j.pragma.2014.01.006

Marshall, A., & Batten, S. (2004). Researching across cultures: Issues of ethics and power. *Forum Qualitative Sozialforschung / Forum: Qualitative Social Research*, 5(3).

Martínez Lirola, M. (2014). Approaching the representation of sub-Saharan immigrants in a sample from the Spanish press. *Critical Discourse Studies*, 11(4), 482–499. https://doi.org/10.1080/17405904.2014.915382

Maruna, S. (2004). Is rationalization good for the soul?: Resisting "responsibilization" in corrections and the courts. In B. A. Arrigo (Ed.), *Psychological jurisprudence: Critical explorations in law, crime, and society* (pp. 179–199). Albany: State University of New York Press.

Matoesian, G. (2000). Intertextual authority in reported speech: Production media in the Kennedy Smith rape trial. *Journal of Pragmatics*, 32(7), 879–914. https://doi.org/10.1016/S0378-2166(99)00080-6

May, T. (2011). *Social research: Issues, methods and process* (4th ed.). Maidenhead: Open University Press.

May, V. (2004). Narrative identity and the re-conceptualization of lone motherhood. *Narrative Inquiry*, 14(1), 169–189. https://doi.org/10.1075/ni.14.1.08may

McCall, L. (2005). The complexity of intersectionality. *Signs*, 30(3), 1771–1800. https://doi.org/10.1086/426800

McKay, S., & Snyder, P. (2009). Methodological challenges in researching the working experiences of refugees and recent migrants. In S. McKay (Ed.), *Refugees, recent migrants and employment: Challenging barriers and exploring pathways* (pp. 35–49). New York: Routledge.

McKendy, J. P. (2006). 'I'm very careful about that': Narrative and agency of men in prison. *Discourse & Society*, 17(4), 473–502. https://doi.org/10.1177/0957926506063128

McSpadden, L. A., & Moussa, H. (1993). I have a name: The gender dynamics in asylum and in resettlement of Ethiopian and Eritrean refugees in North America. *Journal of Refugee Studies*, 6, 203–225.

Meadows, B. (2009). Capital negotiation and identity practices: Investigating symbolic capital from the "ground up." *Critical Discourse Studies*, 6(1), 15–30. https://doi.org/10.1080/17405900802560025

Menard-Warwick, J. (2005). Both a fiction and an existential fact: Theorizing identity in second language acquisition and literacy studies. *Linguistics and Education*, 16(3), 253–274. https://doi.org/10.1016/j.linged.2006.02.001

Miglbauer, M. (2017). Workplace conflicts as (re)source for analysing identity struggles in stories told in interviews. In D. van de Mieroop & S. Schnurr (Eds.), *Identity struggles: Evidence from workplaces around the world* (pp. 207–224). Amsterdam: John Benjamins. https://doi.org/10.1075/dapsac.69.11mig

Migration Research Network. (2018). Migration research network. Retrieved November 25, 2018, from https://www.esocsci.org.nz/networks-connect/migration-research-network/

Milford, P. (1980). Laughter as communication: Some intercultural implications. Retrieved November 30, 2018, from Institute of Education Sciences website: https://eric.ed.gov/?id=ED188278

Miller, E., & Kubota, R. (2013). Second language identity construction. In J. Herschensohn & M. Young-Scholten (Eds.), *The Cambridge handbook of second language acquisition* (pp. 230–250). New York: Cambridge University Press. https://doi.org/10.1017/CBO9781139051729.015

Mills, M. A. (1997). Narrative identity and dementia: A study of emotion and narrative in older people with dementia. *Ageing and Society*, 17(6), 673–698. https://doi.org/10.1017/S0144686X97006673

Milroy, J. (2001). Language ideologies and the consequences of standardization. *Journal of Sociolinguistics*, 5(4), 530–555. https://doi.org/10.1111/1467-9481.00163

Ministry of Business, Innovation and Employment. (2007). New Zealand refugee quota programme. Retrieved June 19, 2017, from https://www.immigration.govt.nz/about-us/what-we-do/our-strategies-and-projects/supporting-refugees-and-asylum-seekers/refugee-and-protection-unit/new-zealand-refugee-quota-programme

Ministry of Health. (2012). *Long-term residential care for older people: What you need to know*. Wellington: Ministry of Health. Retrieved from http://www.health.govt.nz/system/files/documents/publications/long-term-residential-care-older-people-2012.pdf

Minks, A. (2007). "Goblins like to hear stories": Miskitu children's narratives of spirit encounters. In M. Bamberg, A. De Fina, & D. Schiffrin (Eds.), *Selves and identities in narrative and discourse* (pp. 9–39). Amsterdam: Benjamins. https://doi.org/10.1075/sin.9.03min

Mithen, J., Aitken, Z., Ziersch, A., & Kavanagh, A. M. (2015). Inequalities in social capital and health between people with and without disabilities. *Social Science & Medicine*, 126, 26–35. https://doi.org/10.1016/j.socscimed.2014.12.009

Mohanty, C. (1988). Under Western eyes: Feminist scholarship and colonial discourses. *Feminist Review*, 30(1), 61–88. https://doi.org/10.1057/fr.1988.42

Mohnen, S. M., Völker, B., Flap, H., Subramanian, S. V., & Groenewegen, P. P. (2015). The influence of social capital on individual health: Is it the neighbourhood or the network? *Social Indicators Research*, 121(1), 195–214. https://doi.org/10.1007/s11205-014-0632-8

Moissinac, L. (2007). "Mr. Lanoe hit on my mom": Reestablishment of believability insequential 'small stories' by adolescent boys. In M. Bamberg, A. De Fina, & D. Schiffrin (Eds.), *Selves and identities in narrative and discourse* (pp. 229–252). Amsterdam: Benjamins. https://doi.org/10.1075/sin.9.11moi

Møllegaard, S., & Jæger, M. M. (2015). The effect of grandparents' economic, cultural, and social capital on grandchildren's educational success. *Research in Social Stratification and Mobility*, 42, 11–19. https://doi.org/10.1016/j.rssm.2015.06.004

Monkman, K., Ronald, M., & Théramène, F. D. (2005). Social and cultural capital in an urban Latino school community. *Urban Education*, 40(1), 4–33. https://doi.org/10.1177/0042085904270416

Montgomery, E. (2010). Trauma and resilience in young refugees: A 9-year follow-up study. *Development and Psychopathology*, 22, 477–489. https://doi.org/10.1017/S0954579410000180

Moreau, M.-P., & Leathwood, C. (2006). Graduates' employment and the discourse of employability: A critical analysis. *Journal of Education and Work*, 19(4), 305–324. https://doi.org/10.1080/13639080600867083

Morita, N. (2004). Negotiating participation and identity in second language academic communities. *TESOL Quarterly*, 38(4), 573–603. https://doi.org/10.2307/3588281

Morning Report. (2018, October 1). NZ First members vote for migrants to sign "NZ values" contract. Retrieved October 3, 2018, from https://www.radionz.co.nz/national/programmes/morningreport/audio/2018664821/nz-first-members-vote-for-migrants-to-sign-nz-values-contract

Morrice, L. (2007). Lifelong learning and the social integration of refugees in the UK: The significance of social capital. *International Journal of Lifelong Education*, 26(2), 155–172. https://doi.org/10.1080/02601370701219467

Morrice, L. (2009). Journeys into higher education: The case of refugees in the UK. *Teaching in Higher Education*, 14(6), 661–672. https://doi.org/10.1080/13562510903315282

Morris, M. W., Leung, K., Ames, D., & Lickel, B. (1999). Views from inside and outside: Integrating emic and etic insights about culture and justice judgement. *Academy of Management Review*, 24(4), 781–796. https://doi.org/10.5465/amr.1999.2553253

Moulin, C. (2012). Ungrateful subjects? Refugee protests and the logic of gratitude. In Peter Nyers & K. Rygiel (Eds.), *Citizenship, migrant activism and the politics of movement* (pp. 54–72). London: Routledge.

Moussa, H. (1993). *Storm and sanctuary: The journey of Ethiopian and Eritrean women refugees*. Dundas: Artemis Enterprises.

Navarro, D. (2016). Language learner cognition: Exploring adult migrants' L2 activity beyond the classroom (Doctoral Dissertation). Victoria University of Wellington, Wellington.

Navarro, D., & Macalister, J. (2017). Adrift in an Anglophone world: Refugee families' language policy challenges. In J. Macalister & S. H. Mirvahedi (Eds.), *Family language policies in a multilingual world: Opportunities, challenges, and consequences* (pp. 115–132). London: Routledge.

Nawyn, S. J., Gjokaj, L., LaFa Agbényiga, D., & Grace, B. (2012). Linguistic isolation, social capital, and immigrant belonging. *Journal of Contemporary Ethnography*, 41, 255–282. https://doi.org/10.1177/0891241611433623

Nayeri, D. (2017, April 4). The ungrateful refugee: 'We have no debt to repay.' *The Guardian Online*. Retrieved from https://www.theguardian.com/news/series/the-long-read?page=2

Ng, S. H., & McCreanor, T. (1999). Patterns in discourse about elderly people In New Zealand. *Journal of Aging Studies*, 13(4), 473–489. https://doi.org/10.1016/S0890-4065(99)00022-5

Ngo, B., & Hansen, S. (2013). Constructing identities in UN refugee camps: The politics of language, culture and humanitarian assistance. *Critical Inquiry in Language Studies*, 10(2), 97–120. https://doi.org/10.1080/15427587.2013.753843

Nguyen, V. (2013). Refugee gratitude: Narrating success and intersubjectivity in Kim Thúy's Ru. *Canadian Literature*, (219), 17–36.

Nissenbaum, A., & Shifman, L. (2017). Internet memes as contested cultural capital: The case of 4chan's /b/ board. *New Media & Society*, 19(4), 483–501. https://doi.org/10.1177/1461444815609313

Norrick, N. R. (2001). Discourse markers in oral narrative. *Journal of Pragmatics*, 33, 849–878. https://doi.org/10.1016/S0378-2166(01)80032-1

Norton, B. (2000). *Identity and language learning*. New York: Longman.

Norton, B. (2001). Non-participation, imagined communities and the language classroom. In M. Breen (Ed.), *Learner contributions to language learning: new directions in research* (pp. 159–171). Harlow: Pearson Education.

Norton, B. (2013). *Identity and language learning: Extending the conversation* (2nd ed.). Bristol: Multilingual Matters. https://doi.org/10.21832/9781783090563

Norton, B. (2017). Learner investment and language teacher identity. In G. Barkhuizen (Ed.), *Reflections on language teacher identity* (pp. 80–86). London: Routledge.

Norton, B., & McKinney, C. (2011). An identity approach to second language acquisition. In D. Atkinson (Ed.), *Alternative approaches to second language acquisition* (pp. 73–94). New York: Routledge.

Norton, B., & Toohey, K. (2011). Identity, language learning, and social change. *Language Teaching*, 44(4), 412–446. https://doi.org/10.1017/S0261444811000309

Nyers, P. (2006). *Rethinking refugees*. New York: Routledge.

NZ Herald. (2015, June 19). Settlers grateful for safer lives and careers in New Zealand. *New Zealand Herald*.

Ochs, E., & Capps, L. (2001). *Living narrative*. Massachusetts: Harvard University Press.

O'Conner, B. P., & St. Pierre, E. S. (2004). Older persons' perceptions of the frequency and meaning of elderspeak from family, friends, and service workers. *Aging and Human Development*, 58(3), 197–221. https://doi.org/10.2190/LY83-KPXD-H2F2-JRQ5

O'Connor, C. (1999). Race, class, and gender in America: Narratives of opportunity among low-income African American youths. *Sociology of Education*, 72(3), 137–157. https://doi.org/10.2307/2673226

O'Connor, S. (2014). Linguistic socialization in the refugee assimilation process: Transmitting cultural capital for self-sufficiency. *Undergraduate Student Research Awards*, (Paper 17), 1–19.

O'Higgins, A. (2012). Vulnerability and agency: Beyond an irreconcilable dichotomy for social service providers working with young refugees in the UK. *New Directions for Child and Adolescent Development*, 2012(136), 79–91. https://doi.org/10.1002/cad.20012

Oikonomidoy, E. (2010). Zooming into the school narratives of refugee students. *Multicultural Perspectives*, 12(2), 74–80. https://doi.org/10.1080/15210960.2010.481186

Oliphant, T. (2014). An introduction to discourse analysis. Retrieved November 27, 2017, from https://iiqm.wordpress.com/2014/09/08/an-introduction-to-discourse-analysis/

Olive, J. L. (2014). Reflecting on the tensions between emic and etic perspectives in life history research: Lessons Learned. *Forum Qualitative Sozialforschung / Forum: Qualitative Social Research*, 15(2).

Oo Jin Lee, E., & Brotman, S. (2011). Identity, refugeeness, belonging: Experiences of sexual minority refugees in Canada. *Canadian Review of Sociology/Revue Canadienne de Sociologie*, 48(3), 241–274. https://doi.org/10.1111/j.1755-618X.2011.01265.x

Oppenheim, A. N. (1992). *Questionnaire design, interviewing and attitude measurement*. London: Pinter Publishers.

Opsahl, T. (2009). *Wolla I swear* this is typical for the conversational style of adolescents in multiethnic areas in Oslo. *Nordic Journal of Linguistics*, 32(2), 221–244. https://doi.org/10.1017/S0332586509990059

O'Reilly, K. (2009). *Key concepts in ethnography*. London: Sage Publications. https://doi.org/10.4135/9781446268308

Ortega, L., & Iberri-Shea, G. (2005). Longitudinal research in second language acquisition: Recent trends and future directions. *Annual Review of Applied Linguistics*, 25, 26–45. https://doi.org/10.1017/S0267190505000024

Ortner, S. B. (1989). *High religion: A cultural and political history of Sherpa Buddhism*. Princeton: Princeton University Press.

Ortner, S. B. (2006). *Anthropology and social theory: Culture, power, and the acting subject*. Durham: Duke University Press. https://doi.org/10.1215/9780822388456

O'Shea, S., Stone, C., Delahunty, J., & May, J. (2018). Discourses of betterment and opportunity: Exploring the privileging of university attendance for first-in-family learners. *Studies in Higher Education*, 43(6), 1020–1033. https://doi.org/10.1080/03075079.2016.1212325

Paltridge, B. (2012). *Discourse analysis* (2nd ed.). London: Bloomsbury.

Paoletti, I., & Johnson, G. C. (2007). Doing "being ordinary" in an interview narrative with a second generation Italian-Australian woman. In M. Bamberg, A. De Fina, & D. Schiffrin (Eds.), *Selves and identities in narrative and discourse* (pp. 89–105). Amsterdam: Benjamins. https://doi.org/10.1075/sin.9.06pao

Partington, A. (2006). *The linguistics of laughter: A corpus-assisted study of laughter-talk*. Abington: Routledge. https://doi.org/10.4324/9780203966570

Patton, M. Q. (2002). *Qualitative research and evaluation methods* (3rd ed.). Thousand Oaks: Sage.

Pavlenko, A. (2000). Access to linguistic resources: Key variable in second language acquisition research, 1(2), 85–105. *Estudios de Sociolinguistica*, 1(2), 85–105.

Pavlenko, A. (2001). "In the world of the tradition, I was unimagined": Negotiation of identities in cross-cultural autobiographies. *International Journal of Bilingualism*, 5(3), 317–344. https://doi.org/10.1177/13670069010050030401

Pavlenko, A. (2002). Bilingualism and emotions. *Multilingua – Journal of Cross-Cultural and Interlanguage Communication*, 21, 45–78. https://doi.org/10.1515/mult.2002.004

Pavlenko, A., & Blackledge, A. (2004). *Negotiation of identities in multilingual contexts*. Clevedon: Multilingual Matters.

Pavlenko, A., & Lantolf, J. (2000). Second language learning as participation and the (re)construction of selves. In J. Lantolf (Ed.), *Sociocultural theory and second language learning* (pp. 155–177). Oxford: Oxford University Press.

Peeters, B. (2004). "Thou shalt not be a tall poppy": Describing an Australian communicative (and behavioral) norm. *Intercultural Pragmatics*, 1(1), 71–92. https://doi.org/10.1515/iprg.2004.008

Pérez, P. A., & McDonough, P. M. (2008). Understanding Latina and Latino college choice: A social capital and chain migration analysis. *Journal of Hispanic Higher Education*, 7(3), 249–265. https://doi.org/10.1177/1538192708317620

Piller, I. (2016). *Linguistic diversity and social justice: An introduction to applied sociolinguistics*. New York: Oxford University Press. https://doi.org/10.1093/acprof:oso/9780199937240.001.0001

Pinxten, W., & Lievens, J. (2014). The importance of economic, social and cultural capital in understanding health inequalities: using a Bourdieu-based approach in research on physical and mental health perceptions. *Sociology of Health & Illness*, 36(7), 1095–1110. https://doi.org/10.1111/1467-9566.12154

Pittaway, E., & Bartolomei, L. (2001). Refugees, race, and gender: The multiple discrimination against refugee women. *Refuge*, 19(6), 21–32.

Pomerantz, A. (2012). Narrative approaches to second language acquisition. In C. A. Chapelle (Ed.), *The encyclopedia of applied linguistics* (pp. 1–7). Blackwell Publishing Ltd.. https://doi.org/10.1002/9781405198431.wbeal0849

Portes, A. (1998). Social capital: Its origins and applications in modern sociology. *Annual Review of Sociology*, 24, 1–24. https://doi.org/10.1146/annurev.soc.24.1.1

Pupavac, V. (2008). Refugee advocacy, traumatic representations and political disenchantment. *Government and Opposition*, 43(2), 270–292. https://doi.org/10.1111/j.1477-7053.2008.00255.x

Purcell, K., & Purcell, J. (1998). In-sourcing, outsourcing, and the growth of contingent labour as evidence of flexible employment strategies. *European Journal of Work and Organizational Psychology*, 7(1), 39–59. https://doi.org/10.1080/135943298398952

Puvimanasinghe, T., Denson, L. A., Augoustinos, M., & Somasundaram, D. (2014). Narrative and silence: How former refugees talk about loss and past trauma. *Journal of Refugee Studies*, 28(1), 69–92. https://doi.org/10.1093/jrs/feu019

Raddon, A. (2002). Mothers in the academy: Positioned and positioning within discourses of the "successful academic" and the "good mother." *Studies in Higher Education*, 27(4), 387–403. https://doi.org/10.1080/0307507022000011516

Rampton, B. (2017). Interactional sociolinguistics. *Tilburg Papers in Cultural Studies*, (175), 1–15.

Rampton, B., Maybin, J., & Roberts, C. (2014). Methodological foundations in linguistic ethnography. In *Working papers in urban language & literacies* (Vol. 125, pp. 1–24). King's College London.

Reeves, S., Kuper, A., & Hodges, B. D. (2008). Qualitative research methodologies: Ethnography. *British Medical Journal*, 337, 512–514. https://doi.org/10.1136/bmj.a1020

Reissner-Roubicek, S. (2017). Juggling "I"s and "we"s with "he"s and "she"s: Negotiating novice professional identities in stories of teamwork told in New Zealand job interviews. In D. van de Mieroop & S. Schnurr (Eds.), *Identity struggles: Evidence from workplaces around the world* (pp. 57–78). Amsterdam: John Benjamins. https://doi.org/10.1075/dapsac.69.04rei

Rescher, N. (1992). Moral obligation and the refugee. *Public Affairs Quarterly*, 6(1), 23–30.

Revis, M. (2015). Family language policies of refugees: Ethiopians and Colombians in New Zealand (Doctoral Dissertation). Victoria University of Wellington, Wellington.

Ricento, T. (2015). Refugees in Canada: On the loss of social capital. In B. Spolsky, O. Inbar, & M. Tannenbaum (Eds.), *Challenges for language education and policy: Making space for people* (pp. 135–148). New York: Routledge.

Riessman, C. K. (2003). Performing identities in illness narrative: Masculinity and multiple sclerosis. *Qualitative Research*, 3(1), 5–33. https://doi.org/10.1177/146879410300300101
Riessman, C. K. (2004). Narrative analysis. In M. S. Lewis-Beck, A. Bryman, & T. Futing Liao (Eds.), *The SAGE encyclopedia of social science research methods* (pp. 705–709). Thousand Oaks: Sage.
RNZ. (2018, September 21). Refugee quota to rise from 1000 to 1500. *RNZ*. Retrieved from https://www.radionz.co.nz/news/political/366801/refugee-quota-to-rise-from-1000-to-1500
Rose, N. (1999). *Governing the soul: The shaping of the private self*. London: Free Association.
Rosenwald, G. C., & Ochberg (Eds.). (1992). *Storied lives: The cultural politics of self-understanding*. New Haven: Yale University Press.
Rubin, H. J., & Rubin, I. S. (2005). *Qualitative interviewing: The art of hearing data* (2nd ed.). Thousand Oaks: Sage Publications. https://doi.org/10.4135/9781452226651
Salahshour, N. (2016). Liquid metaphors as positive evaluations: A corpus-assisted discourse analysis of the representation of migrants in a daily New Zealand newspaper. *Discourse, Context & Media*, 13, 73–81. https://doi.org/10.1016/j.dcm.2016.07.002
Salahshour, N. (2017). Representation of immigrants in New Zealand print media: A critical discourse analysis (Doctoral Dissertation). Victoria University of Wellington, Wellington.
Sarbin, T. R. (1986). The narrative as root metaphor for psychology. In T. R. Sarbin (Ed.), *Narrative psychology: The storied nature of human conduct* (pp. 3–21). New York: Praeger.
Sass, J. S. (2000). Emotional labor as cultural performance: The communication of caregiving in a nonprofit nursing home. *Western Journal of Communication; Salt Lake City*, 64(3), 330–358. https://doi.org/10.1080/10570310009374679
Scheyvens, R., Scheyvens, H., & Murray, W. E. (2003). Working with marginalised, vulnerable or privileged groups. In R. Scheyvens & D. Storey (Eds.), *Development fieldwork: A practical guide* (pp. 167–193). London: Sage Publications. https://doi.org/10.4135/9781849208864.n9
Schieffelin, B. B., & Ochs, E. (1986). Language socialisation. *Annual Review of Anthropology*, 163–191. https://doi.org/10.1146/annurev.an.15.100186.001115
Schiffrin, D. (1987). *Discourse markers*. Cambridge: Cambridge University Press. https://doi.org/10.1017/CBO9780511611841
Schiffrin, D. (1996a). Interactional sociolinguistics. In S. L. McKay & N. H. Hornberger (Eds.), *Sociolinguistics and language teaching* (pp. 307–328). Cambridge: Cambridge University Press.
Schiffrin, D. (1996b). Narrative as self-portrait: Sociolinguistic constructions of identity. *Language in Society*, 25(2), 167–203. https://doi.org/10.1017/S0047404500020601
Schiffrin, D. (2001). Discourse markers: Language, meaning, and context. In D. Schiffrin, D. Tannen, & H. E. Hamilton (Eds.), *The handbook of discourse analysis 1* (pp. 54–75). Oxford: Blackwell.
Schnurr, S. (2011). Exploring another side of co-leadership: Negotiating professional identities through face-work in disagreements. *Language in Society*, 40(2), 187–209. https://doi.org/10.1017/S0047404511000030
Schori, D., Hofmann, K., & Abel, T. (2014). Social inequality and smoking in young Swiss men: Intergenerational transmission of cultural capital and health orientation. *International Journal of Public Health*, 59(2), 261–270. https://doi.org/10.1007/s00038-013-0537-3
Schwartz, B. (1967). The social psychology of the gift. *American Journal of Sociology*, 73(1), 1–11. https://doi.org/10.1086/224432

Schwöbel-Patel, C. (2015, August 5). Nils Christie's 'ideal victim' applied: From lions to swarms. Retrieved January 26, 2018, from http://criticallegalthinking.com/2015/08/05/nils-christies-ideal-victim-applied-from-lions-to-swarms/

Schwöbel-Patel, C. (2016). Spectacle in international criminal law: The fundraising image of victimhood. *London Review of International Law*, 4(2), 247–274. https://doi.org/10.1093/lril/lrw014

Schwöbel-Patel, C., & Ozkaramanli, D. (2017). The construction of the "grateful" refugee in law and design. *Queen Mary Human Rights Review*, 4(1), 1–10.

Seals, C. A. (2010). Gender and memory: How Symbolic capital and external evaluation affect who receives the credit in discourse. In *IGALA 6* (pp. 362–382). Tokyo.

Seals, C. A. (2017). Positive and negative identity practices in heritage language education. *International Journal of Multilingualism*, 1–20. https://doi.org/10.1080/14790718.2017.1306065

Seals, C. A., & Peyton, J. K. (2017). Heritage language education: Valuing the languages, literacies, and cultural competencies of immigrant youth. *Current Issues in Language Planning*, 18(1), 87–101. https://doi.org/10.1080/14664208.2016.1168690

Searle, W., Prouse, E., L'Ami, E., Gray, A., & Gruner, A. (2012). *New land, new life: Long-term settlement of refugees in New Zealand*. Wellington: Ministry of Business, Innovation, and Employment.

Sensoy, O., & DiAngelo, R. (2006). "I wouldn't want to be a woman in the Middle East": White female student teachers and the narrative of the oppressed Muslim woman. *Radical Pedagogy*, 8(1), 1–14.

Sewell, W. H. (1992). A theory of structure: Duality, agency, and transformation. *American Journal of Sociology*, 98(1), 1–29. https://doi.org/10.1086/229967

Sharkin, B. S. (1993). Anger and gender: Theory, research, and implications. *Journal of Counseling and Development*, 71(4), 386. https://doi.org/10.1002/j.1556-6676.1993.tb02653.x

Shuttleworth, K. (2017, September 2). Jacindamania: rocketing rise of New Zealand Labour's fresh political hope. *The Guardian Online*.

Skeggs, B. (2004). *Class, self, culture*. London: Routledge.

Smith, B. (2007). The state of the art in narrative inquiry: some reflections. *Narrative Inquiry*, (17), 391–398. https://doi.org/10.1075/ni.17.2.13smi

Smith, S. W., & Jucker, A. H. (2000). *Actually* and other markers of an apparent discrepancy between propositional attitudes of conversational partners. In G. Anderson & T. Fretheim (Eds.), *Pragmatic markers and propositional attitude* (pp. 207–237). Amsterdam: John Benjamins. https://doi.org/10.1075/pbns.79.10smi

Smith, V. (2010). Enhancing employability: Human, cultural, and social capital in an era of turbulent unpredictability. *Human Relations*, 63(2), 279–300. https://doi.org/10.1177/0018726709353639

Sontag, S. (2003). *Regarding the pain of others*. New York: Picador. https://doi.org/10.3917/dio.201.0127

Sotirin, P. (2000). "All they do is bitch bitch bitch": Political and interactional features of women's officetalk. *Women and Language*, 23(2), 19–25.

Spaaij, R. (2012). Beyond the playing field: Experiences of sport, social capital, and integration among Somalis in Australia. *Ethnic and Racial Studies*, 35(9), 1519–1538. https://doi.org/10.1080/01419870.2011.592205

Spector-Mersel, G. (2011). Mechanisms of selection in claiming narrative identities: A model for interpreting narratives. *Qualitative Inquiry*, 17(2), 172–185. https://doi.org/10.1177/1077800410393885

Spellerberg, A. (2001). *Framework for the measurement of social capital in New Zealand.* Wellington: Statistics New Zealand.

Spoonley, P., & Butcher, A. (2009). Reporting superdiversity. The mass media and immigration in New Zealand. *Journal of Intercultural Studies*, 30(4), 355–372. https://doi.org/10.1080/07256860903213638

Spouse, L. (1999). The trauma of being a refugee. *Medicine, Conflict and Survival*, 15(4), 394–403. https://doi.org/10.1080/13623699908409481

Starfield, S. (2010). Ethnographies. In B. Paltridge & A. Phakiti (Eds.), *Continuum companion to research methods in applied linguistics* (pp. 50–65). London: Continuum International.

Statistics New Zealand. (2004). *Degrees of difference: The employment of university-qualified immigrants in New Zealand.* Wellington: Statistics New Zealand.

Strategic Social Policy Group. (2008). *Diverse communities – Exploring the migrant and refugee experience in New Zealand.* Wellington: Ministry of Social Development.

Stubbe, M. (2001). From office to production line: Collecting data for the Wellington Language in the Workplace Project. *Language in the Workplace Occasional Papers*, 2, 1–26.

Stubbe, M., & Holmes, J. (1995). *You know, eh*, and other "exasperating expressions": An analysis of social and stylistic variation in the use of pragmatic devices in a sample of New Zealand English. *Language & Communication*, 15(1), 63–88. https://doi.org/10.1016/0271-5309(94)00016-6

Stubbe, M., Holmes, J., Vine, B., & Marra, M. (2000). Forget Mars and Venus, let's get back to Earth! Challenging gender stereotypes in the workplace. In J. Holmes (Ed.), *Gendered speech in social context: Perspectives from gown and town* (pp. 231–258). Wellington: Victoria University Press.

Stubbe, M., & Ingle, M. (1999). Collecting natural interaction data in a factory: Some methodological challenges. Presented at the Murdoch Symposium on Talk-in-Interaction, Perth. Retrieved from http://www.victoria.ac.nz/lals/centres-and-institutes/language-in-the-workplace/docs/articles/Stubbe-and-Ingle-1999.pdf

Sulaiman-Hill, C. M. R., Thompson, S. C., Afsar, R., & Hodliffe, T. L. (2011). Changing images of refugees: A Comparative analysis of Australian and New Zealand print media 1998–2008. *Journal of Immigrant & Refugee Studies*, 9(4), 345–366. https://doi.org/10.1080/15562948.2011.616794

Sunstein, B. S., & Chiseri-Strater, E. (2007). *Field working* (3rd ed.). Boston: Bedford/St. Martin's.

Swartz, D. (1997). *Culture and power: The sociology of Pierre Bourdieu.* Chicago: Chicago University Press.

Tainio, L. (2002). Negotiating gender identities and sexual agency in elderly couples' talk. In P. McIlvenny (Ed.), *Talking gender and sexuality* (pp. 181–206). Amsterdam: John Benjamins. https://doi.org/10.1075/pbns.94.08tai

Talmy, S. (2010). Qualitative interviews in applied linguistics: From research instrument to social practice. *Annual Review of Applied Linguistics*, 30, 128–148. https://doi.org/10.1017/S0267190510000085

Tannen, D. (1985). Cross-cultural communication. In T. A. van Dijk (Ed.), *Handbook of discourse analysis* (pp. 203–216). New York: Academic Press.

Tannen, D. (1986). Introducing constructed dialogue in Greek and American conversational and literary narrative. *Direct and Indirect Speech*, 3, 11–32.

Tannen, D. (1987). Remarks on discourse and power. In L. Kedar (Ed.), *Power through discourse* (pp. 3–10). Norwood: Ablex.

Tannen, D. (1992). Interactional sociolinguistics. In W. Bright (Ed.), *Oxford international encyclopedia of linguistics* (Vol. 4, pp. 9–12). Oxford: Oxford University Press.

Tannen, D. (2005). Interactional sociolinguistics as a resource for Intercultural Pragmatics. *Intercultural Pragmatics*, 2(2), 205–208. https://doi.org/10.1515/iprg.2005.2.2.205

Tanyas, B. (2016). Gendering migration narratives: A qualitative inquiry on language use and agency in adaptation stories. *Gender & Language*, 10(1), 85–105. https://doi.org/10.1558/genl.v10i1.17495

The Guardian. (2019, March 28). Jacinda Ardern's speech at Christchurch memorial – full transcript. Retrieved July 26, 2019, from The Guardian website: https://www.theguardian.com/world/2019/mar/29/jacinda-arderns-speech-at-christchurch-memorial-full-transcript

The Nelson Mail. (2015, December 18). Grateful refugee turned scholar. *The Nelson Mail.*

Thompson, J. B. (1991). Editor's introduction. In P. Bourdieu, G. Raymond & M. Adamson (Trans.), *Language and symbolic power* (pp. 1–31). Cambridge: Polity Press.

Tilbury, F., & Colic-Peisker, V. (2006). Deflecting responsibility in employer talk about race discrimination. *Discourse & Society*, 17(5), 651–676. https://doi.org/10.1177/0957926506066349

Tomlinson, F. (2010). Marking difference and negotiating belonging: Refugee women, volunteering and employment. *Gender, Work and Organization*, 17(3), 278–296. https://doi.org/10.1111/j.1468-0432.2008.00399.x

Tomlinson, M. (2010). Investing in the self: Structure, agency and identity in graduates' employability. *Education, Knowledge and Economy*, 4(2), 73–88. https://doi.org/10.1080/17496896.2010.499273

Tracy, S. J., Lutgen-Sandvik, P., & Alberts, J. K. (2006). Nightmares, demons, and slaves: Exploring the painful metaphors of workplace bullying. *Management Communication Quarterly*, 20(2), 148–185. https://doi.org/10.1177/0893318906291980

Tranekjær, L. (2017). Laughables as a resource for foregrounding shared knowledge and shared identities in intercultural interactions in Scandinavia. In D. van de Mieroop & S. Schnurr (Eds.), *Identity struggles: Evidence from workplaces around the world* (pp. 185–205). Amsterdam: John Benjamins. https://doi.org/10.1075/dapsac.69.10tra

Trester, A. M. (2009). Discourse marker 'oh' as a means for realizing the identity potential of constructed dialogue in interaction. *Journal of Sociolinguistics*, 13(2), 147–168. https://doi.org/10.1111/j.1467-9841.2009.00402.x

Trudgill, P. (1974). *The social differentiation of English in Norwich.* Cambridge: Cambridge University Press.

Trueba, H. T. (2002). Multiple ethnic, racial, and cultural identities in action: From marginality to a new cultural capital in modern society. *Journal of Latinos and Education*, 1(1), 7–28. https://doi.org/10.1207/S1532771XJLE0101_2

Turner, D. (2010). Qualitative interview design: A practical guide for novice investigators. *The Qualitative Report*, 15(3), 754–760.

UNHCR. (2002). Refugee resettlement: An International handbook to guide reception and integration. Retrieved October 20, 2014, from http://www.unhcr.org/4a2cfe336.html

UNHCR. (2011). *UNHCR Resettlement Handbook.* Geneva: United Nations High Commissioner for Refugees.

UNHCR. (2017). Somali refugee mother searches for a better life for her children. Retrieved February 2, 2018, from https://www.unrefugees.org/news/all-i-want-is-a-better-life-for-my-children/

UNHCR. (2018a). Asylum in the UK. Retrieved September 27, 2018, from http://www.unhcr.org/asylum-in-the-uk.html

UNHCR. (2018b). Figures at a glance. Retrieved October 8, 2018, from http://www.unhcr.org/figures-at-a-glance.html

UNHCR. (2018c). Refugee definition. Retrieved October 1, 2018, from https://emergency.unhcr.org/entry/114761/refugee-definition

Utas, M. (2005). Victimcy, girlfriending, soldiering: Tactic agency in a young woman's social navigation of the Liberian war zone. *Anthropological Quarterly*, 78(2), 403–430. https://doi.org/10.1353/anq.2005.0032

van de Mieroop, D. (2009). A rehearsed self in repeated narratives? The case of two interviews with a former hooligan. *Discourse Studies*, 11(6), 721–740. https://doi.org/10.1177/1461445609347236

van de Mieroop, D., & Schnurr, S. (2017a). Epilogue: Identity struggles as a reflection of knowledge, competing norms, and attempts for social change. In D. van de Mieroop & S. Schnurr (Eds.), *Identity struggles: Evidence from workplaces around the world* (pp. 445–454). Amsterdam: John Benjamins. https://doi.org/10.1075/dapsac.69.24van

van de Mieroop, D., & Schnurr, S. (2017b). Introduction: A kaleidoscope view of identity struggles at work. In D. van de Mieroop & S. Schnurr (Eds.), *Identity struggles: Evidence from workplaces around the world* (pp. 1–18). Amsterdam: John Benjamins. https://doi.org/10.1075/dapsac.69

van Dijk, T. A. (1993). Principles of critical discourse analysis. *Discourse & Society*, 4(2), 249–283. https://doi.org/10.1177/0957926593004002006

van Dijk, T. A. (2000). New(s) racism: A discourse analytical approach. In S. Cottle (Ed.), *Ethnic minorities and the media* (pp. 33–49). Buckingham: Open University Press.

van Wees, H. (1998). The law of gratitude: Reciprocity in anthropological theory. In C. Gill, N. Postlethwaite, & R. Seaford (Eds.), *Reciprocity in ancient Greece* (pp. 13–49). New York: Oxford University Press.

Vásquez, C. (2007). Moral stance in the workplace narratives of novices. *Discourse Studies*, 9(5), 653–675. https://doi.org/10.1177/1461445607081270

Vertovec, S. (2001). Transnationalism and identity. *Journal of Ethnic and Migration Studies*, 27(4), 573–582. https://doi.org/10.1080/13691830120090386

Vervliet, M., De Mol, J., Broekaert, E., & Derluyn, I. (2013). 'That I live, that's because of her': Intersectionality as framework for unaccompanied refugee mothers. *British Journal of Social Work*, 1–19.

Victoria University of Wellington. (2018, April 17). *Human ethics policy*. Victoria University of Wellington.

Vine, B. (2017). *Just* and *actually* at work in New Zealand. In E. Friginal (Ed.), *Studies in corpus-based sociolinguistics* (pp. 199–219). New York: Routledge.

Vine, B., Holmes, J., Marra, M., Pfeifer, D., & Jackson, B. (2008). Exploring co-leadership talk through interactional sociolinguistics. *Leadership*, 4(3), 339–360. https://doi.org/10.1177/1742715008092389

Vine, B., Johnson, G., O'Brien, J., & Robertson, S. (2002). Wellington archive of New Zealand English transcriber's manual. *Language in the Workplace Occasional Papers*, 5, 1–16.

Vitanova, G. (2005). Authoring the self in a non-native language: A Dialogic approach to agency and subjectivity. In J. Kelly Hall, G. Vitanova, & L. Marchenkova (Eds.), *Dialogue with Bakhtin on second and foreign language learning* (pp. 149–169). London: Lawrence Erlbaum.

Wallace, D. (2017). Reading 'race' in Bourdieu? Examining Black cultural capital among Black Caribbean youth in south London. *Sociology*, 51(5), 907–923. https://doi.org/10.1177/0038038516643478

Ward, T., & Marshall, B. (2007). Narrative identity and offender rehabilitation. *International Journal of Offender Therapy and Comparative Criminology*, 51(3), 279–297. https://doi.org/10.1177/0306624X06291461

Warner-Garcia, S. (2014). Laughing when nothing's funny: The pragmatic use of coping laughter in the negotiation of conversational disagreement. *Pragmatics*, 24(1), 157–180. https://doi.org/10.1075/prag.24.1.07war

Warren, P. (2016). *Uptalk: The phenomenon of rising intonation*. Cambridge: Cambridge University Press. https://doi.org/10.1017/CBO9781316403570

Warriner, D. (2004). "The days now is very hard for my family": The negotiation and construction of gendered work identities among newly arrived women refugees. *Journal of Language, Identity & Education*, 3(4), 279–294. https://doi.org/10.1207/s15327701jlie0304_4

Watts, R. J. (1988). A relevance-theoretic approach to commentary pragmatic markers: The case of *actually, really* and *basically*. *Acta Linguistica Hungarica*, 38(1–4), 235–260.

Weicht, B. (2013). The making of 'the elderly': Constructing the subject of care. *Journal of Aging Studies*, 27(2), 188–197. https://doi.org/10.1016/j.jaging.2013.03.001

Weininger, E. B., & Lareau, A. (2007). Cultural capital. In G. Ritzer (Ed.), *Encyclopaedia of sociology*. Oxford: Blackwell. https://doi.org/10.1002/9781405165518.wbeosc169

Wetherell, M. (1998). Positioning and interpretative repertoires: Conversation analysis and post-structuralism in dialogue. *Discourse & Society*, 9(3), 387–412. https://doi.org/10.1177/0957926598009003005

White, C. J. (2016). Agency and emotion in narrative accounts of emergent conflict in an L2 classroom. *Applied Linguistics*, 39(4), 579–598.

Whitley, M. S. (1986). *Spanish/English contrasts: A course in Spanish linguistics*. Washington: Georgetown University Press.

Williams, A. M. (2009). Employability and international migration: Theoretical perspectives. In S. MacKay (Ed.), *Refugees, recent migrants and employment: Challenging barriers and exploring pathways* (pp. 23–24). Oxford: Routledge.

Winn, M. (2005). Collecting target discourse: The case of the US naturalization interview. In M. H. Long (Ed.), *Second language needs analysis* (pp. 265–304). Cambridge: Cambridge University Press. https://doi.org/10.1017/CBO9780511667299.010

Wodak, R. (2011). Critical discourse analysis. In K. Hyland & B. Paltridge (Eds.), *The Continuum companion to discourse analysis*. London: Bloomsbury. https://doi.org/10.4324/9781315852515.ch20

Wodak, R., de Cillia, R., Reisigl, M., & Liebhart, K. (2010). *The discursive construction of national identity* (2nd ed.). Edinburgh: Edinburgh University Press.

Wooden, M. (1991). The experience of refugees in the Australian labor market. *International Migration Review*, 25(3), 514–535. https://doi.org/10.2307/2546758

Woodhams, J. (2015). A critical realist study of political identity in Aotearoa New Zealand: Materiality, discourse and context (Doctoral Dissertation). Victoria University of Wellington, Wellington.

Woods, A. (2009). Learning to be literate: Issues of pedagogy for recently arrived refugee youth in Australia. *Critical Inquiry in Language Studies*, 6(1–2), 81–101. https://doi.org/10.1080/15427580802679468

Yap, S. Y., Byrne, A., & Davidson, S. (2010). From refugee to good citizen: A discourse analysis of volunteering. *Journal of Refugee Studies*, 24(1), 157–170. https://doi.org/10.1093/jrs/feq036

Young, R. A., & Collin, A. (2004). Introduction: Constructivism and social constructionism in the career field. *Journal of Vocational Behavior*, 64(3), 373–388. https://doi.org/10.1016/j.jvb.2003.12.005

Yuval-Davis, N. (2006). Intersectionality and feminist politics. *European Journal of Women's Studies*, 13(3), 193–209. https://doi.org/10.1177/1350506806065752

Yuval-Davis, N. (2007). Intersectionality, citizenship and contemporary politics of belonging. *Critical Review of International Social and Political Philosophy*, 10(4), 561–574. https://doi.org/10.1080/13698230701660220

Zetter, R. (2007). More labels, fewer refugees: Remaking the refugee label in an era of globalization. *Journal of Refugee Studies*, (2), 172–192. https://doi.org/10.1093/jrs/fem011

Index